THREE MEN IN A HUPP

THREE MEN IN A HUPP

Around the World by Automobile,

1910-1912

James A. Ward

STANFORD GENERAL BOOKS
Stanford University Press
Stanford, California 2003

Stanford University Press
Stanford, California

Printed in the United States of America
on acid-free, archival-quality paper.

Library of Congress Cataloging-in-Publication Data

Ward, James Arthur.
    Three men in a Hupp : around the world by automobile, 1910–1912 /
James A. Ward.
        p. cm.
    Includes bibliographical references and index.
    ISBN 0-8047-3460-7 (alk. paper)
    1. Automobile travel.   2. Voyages around the world.   3. Hupp automobile—History.
I. Title.
GV1021 .W27   2003
796.7—dc21   2003009923

Original Printing 2003

Typeset in 12/16 Granjon

For Roberta

CONTENTS

ACKNOWLEDGMENTS

It would be easiest to say that I was beholden to nobody and that everything sprang full-blown from my own mind and resources. At the very least, that would ensure that I did not hurt anyone's feelings by leaving him or her out. Unfortunately, however, this is a fantasy.

I cannot even claim to have come up with the idea for this book—Don Jeffery, Jr., the grandson of Thomas Hanlon, the Hupmobile's driver-mechanic, did that. A half a dozen years ago, Don wrote to me to say that he had enjoyed my book *The Fall of the Packard Motor Car Company* (Stanford University Press, 1995) and mentioned that his grandfather had driven around the world in a Hupp in 1910–12 and that he had the photos. I was hip-deep at the time in what became *Ferrytale: The Career of W. H. "Ping" Ferry* (Stanford University Press, 2001) and I thanked Don for his kind remarks and suggested he ought to "do something" with the photos. We exchanged several letters over the next eighteen months or so, and I finally recommended that he write up his grandfather's trip and see if he could get it published. He demurred, and after some discussion, I offered to do it after I was done with my biography of Ferry.

Don has been a great help; he never turned down a request. He allowed me full access to his photographs, lent me several originals that had become separated from the album over the years, dug out his mother's negatives, and rounded up a small parcel of material his grandfather had left. He copied photos for me, answered innumerable questions, and even drove from Livonia to Albion to enable me to check all Hanlon's pictures before I sent the manuscript to Stanford University Press. His wife,

Julie, provided the space, platters of food, and a comfortable ambiance that made it easy for my wife Roberta and me to work at the Jefferys' house.

Jeffery also put me in touch with his mother, Mariann Hanlon Jeffery, a lively septuagenarian, who spun numerous stories her father had told her about his trip and gave me vivid thumbnail sketches of family members. She also lent me 155 negatives taken on the trip and a few showing her father's adventure with General J. J. ("Black Jack") Pershing when the latter invaded Mexico in 1916. Mariann endured three hours of constant questions with unfailing patience and sparkling humor; she's quite a character.

Much of the technical information on the Hupp Model 20 I owe to William Cuthbert, who not only owns and drives a Model 20 but is the technical advisor to the Hupp Club on all matters relating to the car. A well-known automotive writer, Cuthbert shared his specific knowledge and his publications and is responsible for making the chapter on the Hupmobile's technical aspects as definitive as possible.

Everyone who dabbles in automotive history knows that the National Automotive History Collection at the Detroit Public Library has the nation's premier holdings in the field. Mark A. Patrick, the collection's curator, was indispensable. Patrick walked miles to bring sources to the reading room for me to examine, suggested materials I had overlooked, fielded numerous phone calls later to look up facts and sources, photocopied materials I needed, and took an enthusiastic interest in the Hupp project. I thank him for his help.

Karl J. Hetzel, the former editor of the *Hupp Herald,* supplied text and photos of the journey that had previously been published in his journal, gave liberally of his knowledge and advice, and was from the start a cheerleader for this project. And besides all his help, he is a genuinely nice fellow.

At the Frederick C. Crawford Museum of Transportation & Industry, where the little globe-girdling Hupp now reposes, Christopher P. Grasso, assistant curator of Urban & Industrial History–Transportation, combed the museum's archives to find the correspondence between Hupp and the Crawford Museum that brought the car to the museum. Moreover, he gave me what history the Crawford Museum had on the car and some idea about its plans for the Hupp's future.

Out in California, Tracy Montee, the grandson of the expedition's leader, Joseph Drake, pointed me toward the American Heritage Center at the University of Wyoming, where Drake's papers had gravitated. He also gave me much helpful knowledge about the Drake family, which was so instrumental in all the Hupp Motor Car Company's affairs.

Drake could not have been luckier than to have his papers wind up at the American Heritage Center. Carl Hallberg, assistant archivist, reference, was a great help in perusing the material to find those documents that had some bearing on Drake's first two globe-circling adventures.

Relatives of Tom Jones were more difficult to locate, because his mother remarried and he was raised with her second husband's family, the Owens. But Mrs. Holly Broadbent, his niece, if I understand the family's relationships, and David Owen, whose father was Jones's stepbrother, gave me a great deal of insight into the family and shared with me what they knew about Jones's personality and career.

I would be remiss if I did not mention the good folks at the Western Reserve Historical Society's library, who did a thorough search for Hupp company material and unearthed much key information that gave me a solid background on the company and its cars.

While working on this book, I felt the need to drive a 1911 Hupp to experience what it must have been like to spend fourteen months going around the globe in one. I located a Model 20 in Dalton, Georgia, owned by Judson Manly, but unfortunately, as is often the case with such elderly autos, it was not in running condition. Manly invited me down to examine the car, however, and we had a long conversation about its technical aspects and the history of the one he owns. Just after completing the book, I located Steve Speth in Orchard Lake, Michigan, whose wife is a grandniece of Robert C. Hupp. His 1911 tourer was in running condition, and he allowed me to ride, drive, and photograph his car to get a feel for it. The experience convinced me that the 1911 trip had been harder than I had imagined and provided the material for the postscript.

Curt McConnell, who wrote a wonderful book, *Coast to Coast by Automobile: The Pioneer Trips, 1899–1908*, read the manuscript for Stanford University Press and came up with hundreds of good suggestions that improved its content and style; he saved me from many embarrassments.

I owe thanks to Norris Pope, the program director of the Stanford University Press, who, although a Victorian English scholar, harbors a secret love for photography and old cars, particularly when they intersect. From the first, Norris encouraged this book with an advance contract, urged me to include as many photos as possible, and with his usual good humor and dry wit bore with me when I missed my deadline by a year.

Closer to home, the University of Tennessee at Chattanooga's Faculty Research

Committee came through with a timely grant that helped to defray my costs of research. I also have to thank Neal Coulter, possibly the world's most resourceful librarian, for his help in finding the most obscure minutiae. He always complained and will undoubtedly not read the book to see this acknowledgment, but I am greatly indebted to him. Beatrice Talley, the interlibrary loan guru at UTC, spent hours tracking down foreign newspapers for me and did not complain once. In an undergraduate institution's library, she is a jewel.

And, much, much closer to home, I shall be a dead man if I do not thank my wife, Roberta Shannon Ward, for accompanying me on research trips, suffering through more conversations on Hupp than any mortal ought to endure, reading the manuscript, offering her always unvarnished critical comments, looking at several hundred pictures of the same three men with a car, and remaining my best friend through it all. She did ride in a 1911 Hupp, however, met the folks mentioned above, and has her own page herein.

Chattanooga, Tennessee
June 9, 2002

THREE MEN IN A HUPP

INTRODUCTION

The Little Corporal

THREE AMERICANS cranked their 1911 Hupmobile in Detroit on the afternoon of November 3, 1910, and drove around the world, returning to the Motor City on January 25, 1912. They were not the first to circle the globe in an automobile; at least three others had already done it. They were not in a race, and they were not Phileas Foggs trying to set a speed record. They took their time, detoured to see points of interest, stopped to enjoy the sights, talked to local inhabitants, showed off their car, and took hundreds of people on demonstration rides. Afterwards, the three men returned to resume normal, prosaic lives, albeit with endless stories to tell their children and grandchildren.

Their adventure was wondrous. They burst into remote parts of the world that had never seen the wonders of the dawning automotive age. Many native people initially shied away from the little car only to advance cautiously to try to see where the beast hid that gave it motion. The men coaxed their Hupp up mountains to look into volcanoes and down into deep valleys and gorges, where they drove alongside coursing rivers. They crossed swamps, high plains, deserts, swollen streams, and oceans, and sometimes even found smooth roads that enabled them to accelerate to breathtaking speeds, perhaps as high as forty miles per hour. They hobnobbed with princes, sultans, politicians, royal retainers, geishas, headhunters, local nabobs, businessmen, a pope, ship captains, ambassadors, journalists, former guerrillas, and hordes of curious onlookers, especially children. They suffered through snow, sleet, and rain, endured tropical heat, below-zero temperatures, and raw winds. They spent some days

1

A smiling Thomas Jones fording an overflowing stream near Launceston, Tasmania, accompanied by two well-dressed women. HPA/DJC.

soaking wet, for their car had neither top nor windshield, and others parched for water, or at least a little humidity to keep their throats moist and their skin from cracking. Sunburned, windburned, sometimes close to frostbitten, they returned home with the leathery look of explorers. They ate strange native foods, recorded unfamiliar customs, coped with a half a dozen colonial bureaucracies, raced to meet steamship schedules, played baseball on the high seas, saw great wealth and soul-searing poverty firsthand, established Hupp dealerships wherever they went, negotiated dozens of utterly unfamiliar local tongues, gave hundreds of people their first ride in a motorcar, smiled in twenty languages, and did it all with gusto.

They were twentieth-century road versions of Mark Twain's innocents abroad. They combined an awe of much of what they saw with an inborn confidence that they and their car could overcome any obstacles remote corners of the world could throw in their path. The Hupp's odometer read 47,777 miles when it returned to Detroit. The three autoists had traveled almost seven times the diameter of the planet, over one and two-thirds times around the globe.[1]

Their jaunt did not occur in a vacuum; the little-known automobile and its drivers symbolized the emergence of a new industrial giant. Just sixteen years before the Hupp putted westward out of Detroit, the United States had emerged as the world's largest industrial power in place of Great Britain, and the little silk American flag proudly tied to the Hupp's radiator cap signaled a new kind of industrial imperialism America was spreading across the world. The car advertised both Hupp and the wonders of American business.

The Hupp Motor Car Company sponsored the grueling test of its auto and men. It was no billion dollar U.S. Steel or Standard Oil Company; Hupp was barely two years old in 1910 and had manufactured only a few thousand cars when it staked its reputation before the glare of world publicity on a gamble that its product could endure the rigors of such a trip.

Hupp officials were infected with the peculiar American penchant for such an advertising stunt. The other three global odysseys were American as well, even though Europeans had invented the automobile and built the best ones at the turn of the century. Daimler-Benz had already acquired a reputation for quality, engineering, and speed when the first Hupp rolled out of the factory. The French claimed automotive excellence for their De Dions, Renaults, and Panhard and Levassors; the English touted their Daimlers, Napiers, and Rolls-Royces; and the Italians bragged about their Fiats and Italas. Built with care by hand, in limited numbers, these and other cars were aristocratic toys, designed for the spunky who had enough money to indulge their whims. They were energetically exported to the United States, where they displayed their superiority in endurance runs, hill climbs, and races.

Their heyday on American shores was short. Starting with Ransom E. Olds's curved-dash Oldsmobile in 1901, American inventors and tinkerers pursued the dream of a car for the masses, a serviceable machine available at a price most people could afford. By the time the world-touring Hupp left Detroit, Henry Ford's Model T, the car that would reposition the automobile in the American social fabric, had been in production for over two years. Hupp was busily exploiting the same market, influenced by the prevailing national industrial thinking, in which businessmen believed that bigness, lowered production costs, and intense marketing at home and abroad were the keys to profitability.

American auto companies were not coy about their ambitions. Newspapers at the end of the new century's first decade blared headlines promising "World to Ride in American Cars." U.S. auto executives believed, they reported, that "no other country can supply the demands at economical cost." One manager calculated that the domestic economy could absorb 150,000 new autos in 1911, and that the rest of the world would buy another 30,000. "America," he said, "is therefore the only country having a sufficiently large market to permit of manufacturing in quantities to bring the prices down to the lowest figures." He explained that "an English automobile factory with a national reputation will make 300 cars a year," while "an American factory with a name of the same standard will make 10,000." The French were in worse shape; although large concerns might turn out between 1,000 and 2,000 cars a year, they built as many as twenty to thirty different "classes" of cars, thus losing efficiencies of size.[2]

Like other auto makers, Hupp executives looked to overseas markets to supplement their domestic sales, even though by 1910 the U.S. auto market appeared unlimited. Ten years earlier, only 8,000 automobiles had been registered in the nation, many of them imported. By 1905, ownership had increased almost tenfold, to 77,400, and when the three men set off on their adventure in 1910, they joined almost a half a million autos already on American roads, 458,377 to be exact. The industry was still in flux; firms like Hupp stood a reasonable chance of breaking out of the pack of hundreds of automobile producers. In 1910, Henry Ford built only 32,053 Model T's, and the number two, Buick, 1,500 fewer cars. Willys-Overland and Studebaker-E.M.F., each of which assembled about 15,000 units that year, followed. Cadillac, Maxwell, and Brush, companies that built around 10,000 cars a year, occupied the third level. Hupp, a brand-new competitor, was already producing 5,000 to 6,000 autos a year, making it the nation's tenth-largest automobile company in 1910.[3]

The journey was a huge gamble for Hupp. With the widespread publicity and press coverage in the United States and abroad before the expedition set out, any major mechanical malfunction threatened to make headlines everywhere. Failure, for whatever reason, to complete the journey as advertised would adversely, perhaps fatally, affect the firm's sales in an era when reliability was more important than styling, speed, color, and body type. With typical American bravado, however, company managers determined to road test their new automobile in the toughest manner possible, confident it would not fail.

Hupp's confidence and sense of invincibility reflected the national tenor. America had emerged from its post–Civil War isolation to spread its corporate logos and flag around the globe. At the end of the nineteenth century, the country had watched Britain, France, Germany, Belgium, and Russia expand into Asia and Africa, where they planted their flags at gunpoint, enlarged their markets, and captured control of

raw materials. America had not been entirely asleep, however: it had acquired Alaska in 1867 (thus excluding Russia from the Western Hemisphere); taken its first tentative step to compete seriously in the China trade with a treaty establishing a U.S. naval coaling base on Samoa in 1878; leased an important Pacific port, Pearl Harbor, in 1887; and built railroads and exploited mineral deposits in Central and South America.

Admiral Alfred Thayer Mahan, at the Naval War College in Rhode Island, proclaimed in several books, avidly read by world leaders, that all great nations had controlled the seas, a notion that accelerated a naval arms race. The United States, with its newfound industrial might, began laying keels and by 1898 boasted the third-largest navy in the world. Internal conflict in Cuba and a social Darwinist belief in national superiority had prodded the United States to declare war on Spain. In a series of summer campaigns, America stumbled into a small empire that included Puerto Rico, Guam, and the Philippines. During the fighting, it also acquired Hawaii. In less than two years, American troops were waging a savage guerrilla war in the Philippines and marching into China to help suppress the so-called Boxer re-

The Overland & Hupp dealer in Auckland proudly posed three Hupps he had already sold alongside Hanlon and his Little Corporal. HPA/DJC.

bellion. These military ventures later influenced Hupp's plans; its global auto expedition followed American troops to Hawaii, the Philippines, and China, motoring along the periphery of the new American empire.

Although there was not a great deal of territory left for Americans to conquer, expansionist fever at home scarcely abated. Teddy Roosevelt seized a portion of Columbia to build the Panama Canal, which enabled the United States to increase its trade with its new colonies and the Far East. In a show of technological mastery and newly launched military might, Roosevelt sent the "Great White Fleet" around the world. For many of the same reasons, Hupp three years later dispatched a single black version of its technical mastery to wow foreigners.

Other private Americans also dreamed global dreams; in 1908, E. H. Harriman, master of the Union Pacific, Central Pacific, and Southern Pacific railroads, decided to build a railway around the world and besieged the State Department to pressure foreign governments to allow him the necessary rights of way. Only his premature death ended the effort. While the Hupp was tootling down back roads in Asia, the United States invaded Nicaragua, a favorite pastime for several administrations, and just four years after the automotive sojourners returned, U.S. troops under General J. J. ("Black Jack") Pershing invaded Mexico to find Pancho Villa, who had raided a New Mexico town. Pershing took with him Hupp trucks and automobiles and Thomas Hanlon, one of the three men who had encircled the globe in 1911.

Stymied by European powers' earlier and more energetic conquest of African and Asian portions of the world, the United States concentrated on a more remunerative form of expansion—economic imperialism. With the State Department's full approbation, private American companies extended their growing economic might and American culture to many of the world's remoter regions. When George V, newly crowned king of England, journeyed to India for his Durbar in December 1911, for example, he found that the traditional royal elephant and horse procession was no more. He and Indian royalty paraded in thirty-three American-built Model T Fords.[4]

Spurred on by President William Howard Taft (1909–13), who believed economic domination was far less costly than the traditional military means of acquiring colonies, the State Department cajoled leading U.S. business figures to invest overseas, emphasizing the huge, virtually untapped Asian markets where the Hupp travelers spent so much of their time. Taft was blunt about his foreign policy priorities; he believed in the "glut theory," the need for foreign outlets to absorb the excess goods of capitalist nations, which the British economist J. A. Hobson had elaborated around the turn of the century.

In his 1912 state of the union message, delivered less than a year after the Hupp's expedition returned, the president told Congress, "the diplomacy of the present administration . . . has been characterized as substituting dollars for bullets." Such "dollar diplomacy," he thought, appealed "alike to idealistic humanitarian sentiments, to the dictates of sound policy and strategy, and to legitimate commercial aims." He neglected to say that it was cheaper both initially and in the long term, and that, if history was any guide, the flag always followed trade anyway.[5]

The Hupp trip was a tool in Taft's diplomatic kit bag. Just prior to the autoists' noisy Detroit send-off, a local newspaper reported that "John E. Baker, secretary of the Hupp Motor Car Company, has been in communication with the United States consulates along the itinerary," and that everywhere Baker had been assured "that the world touring Hupmobile will receive official encouragement in the furtherance of American trade in foreign countries." The paper assured its readers that "the little machine which is to make the long trip never before attempted in an automobile, will be decorated in the national colors." That was as good as showing the flag; the Hupp, however, sped off into the gray winter mists sporting the anarchists' favorite hue.[6]

Whiffs of industrial invincibility, the race for great empires, America's rearmament, and Taft's "dollar diplomacy" swirled through Hupp's executive suites. Local newspapers grandly proclaimed in headlines such information as "Latin Republics Need Educating; They Do Not Appreciate High-Class American Automobiles as They Ought," and "American Cars Covering the World," with an article pointing to increasing evidence "that America is educating the world to the automobile is becoming more and more evident." Lest its readers be slow to catch the point, James Couzens of the Ford Motor Company was quoted as promising that "should Congress provide a ship subsidy [to lower shipping costs and encourage construction of more ships], American competition would push everything before it in Europe as it is already doing in other parts of the globe." In evidence, Couzens noted that "the King of Siam who is much of an automobile enthusiast" had just ordered a Ford.[7]

Others in the automobile manufacturers' galaxy agreed with Couzens. George Keller, general sales manager of the E.M.F. Company, publicly declared: "America leads the auto world." He admitted that his country had been late in entering the fray but was confident that its combination of "new industrial captains, great engineers, skilled workmen and the finest of machinery have all contributed to the almost perfect car of today." Such commonly held views convinced the Hupp company's managers that a grand expedition cloaked in the language and symbols of America's new world mission would attract splendid corporate attention, demonstrate their auto's durability, and pay dividends in future sales. Their language showed that they fully understood the conjoining of public and private economic impulses with nationalistic overtones represented by the Hupp's jaunty little American flag. In a day when corporate press releases were printed verbatim, a paper quoted Hupp officials as saying their "three soldiers of commerce—Drake, Hanlon, Jones,—are carrying the conquest of the Hupmobile into almost every country where motor cars are known."[8]

The Hupp Company's sales plan was a foreign policy every bit as complex as Taft's and more risky. Its overt scheme to increase world sales demanded that the small, shakily capitalized firm mount its international assault for little more than the cost of keeping its expedition in the field for over a year. Joseph R. Drake, corporate treasurer, who hated to smile for photographers, went along on the expedition to solicit foreign distributors. He judged the trip's success by how much Hupp's sales increased. Virtually every newspaper article printed after the travelers returned to Detroit mentioned Hupp's international sales, their stock refrain being that "the direct result of this tour is claimed to be an increase of 400 per cent. in foreign business for Hupmobile." The company's own account of the trip, published in 1911, when the travelers were barely one-third through their journey, bragged that "from every port that the little car has visited, additional orders to [the] regular schedule of shipments have followed" and claimed this showed "circumstantial evidence of the educational effect of the world-demonstration."[9]

Presumably, proof of the car's durability welded Hupp's corporate claims for its automobiles to America's growing reputation for industrial quality. The trek was a visible statement that Hupp was the best of the best, and the company made frequent mention in news releases of its autos' superior cooling capabilities, tires, oil and gas consumption, electrical apparatus, and chassis. Drivers in 1911 had to be able to make frequent roadside repairs and therefore were interested in their automobiles' inner workings.

Those workings were packaged in what reporters persisted in calling the "little car." Everywhere, the standard story pitted the "little Hupp" against great odds, a David and Goliath drama acted out on the world stage. Hupp advertised its "lighter and smaller technology" as superior to bigger and heavier competitors, exactly what Ford was saying about the two Model T's he entered in the 1909 New York–to–Seattle race. By the standards of the day, the Hupmobile was small; it weighed only 1,600 pounds, sat low to the ground, and advertised only twenty horsepower. By emphasizing the car's diminutive aspects, Hupp officials firmly identified it with the national penchant for cheering for the underdog. Culturally insecure Americans had long seen themselves as underdogs, less developed, out of the mainstream of international affairs, fearing entanglement in more powerful nations' conflicts. The little Hupp sallied forth with the Stars and Stripes waffling in the wind to prove that even the smallest American motorcar was superior to other nations' best, no matter their size. A century or so earlier, Napoleon, who stood only five feet two inches tall, had conquered most of Europe, and an imaginative newspaperman saw a parallel with the Hupmobile, which he dubbed "the little Corporal of motor cars," a moniker other papers quickly adopted.[10]

The little Hupp and its three charioteers, who churned through alkali dust, mud, and snow, and threw themselves up steep mountain roads heedless of precipitous drops, were mobbed by the curious in Bombay and Calcutta, stood next to the Sphinx at dawn, and pitched along the stone-lined Appian Way, symbolized many of the attributes Americans commonly used to differentiate themselves from their European cousins. The men and their machine stood for the national hustle and drive; they took a year of their lives to partake in an adventure most could only dream about. They exhibited a mad-cap derring-do and disdain for danger in their rush to taste the world's offerings, lusting to see what lay around the next curve or over the approaching hill in their mad determination to complete their task. They were a modern-day Ulysses, fated to journey, to confront, to taste the exotic, to overcome, as immigrants to America had done for centuries. The three ventured forth in their untried machine without fear, confident they could fix anything. They hailed from a race of tinkerers, inventors, and producers, people who understood and loved the power of machinery nearly as much as they adored the power of money. None of the three was promised immediate riches, but they understood that if their company prospered, they would too. They represented a classic American paradox, three very different individuals, with dissimilar motivations, yoked to the same machine, working together—teamwork as a product of individualism. They were road warriors clad in America's self-defined ethos, an ensemble compounded of the Protestant work ethic, dash, daring, salesmanship, productive talents, and capitalism's inevitable quest for profits.

At Hupp, most of those symbols were secondary considerations. The auto manufacturers were hard-headed, pragmatic businessmen who understood the publicity advantages of such an adventure and coolly calculated its potential sales. Other companies had staged similar, though less ambitious, jaunts to grab national headlines. Winton had sponsored the first transcontinental auto crossing in 1903. It took sixty-three days, which a Packard soon thereafter bested by ten days. Many companies advertised their marques, as did Henry Ford, by building race cars or entering production models in hill climbs and endurance competitions. Hupp seemed taken with such public trials; it sent three cars across Ontario to New York City just ten months before the Little Corporal set out. No other company, however, had the audacity to promote the biggest business adventure story of the youthful century. It was a masterful public relations coup; although Hupp avowed it was "not merely a publicity adventure," the operative word here was "merely." The firm wanted its owners and the buying public to understand that "behind the undertaking lay a serious sales mission—a world demonstration of the Hupmobile."[11]

It was a "world demonstration" in the largest meaning of that phrase. The little motor car, "decorated in the national colors," was a wheeled display of America's

Manifest Destiny, sublime national pride that emanated from a God-given mandate to extend America's borders from ocean to ocean—and beyond. Most Americans believed God had decreed that speed was of the essence and had endowed them with the restless urge to sprawl across the continent. Thomas Jefferson had confidently predicted that it would take his fellow countrymen 300 years to settle the vast "American Desert"; they had proved him wrong by more than two centuries. Manifest Destiny did not end on the Pacific Coast. The more ebullient Americans believed that if God had decreed that the United States should control the Western Hemisphere, he must also favor extending its beneficent dominance over the rest of the world. The Hupp was in the vanguard of the drive to expose those less fortunate to the twentieth-century wonders of American civilization. These assumptions underlaid Detroit Mayor Philip T. Breitmeyer's thinking as he affixed the flag to the Hupp and "bade the adventurers Godspeed." Destiny had sent U.S. troops into some of these areas only a few years before, and the Little Corporal was to conduct a commercial mopping-up operation, making the tangible benefits of God's industrial world, especially the Hupp, readily available everywhere.[12]

Fewer than a dozen years earlier, Indiana Senator Albert J. Beveridge, a noted jingoist, had stood in the Senate's well and reminded his colleagues that the "American Republic is part of the movement of a race—the most masterful race in history." He was echoing an earlier pronouncement by Josiah Strong, a Congregational minister who had argued that American racial superiority ordained no territorial limits for the American people. Those views, with their social Darwinist overtones, helped precipitate the Spanish-American War and American participation in the international force that smashed the Boxers in Peking. The United States had almost finished legally segregating its own nonwhites, winked at public lynchings, relegated Native Americans to reservations, and toyed with keeping unwanted immigrants out. Detroit was rife with ethnic tensions as Central European immigrants flooded the city to labor in its auto plants and competed with earlier arrivals, especially the Irish, for jobs and political preferment. Americans were convinced that God had reserved the continent, and perhaps the world, for northern Europeans.[13]

The little Hupp represented the assumed superiority of that white world. Its itinerary took it mostly through the "colored world," lands peopled by "near savages!" as its hometown newspaper's headline blared. The three Hupmobilists loved to take photographs of their little car heaped with Igorots, Maoris, Singaporeans, Filipinos, Indians, and Egyptians, natives of all castes and hues. No mobs of Coloradoans, Australians, Italians, or Englishmen sprawled over the Hupp. Presumably they were more reticent in their superiority; they sat primly in the car or behind its wheel. Only a favored few natives, such as Emilio Aguinaldo, who led the Philippine insurrection against the American army, traditionally garbed geishas, and prospective or existing Hupp dealers were treated as whites.

The three men exhibited an almost missionary zeal as they spread the gospel according to Hupp to the preindustrial heathens in backward lands. They had been sent to save them from themselves, to uplift them, to bring salvation in the form of the motorcar. Drake was ordained to sell Hupps to prosperous natives or their colonial overlords, some of whom were now Americans. In foreign colonies, especially English-speaking Australia and New Zealand, Drake found "displaced" whites eager to embrace the Northern Hemisphere's symbols of civilization. The little cars sold so well there that Hupmobile rallies were still well attended in the Southern Hemisphere at the end of the twentieth century.

The Hupp's route traced the outlines of America's new empire. Domestic newspapers assured their readers that "the Hupmobile and its sturdy crew . . . have been welcomed in Uncle Sam's two colonies across the Pacific" by the happy American colonists. The new technology, crewed by "sturdy" whites, was "welcomed" by the nation's new colonial subjects, lusting to share the benefits of their masters' affluence. The Huppers, however, did not have to venture overseas to impress Americans. At home, the intrepid travelers showed the flag in regions only recently "liberated." From Detroit to San Francisco, they motored through states where the Indian wars had ended just twenty years earlier. Hawaii had been a U.S. territory for only thirteen years when the three men gave a ride to Queen Liliuokalani, who in 1893 had attempted to overthrow white rule in her islands. Likewise, the United States had subdued the Philippines only seven years earlier.[14]

Elsewhere, the Hupp toured the periphery of its country's economic reach. Australia and New Zealand were secure stepping-stones to teeming Asian markets. Hong Kong, Canton, and Shanghai were commercial ports where American businessmen were scrapping for a toehold. The Huppers extensively toured Japan, another elusive market, island-hopped through Borneo, Java, and Sumatra, with their valuable natural resources, and showed the flag and investigated sales possibilities in India and Egypt.

The juxtaposition of the Hupp next to the Sphinx and the pyramids powerfully evoked the stark contrasts between ancient societies and America's modern industrial triumphs. The world travelers' convictions that they were conquerors in the name of progress must have been heightened as they drove into the Vatican, once a symbol of civilized unity, and bumped along the Appian Way, where some twenty-two hundred years earlier Roman legions had marched out to conquer the known world. The Hupp's appearance in the industrial center of Europe reminded Europeans that Americans had arrived; the little car and everything it represented threatened continental notions of hegemony and superiority. European nations might control most of the world, and several ruled empires on which the sun never set, but the Hupp had, seemingly without effort, penetrated their colonies, leaving in its wake the sinister realization that commercial imperialism was no respecter of borders.

The small contrivance of cast iron, brass, copper, steel, leather, and rubber presaged worldwide business empires that would break down artificial political and age-old regional peculiarities and later in the century force cultural, political, and economic homogenization. While Hupp never became a powerful player on the world's stage—it remained a mid-sized American auto producer until 1941—several of its competitors did. Henry Ford became the first auto manufacturer in Japan a year after the Hupp toured the islands, moved into the English market as the three men steered their Hupp down the left sides of British roads, and soon diversified into tractors and farm implements. Ford's company accelerated its worldwide expansion and was still at it at century's end, when it acquired Jaguar and Volvo. Those who sent the Hupp to girdle the globe hoped the "little Hupp's" exploits would bring their company worldwide recognition and the commercial domination that Ford, General Motors, and Chrysler later achieved.

By 1910, American corporate officials were beguiled by the lure of overseas profits. While they gave only lukewarm support to efforts to secure colonies and territories, they were interested in exporting American capital, technology, and know-how; they had to find new markets to absorb their country's excess productive capacity. Theirs was a more efficient, less costly, and potentially profitable form of imperialism, in which they could exploit raw materials and cheap labor and reap the benefits of a colonial power without assuming its responsibilities. Hupp's aims were more modest: it wanted to advertise and sell its wares freely within everyone's empire, to create a supranational corporation whose sales would depend to some extent on the dollars American companies floated worldwide. The nation's public and private commercial empire-building efforts were deeply symbiotic.

The Little Corporal's journey was a corporate economic sally at national and international levels. Accepting Adam Smith's hypothesis that competition and supply and demand drove capitalism, Hupp strategists plotted to increase the company's worldwide sales and profits to weaken its overseas competitors, which would strengthen their competitive edge at home.

Bristling with metaphorical armaments, the little auto helped redefine world power. Terrible mechanized armed warfare lurked only four years in the future, and national industrial and economic power had become the fundamental underpinnings of military might. The United States, with the entrepreneurial bustle that Hupp exemplified, emerged as a military power. The Hupp Company was a component of this. It boosted America's gross national product, the measure of world standing, and in an emergency employed its capital and talents to redirect its efforts to manufacture war products. Moreover, its experience in selling and maintaining its cars all over the world meant that it had the measure of the environments where its war production was used.

THE GENESIS

1

When Hupp sent its motorcar around the world, the company was not much bigger or older than the Little Corporal. In an America hell-bent on corporate consolidations, and one that spawned behemoths such as Standard Oil, United States Steel, and the Northern Securities Corporation, Hupp was a midget; John D. Rockefeller, Andrew Carnegie, or E. H. Harriman could have bought it out with their spare change.

The Hupp Motor Car Company's beginnings were similar to those of numerous Motor City auto firms. A few men, hailing from diverse professions, shared an enthusiasm for the automobile's prospects and, lured by a vision of large profits, combined to design and make their own car. As was common in the industry's early years, several of Hupp's founders had learned the automobile trade at other motor car companies and joined forces because they believed they could build a better machine.

The idea for a Hupp Company originated with Robert Craig Hupp, a man with many of the talents and proclivities of his more famous contemporaries Henry Ford and Ransom E. Olds. Like them, he brought little to the business other than his drive and energy, a mechanical knack, a novel view of the market, and an ability to inspire others. Short of capital, and without formal education past high school, he quickly emerged as one of the city's leading automobile producers.

Hupp had been born in 1878 in Grand Rapids, Michigan, and attended high school in Detroit. Upon leaving school, he took a job on the railroad, "the easiest way to fame and fortune." Being inordinately ambitious, however, he soon quit and started several small businesses in turn, all of which failed. Casting about for a job with possibilities, he signed on in 1902 as a laborer in the Olds Motor Works, where he learned to unload coal from railroad cars, sweep floors, and tote heavy castings. He was soon promoted to the assembly department, where he stayed only long enough to be promoted to assistant in the engine testing room. He loved it, especially the opportunity it offered him to road test the company's products. He soon became a regular tester.[1]

Someone noticed the lad's knack for figures, and he was taken off the road and promoted to manager of the service department. When Olds moved his plant to Lansing, Michigan, in 1905, Hupp went along, but he was soon lured away by a job offer from a Chicago soda fountain manufacturer, a detour that distracted him for only nine months.[2]

When Hupp was at Olds, the master car builder was dedicated to manufacturing a low-priced, dependable, utilitarian car. Olds was a far-sighted businessman, quite out of step with his fellow auto makers, who sought to manufacture quality, hand-crafted cars for the well-to-do. His curved-dash runabout was lightweight and powered by a relatively simple one-cylinder, five-horsepower motor. In 1903, two men drove one from San Francisco to New York City, 4,225 miles, in only fifty-five running days, at an average speed of 2.41 miles per hour. The reliability and price of his vehicles made Olds the largest car maker from 1903 through 1905, when he rolled out between 4,000 and 6,500 of his "Merry Oldsmobiles" a year. Equally important, he taught the business to a younger generation of auto executives: Jonathan D. Maxwell, who soon manufactured his own car; Roy Chapin, who led Hudson through some of its best years; and Howard Coffin, who founded and presided over the Society of Automotive Engineers (SAE), which pushed for industry standardization, were all distinguished graduates of Olds's finishing school. In a move Hupp would later emulate, Olds left his company in 1905, to start the Reo Motor Car Company, while his former firm moved upscale in the auto market.[3]

Hupp quit the soda fountain business to take a job in Detroit as head of the repair, claims, and accessory departments at the recently organized Ford Motor Company. While there, he examined the firm's manufacturing practices, and he later claimed to have been involved in the final production planning for the Ford Model K, a big six-cylinder car that Ford brought out in 1905, which sold for a whopping $2,500. Hupp worked on the car with John Dodge, who years afterwards joined his brother to form their own auto company. The Model K was a flop, and Ford followed it the next year with his Model N, a much smaller four-cylinder car, which sold for only $500.[4]

Never shy about changing jobs in the fluid auto business, Hupp signed on with the Regal Motor Car Company, then only a year old, in 1908. Regal manufactured an underslung car with its frame below the axles, giving it a racy look and a lower center of gravity. Powered by a twenty-horsepower, four-cylinder engine, the Regal's car shared many similarities with Hupp's first effort. Regal turned out only fifty cars in 1907, but they were not very good, and the company exchanged them free for its new 1908 models—a total recall.[5]

In his half dozen years in the industry, Hupp became intimately acquainted with almost every process involved in car design, manufacture, and merchandising. And he had reached some definite conclusions about the car the country needed; like Henry Ford, he was convinced the future lay in the lower-priced end of the business. He wanted to manufacture a lightweight, sporty-looking four-cylinder runabout he could sell for well below $1,000 and still turn a tidy profit.

In 1908, Hupp left Regal to design and build a prototype of such a car, which he had completed by November 1. Roughly constructed, it embodied elements of Olds's curved-dash car, hints of Ford's Model T, which appeared the same year, and kinship with the Regal's stylishness. Hupp carefully designed his auto to sell in the lower-priced market. Most cars were what he called "30s," featuring about thirty horsepower, which sold in the medium price range, for between $1,000 and $1,500—less than the $1,719 that the average car commanded in 1909. They were fairly heavy, weighing about three-quarters of a ton, and expensive to manufacture. Hupp wanted to push down below Ford's Model T, priced at $850 in 1908, with a vehicle in the twenty-horsepower range that weighed no more than a half a ton, a car he dubbed the "20." The Dodge Brothers, who built Ford's engines, probably designed and built Hupp's first motors, which were remarkably similar to those the Dodges delivered to Ford.[6]

That fall, Hupp, an engineer friend of his named Emil A. Nelson, and others put the new car through its paces on Detroit's chilly streets. The city's auto show was scheduled for February 15–20, 1909, and they had to shake their new car down and construct a copy with much better fit and finish to impress buyers and potential dealers at the motor world's extravaganza.

Robert Hupp and his friends all pitched in to build the show car in an unheated shed, working nights as winter descended on the city and cold blasts of wind and snow ripped through the shack's cracks. They completed their demonstration model the night before the show opened. The second Hupp, a sporty Model 20 runabout, was the talk of the show. It was not underslung, but Hupp achieved the same jaunty effect by dropping the center of the front axle to give the little two-seater a rakish downward tilt, and it was painted bright red to contrast with its black leather upholstery.[7]

Throughout the shakedown process, Hupp frantically sought money to put the car into production. On November 8, 1908, he incorporated the Hupp Motor Car Company, a shoestring venture that paled even in comparison with other infant auto companies. The firm's capitalization was only $25,000, and very little of that was in its till. Olds had begun with $200,000, to which he contributed a munificent $400. Jonathan Maxwell, who teamed up with Benjamin and Frank Briscoe to manufacture the Maxwell-Briscoe, raised $100,000 to get started. Hugh Chalmers was positively wealthy by comparison after he inveigled $900,000 from J. L. Hudson, owner of the famous Detroit department store, to build a car named for the retailer. Even Ford, with his checkered corporate past, pulled together $30,000 and gave the Dodge brothers a percentage of the company to provide him with chassis, engines, and transmissions. Hupp probably paid for his initial shares in kind with his prototype and labor.[8]

The infant company attracted talented men with diverse skills, overlapping relationships, and a driving enthusiasm that enabled the firm to overcome its lack of liquid assets. The brothers J. Walter and Joseph R. Drake teamed up with John E. Baker to raise the $3,500 needed to finance the first two Hupps. None of the founders was wealthy or well-connected, however. The Drakes were the sons of immigrants; J. Walter, Hupp's president until 1914 and again in 1939, had been born in 1875 in Sturgis, Michigan. Like Hupp, his parents migrated to Detroit, where Drake graduated from public schools and the Detroit College of Law. When he invested in Hupp's dream, he had "a solid though not spectacular [law] practice" in his hometown.[9]

During the Spanish-American War, Drake had served aboard the USS *Yosemite* with Edwin Denby, grandson of a U.S. senator and son of a U.S. ambassador to China. Edwin Denby was born in Evansville, Indiana, in 1870. After graduating from the University of Michigan Law School, he moved to Detroit, where he opened a law practice in 1896. After the war, he served three terms in Congress from 1905 through 1911. In 1908, Congressman Denby joined his former shipmate and invested $7,500 in real money in Hupp's project, although he never became active in its affairs. His career was intertwined with Drake's, however, and both were ardent Republicans. President Warren Harding appointed Denby secretary of the Navy in 1921, and Denby later persuaded President Herbert Hoover to appoint J. Walter Drake as

Several Hupp Motor Car Company founders welcomed Hanlon, Drake, and Jones home outside Windsor, Ontario, on January 24, 1912. From the right: unknown, J. Walter Drake, George Drake, John E. Baker, Joseph Drake, unknown, Hanlon, Jones, unknown wearing two hats, and two more unknowns. HPA/DJC.

chairman of the U.S. delegation at the Second Pan-American Congress of Highways to promote road construction in Latin America.[10]

Another early investor, Charles D. Hastings, provided Hupp with its biggest cash infusion, $8,500. Born in 1859 in Hillsdale, Michigan, he worked for several car companies before he joined Olds, where he met Robert Hupp. Hastings left Olds for the Thomas-Detroit Automobile Company and soon afterwards joined Hupp, a firm with no capital, one car, no factory, and no orders. Although Hastings endured the long, cold nights in the shed, his principal talents were not mechanical; he contributed a badly needed nest egg and exceptional merchandising abilities. Older than his partners, he knew the business well, was a friendly outgoing soul, exuded a surfeit of energy, and served as Hupmobile's president from 1914 through 1926. He remained connected with the firm until its demise in 1941.[11]

Robert Hupp was never president of the company that bore his name. As valuable as his technical talents were, those who provided the capital ran the show. J. Walter Drake was president and legal counsel, while Hupp was named vice president and general manager. John Baker was selected to oversee the firm's anemic finances, and Joseph R. Drake became its secretary. Hastings was appointed assistant general manager for sales, and Nelson became Hupp's first chief engineer. It was a talented group that lacked only the wherewithal to convert its dreams into reality.[12]

Hastings raised badly needed funds at the Detroit auto show. The perky Hupp drew rapt attention, and Hastings, who already knew many dealers, glad-handed them all on the exhibition floor. He also chatted up any prospective purchaser who ventured into his orbit. Even Henry Ford wandered over to examine the new Hupp; he later told a friend, "I recall looking at Bobby Hupp's roadster at the first show where it was exhibited and wondering whether we could ever build as good a car for as little money." This from the man whose Model T revolutionized the auto industry, put the nation on wheels, and brought him one of the largest personal fortunes in the world.[13]

Others at the show agreed with Ford. Promoting an automobile that had not been thoroughly tested or put into production, Hastings sold 500 of them in five days. More important, he collected a $50 deposit from each purchaser and dealer that brought 25,000 precious dollars into the company's coffers. All Hupp had to do was build the cars on time.[14]

Like other fledgling auto manufacturers, the Hupp Company extracted the maximum leverage from its scanty assets. With the $25,000, it rented a small factory at

345 Bellevue Avenue in Detroit and contracted with suppliers to provide parts on credit. The company pushed much of its risk off on its suppliers; they got paid only after Hupp assembled, delivered, and collected the buyers' money. The parts companies did not hazard much, however, for Hupp planned to manufacture only 500 cars in 1909.[15]

The new plant was in production two weeks after the Detroit auto show closed. The company kept the first Hupp built there, named it "Little Pal," and used it for errands; it was one of the three cars to make the winter run to the New York auto show. On March 1, 1909, the factory shipped its first production model, and by mid-August, it had delivered the promised 500. Despite his haste to build cars to collect the desperately needed $750 on each to pay his suppliers and overhead expenses,

The 1909 Hupmobile, on the right, with the Little Corporal outside the Hupmobile factory in 1930. The company claimed the 1909 model was the Detroit Police Department's first car. HPA/DJC

Money Could Not Make Its Power Plant More Perfect

The Hupmobile dealer who also sells some other car of the highest reputation and price, can, with perfect consistency, lift the hoods of both and say to you:

"Compare the two power plants."

Of the power plant in the larger, costlier car, he can say with perfect truth: "This engine is no better and no more efficient than the engine of the Hupmobile."

He can go further than that. He can compare the two plants by progressive steps in the matter of: (a) design; (b) steels and other materials; (c) fineness of measurements; (d) power developed; (e) silence; (f) simplicity; (g) quality of service.

And he is able to say without overstating the case a particle:

"For its purpose and for its type, the Hupmobile power plant is not surpassed by the other.

"It cost, in proportion, just as much to produce.

"It enlisted the same high degree of engineering skill.

"It engaged manufacturing methods just as fine; and careful; and conservative.

"It incorporates the same high grade of material.

"It will render within reason precisely the same quality of service in the proportion of power produced; the quick and easy development of that power; in the matter of speed; in flexibility; in smoothness; and in all-around efficiency on the straight-away or on the grade."

In short, he is justified in saying to you that the Hupmobile is the first car of its type and size made with exactly the same sincerity of purpose (in method and material) as the leaders among cars of the larger class.

The man who owns the two types—the Hupmobile and the heavier, costlier car—will corroborate this estimate to the letter.

Do you wonder that the Hupmobile demand is so widespread and insistent that the facilities of the great new Hupmobile plant are taxed to the uttermost?

Have a demonstration of the car and write for the literature.

Leaving Detroit December 27, 1909—just after the Christmas blizzard and the heaviest snowfall of the winter—three Hupmobiles negotiated the thousand miles between Detroit and New York City by Jan. 6. Over every mile of it was a battle with the snow; and the termination of the trip—with every car fit and ready to turn back at once for Detroit—marked the successful completion of the severest task ever imposed on a car of Hupmobile size and type.

HUPP MOTOR CAR COMPANY   Dept. X, DETROIT, MICHIGAN

Licensed Under Selden Patent

4 cylinders
20 H. P.
Sliding Gears
Bosch Magneto

$750

(F.O.B. Detroit)
Including three oil lamps,
horn and tools.

Hupmobile

Please mention The Automobile when writing to Advertisers

This advertisement in *The Automobile* (n.d.) for the sporty little 1910 Model 20 Runabout emphasized its quality construction, low price, and outstanding driving characteristics.

Robert Hupp still found time to improve his runabout. He altered its rear suspension to add more lateral stability, switched the upholstery from tufted to plain buffed black leather, and moved the horn so that its bell faced forward rather than toward the ground. The few alterations reflected the care Hupp and Nelson had taken with the auto's initial design.[16]

Caught on a financial treadmill, the company had to produce more cars to keep abreast of its constant borrowing. As soon as the last 1909 model was pushed out the door, the factory started manufacturing 1910 models, all runabouts, all Model 20s. The new cars were outwardly similar to their predecessors, but Nelson and Hupp increased their comfort, durability, and handling. Seats were wider and higher; the exterior gas tank was oval, rather than square; the radiator was enlarged for better cooling and its filler neck was extended to create a distinctive Hupp styling feature. Their most important change was to use a new multiple-disk clutch to replace the earlier cone model. The 1910 Hupps also featured better-braced running boards, an I-beam front axle instead of a tubular one, and an adjustable drip-oiler on the engine. The Model 20s were all painted red with black accents.[17]

The cars sold quickly. On November 15, 1909, nine months after Hastings pocketed his first deposits, the company celebrated the production of its 1,000th Hupp. Orders poured in so rapidly that the firm's small factory could not handle them. Hupp built, "to his own specifications," a new plant on Jefferson and Concord avenues, described as a "handsome, day-lighted factory, with every modern equipment of machinery for the special requirements of the Hupmobile." The new facility had 50,000 square feet of floor space, and by December 1909, production there had begun.[18]

Hupp was one of the earliest manufacturers to recognize the relationship between working conditions and productivity. Five months after he opened his new plant, he told a reporter that he was "a stickler for plenty of light and cleanliness," which, along with "an orderly arrangement of tools keep the men in better spirits at their work and . . . added [to their] efficiency." When asked about his theories "of handling men," Hupp was just as opinionated. His guiding principle was, he said, "to get them to handle themselves." That was not a difficult proposition, he quickly added. "I believe in giving a man the responsibility of his particular task and let him work it out his own way [and] as long as he gets results don't interfere with him."[19]

His theories worked; the underfunded firm turned out about 20 cars a day, and in 1909, it manufactured 1,618 automobiles, enough to rank Hupp the twelfth car

Hupp's second factory, located at Jefferson and Concord streets in Detroit, was a major investment for a corporation only slightly more than a year old. *Hupmobile Instruction Book, 1910.*

maker in the nation, just behind Oldsmobile, which built only about eighty more. Henry Ford rolled out 17,771 Model Ts in 1909, an impressive output before the innovation of the moving assembly line, winning Ford first place. All car makers at that time brought their parts together on one large production floor, where crews assembled them into cars; the assemblers moved, the cars remained stationary.[20]

Robert Hupp vowed that he would produce 5,000 cars in 1910, and he exceeded his prediction by 340 units, a 303 percent increase for the year, good enough for tenth place in the manufacturers' sweepstakes. Ford's 55 percent production increase enabled him to slip past Buick by 1,500 units, and not for seventeen years would any company challenge him for the top position. In 1911, his Model T eclipsed its nearest competitor by a three-to-one margin; he had, in fact, captured Hupp's market.[21]

At the end of the automotive century's first decade, Ford and other manufacturers recognized that the car business was seasonal and cyclical; car sales slumped in cold and inclement weather. Robert Hupp noted in January 1911 that the coming year ought to be great for his company, because auto producers had "retrenched" the preceding fall and had not increased production for "the spring business," creating a pent-up demand. His approach to the industry's seasonal nature was to keep his factory operating year round and push overseas sales. He proudly informed Detroit's newspapers that although his company had "had practically no foreign business a year ago," his officers had actively solicited such trade, and "we have recently become obligated to ship a total of about one thousand cars into foreign countries." That was a significant number: "about one-fifth of [our] total output for the next eight months."[22]

Other auto companies were also active in motordom's version of "dollar diplomacy." Newspapers and automotive trade publications were full of stories predicting that American motorcars would soon dominate the world's markets. In late 1910, James Couzens, Ford's secretary, had already been overseas twice seeking markets, examining foreign cars and their production methods. "America is educating the world to the automobile," he said. As proof, Couzens noted that Ford exported to places as diverse as Sardinia, Turkey, Tasmania, Uruguay, and Cuba.[23]

Smaller firms were just as enthusiastic over foreign markets' prospects. The Mitchell-Lewis Motor Company in Racine created a separate export department, whose director believed American dominance of overseas sales was clearly written in the numbers. He estimated domestic demand at 150,000 cars in 1911 and predicted that only U.S. companies had enough capacity to produce that many; English and French manufacturers, he pointed out, built only 300 to 1,000 autos per year. American factories, he forecast, would soak up the rest of the world's demand for 30,000 automobiles.[24]

George Keller, sales manager for the E.M.F. automobile company, took the broader view to reach the same conclusion. Auto shows, he thought, demonstrated that American cars were equal or superior to European ones. "America was a little slow in getting started," he admitted, but "it did not take long for the American designer to catch up with and pass his foreign competitor." This dominant position was owing to the United States's "new industrial captains, great engineers, skilled workmen and the finest of machinery," which had conceived and built "the almost perfect car of today."[25]

General Motors, which despite William Crapo Durant's financial difficulties in 1910, did everything in a big way, organized a separate entity, the General Motors Export Company, to ensure that foreign purchasers enjoyed the same sales and service as domestic buyers. Preliminary statistics for the United States's trade with its new colonies in 1910 supported the car makers' optimism. Hawaiians spent $750,000 on American automobiles, Puerto Ricans about $300,000, and Filipinos $330,000, which may explain why Hupp chose to demonstrate its car in two out of three of the new U.S. island possessions.[26]

Robert Hupp read such predictions and, imbued with the industry's prevailing sense of business imperialism, laid his own plans. He admired the Thomas Flyer's win in a 1908 around-the-world race and envied the shower of publicity the company had enjoyed as a result. Hupp's son recalled that his father had come home one evening shortly afterwards and, while discussing the race, suddenly said, "I believe we'll send a Hupmobile around the world."[27]

THE SEND-OFF

2

As Joseph Drake released the clutch and set out on November 3, 1910 to circumnavigate the world in a Hupmobile, he continued the company's tradition of endurance stunts, staged to demonstrate its autos' reliability and to attract publicity. The Hupp Motor Car Company was not yet two years old and had produced fewer than 7,000 cars, 1,618 of its 1909 model, 5,340 1910s, and a handful of 1911s, the Little Corporal's siblings. Before it dispatched its 1911 Model 20 to conquer the globe, however, the company had already tested its cars on less arduous endurance runs.[1]

Hupp sponsored cars in the Glidden and Munsey tours, well-organized reliability runs, some almost endurance feats, with different itineraries each year, dedicated to demonstrating the feasibility of long-distance travel by car. The company garnered even more publicity when it sent three Hupps from Detroit to New York City in midwinter for exhibit in the Grand Central Palace Automobile Show in early January 1910, a stunt that served as a warm-up for its globe-circling expedition ten months later. Both trips involved severe weather and tested the limits of cars and men alike. The drivers used standard Hupp production models, had photographers on board, and earned the company accolades in newspapers across the country.[2]

News accounts of the winter journey intrigued the reading public. The three cars included the 1909 Model A called the "Little Pal," probably the third Hupmobile built, and two 1910 Model 20 roadsters, which were privately owned and, the company claimed, "had seen a full season's hard service." Four men endured the entire trip, including Joseph R. Drake, Hupp's secretary, who within the year would set out to circumnavigate the globe; John Baker, a company official; Fred Harvey, the firm's purchasing agent; and R. W. Keefe, Hupp's Michigan sales agent. Two other men left Detroit with them, but one dropped out at Niagara Falls to rush ahead to greet the Hupps at the car show, and another, half frozen, switched to a train in Utica, New York.[3]

The weather in the Midwest was abominable over Christmas 1909. Snow fell for two days starting Christmas Eve, and when it stopped, some trains were running six to twelve hours late and scores of others were trapped in huge snowdrifts. A cold front followed across the region, making everyone miserable. Nevertheless, with the thermometer hovering near zero and predicted to fall, the six intrepid Hupp adventurers motored out of Windsor, just across the river from Detroit, a few minutes before 9:00 P.M. on December 27. They were equipped with shovels and tire chains, and they drove and shoveled all night. None of them was familiar with the roads, and with drifting snow covering prominent landmarks, they frequently became lost. They straggled into Blenheim, Ontario, only seventy-two miles from Windsor, at dawn, where they roused the proprietor of the town's only hotel, who gave them beds for an hour and a half nap, fed them breakfast, and sent them on their way. Although the day was clear, "the wind drove the snow merrily and bitingly" as they fairly sped to London, Ontario, where they arrived at nightfall. Lighting their gas lamps, they drove into Thamesford, where they ate before continuing a few more miles up the road to Ingersoll. There, exhausted, they stopped for the night.

They "enjoyed" their best single day's run the following day. The Little Pal left at eleven in the morning, and the driver sighted Niagara Falls by 8:30 that evening. The other two cars left at the same time, promptly got lost, and took three additional hours to reach the Falls. They found one stretch on the day's run where the wind had blown the snow off the frozen road and all three cars raced along at 45 miles per hour. Without windshields, it must have been a bracing dash.[4]

Leaving Niagara Falls the next morning, with the mercury registering zero, they crossed the Niagara River into New York State and drove through Buffalo to Batavia, where they encountered deep snowdrifts. Having skipped lunch, they ate supper in Batavia, where the locals averred that the road to Rochester was in pretty good shape, saying that they had heard sleighs "drag on the ground" over parts of it. The locals, however, "evidently had the good old summer-time in mind." Encountering three-foot snow drifts blocking their way, the automobilists turned around and returned to Batavia; their comments to the locals who had recommended they drive on are not recorded.[5]

They manfully struggled to wrest their cars across the upstate New York snow belt but fell short of making Syracuse the next night; the Hupps chugged into Auburn long after dark on New Year's Eve. They celebrated the holiday by floundering on toward Utica, one of the toughest days on their trip. The snow was four feet deep in places, and one of the cars slid into a ditch, where it tilted at a thirty-degree angle. "The wind cut viciously," and the snow became "deep and heavy." Darkness fell; they had not eaten and were bone-tired. They found a farmer fourteen miles west of Utica who put their cars in his barn and took the freezing men in for the night.[6]

They arrived at Utica near noon the following day, fueled and oiled their cars, and pushed on to Amsterdam, where they spent the night. On January 3, the exhausted travelers dug and pushed their way to Albany. After crossing the Hudson River, they arrived in Kinderhook at nightfall. The next day, they drove to Wappingers Falls, where their luck worsened. Rain turned to sleet, coating the roads with a glare of ice; all three cars kept sliding off them. The four remaining crewmen hoped to make New York City by nightfall, but at dusk they were still miles away; they decided to drive all night. The "bedraggled, forlorn party . . . sped" into town at 7:00 A.M. on January 6, 1910, after having spent ten miserably cold days on the road. The company advertised that although the men were "utterly fagged," their cars "were fine and fit. Their motors ran as smoothly and sweetly and silently as when the start was made." It assured the public that "there was not a rattle or grind or a groan from the mechanism of any of the three," and that they "stood ready to be headed back over the same snowbound route to Detroit." The drivers, "muffled in heavy overcoats, sweaters, fur gloves, and mittens, and . . . hoods and leggings," were not, however. "Arctic exploration could have no terrors for them after their trip through snow covered roads and the ice covered slippery highways," a reporter recorded them saying. The trip was so grueling that the cars averaged only eight to nine miles per gallon, rather than their usual twenty-eight to thirty.[7]

The Hupps were a hit at the New York auto show, which attracted 1,200 dealers to appraise and choose among the latest offerings. The wintry expedition's public acclaim emboldened Hupp to consider an endurance test to top that of any other motorcar manufacturer: sponsor a trip around the world that would dominate press coverage of the auto world, prove its cars' worthiness beyond all doubt, and increase its overseas sales. By early fall 1910, Hupp managers were well along with their planning, but when they made their public announcement on October 6, 1910, many of the trip's details had not been fully worked out. They had chosen the crew: Joseph R. Drake; Thomas Hanlon, a company mechanic and experienced driver; and Will B. Wreford, "formerly a prominent newspaper man connected with the Detroit *Free Press* and at present identified with the automobile industry." The company even distributed a formal photograph of the three men to the newspapers. Their proposed itinerary was generally the one they followed, except for the Cape-to-Cairo segment. The company said that the three men would take only "light baggage," defined as "a few extra parts and such implements and tack as will be needed by the conditions of the road and climate." Hupp's managers calculated, however, that the "light baggage" would be "more than equivalent to the weight of a fourth passenger."[8]

Drake, and probably Baker, who had driven in the earlier trek to New York City, wrote in advance to officials in towns across the United States through which the Hupp was scheduled to pass. Accordingly, they announced, they anticipated that their expedition would "receive an enthusiastic welcome on its trip to the [West] coast." They also contacted the State Department, which promised "official encouragement in the furtherance of American trade in foreign countries." Hupp already had a general European agent, who, even before the trip started, was making "arrangements for receptions of the Hupmobile party in several of the prominent cities of Europe."[9]

Hupp was not shy about admitting its financial expectations from the journey. "The purpose of the tour is to stimulate the interest which has already been created in foreign countries by Hupmobile," the firm told the press. It already had distributors in Manila and Australia and was anxious to open other agencies. To attract new dealers, it noted, "demonstrations of the car will be given in the different cities and where it seems advisable the party may stay for two or three weeks at a time." With so much to do, the world travelers would be kept busy, and "we hardly expect to see them back inside of a year," the firm declared.[10]

Hupp hoped to get the three men on the road by November 1, 1910, and had less than a month to make the final arrangements. At the last minute, moreover, Wreford backed out because his grandfather was ill, and Thomas O. Jones, another *Free Press* reporter, was substituted for him.

Jones and Hanlon first went to New York City to confer with American Automobile Association officials about traveling conditions in remote regions such as the American West and procure road maps. The AAA was of little help, however—it evidently lacked maps even for many parts of the United States. The "scope" of the AAA's touring departments, it was reported with some irony, would, in fact, "be made much more extensive by the reports of the Hupmobile party, for all data in regard to routes and road conditions will be placed at their disposal by the Hupp Motor Car Company upon the party's return."[11]

A dozen or more cars had already driven coast-to-coast, and it is hard to understand why the three men could not find at least sketchy maps detailing feasible routes. Perhaps their planning was too hasty. The Hupp planners announced that they were sending their car over the most direct route to the Pacific and would rely upon Hanlon's driving experience in choosing the roads and trails. The day before the party left Detroit, Hupp reported that its car was in a "race with the snow," because the three men planned to take "the northern route across the continent." To increase their odds of beating the anticipated heavy western snows, the company cut out a few days scheduled for Chicago, which became just another overnight stop. If the rains held off, the automobilists believed, they would find "fair road conditions as far as Omaha," but west of there, they averred, "no one is willing to venture a prediction as to what will be encountered." In other words, like earlier transcontinental drivers, the men planned to follow the Union Pacific Railroad's route as much as possible.[12]

The trip's planners had even less of an idea of what the three would find in remoter parts of the world. For perhaps weeks at a time, the car and its crew would be out of touch—and out of the public eye. They therefore planned to milk the maximum publicity from the tour's start and organized a gala send-off spectacle to celebrate Hupp, the crew, the car, the company's dealers, and the glories of Detroit's and America's latest automotive technology.

Public attention had been drawn to Detroit the day before the scheduled Hupp start when George Miller, a crewman on the Thomas Flyer that had won the 1908 race from New York to Paris, and who had driven from New York to Seattle in 1909, visited Detroit on a cross-country stunt of his own. Driving a new Thomas Flyer from which all the gears in the gearbox except high had been removed, he was tout-ing the car's pulling power by challenging all kinds of rugged terrain. Miller told Detroit newspapermen, "Mr. Thomas told me when I found anything we couldn't negotiate in high gear to come home at once." He had driven 1,800 miles across the East and found nothing that could stop him, and he was off to Chicago the next day to join the Chicago Auto Club's 1,000-mile reliability run. Some of the Thomas Company's cars were three times bigger than the little Hupp, but despite Thomas's racing reputation, its sales had fallen drastically in 1910. Miller's feat with his one-gear car was an attempt to resuscitate the firm. His demonstration was praiseworthy enough, however, to bring out Detroit's Mayor Philip T. Breitmeyer to officially welcome him to the "Motor City," even though Flyers were made in rival Buffalo, New York.[13]

Miller had left Detroit before Hupp held its gala dinner on November 2, 1910, at the Pontchartrain Hotel on Cadillac Square. Hupp executives, forty-two Hupmobile dealers from Indiana, Illinois, and Wisconsin, and the world tourers crowded into the spacious dining room. They ingested a huge meal, drank uncounted toasts, and enjoyed several vaudeville acts from local theaters, after which, the *Free Press* observed, "the Chicago party was ready to quit and get to bed."[14]

Dealers brought to Detroit as the local Hupmobile agent's guests were exhausted even before the party. Early that morning, they had been escorted through the Hupp plant and factories that supplied Hupp's parts. After a lunch at the Lighthouse Inn, they motored over to East Grand Boulevard, where they spent the afternoon inspecting the Packard factory before returning to their hotel for the dinner.[15]

Luckily, the Hupp expedition was not scheduled to leave at dawn the next day; as it was, it missed its advertised noon departure by almost three hours. The dealers drove out to the Hupp plant and escorted the Little Corporal's crew back to the Pontchartrain, where they sat down to a long, hearty lunch. While the anxious adventurers and their escort were eating, a crowd began to swell in the square, despite the overcast 44° F day freshened by a stiff fifteen mile-an-hour wind that drove the wind chill into the thirties. The day was a harbinger of worsening weather that brought Detroit its first snowfall of the year just forty-eight hours after the Hupp expedition's departure.[16]

One hundred hardy Hupmobile owners brought their cars out to join a parade to accompany the little Hupp to the Detroit city limits. Well before the car was ready to leave, some in the "expectant crowd," fleeing the chilly temperatures, "thronged the lobbies of the hotel," while others "lined the sidewalks and parkways of Cadillac Square." When company dignitaries had finished their lunch, they joined the well-

wishers, most of whom were bundled up in woolen overcoats and wore their derbies at rakish tilts apropos of the departure's festive nature. The three explorers were reportedly at "the center of an admiring group" and "kept busy answering questions, many of which were really unanswerable."

At 2:30 P.M., Hanlon, Jones, and Drake climbed into their Hupmobile and the mayor "wormed his way through the crowd" to shake their hands. "He spoke cheeringly to each occupant of the car, and wishing them a warm goodby [sic], sped them on their long jaunt with his message to the mayor of San Francisco." At the ceremony's climax, he presented them with a silk American flag, saying it symbolized "the honor of Detroit's foremost industry." He trusted they would return it safely to Detroit, "to the credit of themselves and the staunch little car which was to represent the city on this trip."[17]

Hanlon labeled this photo "Waiting for the word." A Hupp Torpedo is parked directly behind the Little Corporal. HPA/DJC.

Detroit's Mayor Philip T. Breitmeyer presenting the Hupmobilists with the silk American flag that accompanied them around the world. Drake and Hanlon look anxious to get on the road; Jones peers around from the back seat. HPA/DJC.

For another quarter of an hour, photographers snapped pictures of the cars and the crowd from every possible angle. Most show Drake and Hanlon in the front of the car, smiling broadly; Jones is hunched up in the rear next to the baggage, evidently still feeling the effects of the previous evening. Years later, Hanlon captioned one of the photos he pasted into his scrapbook, "the smiles that came off." All three men were warmly clad in three-quarter-length wool coats, leather boots, long driving gauntlets, and wool hats with earflaps tied across the top. Hanlon's wife and son are in none of the photographs, which show only one woman standing near the car.[18]

At exactly 2:45 P.M. on Thursday, November 3, 1910, "a cheer arose as the car started, surrounded by the smoke from other cars, the crowd pressing in on all sides with policemen trying to keep a clear field." "A young woman rushed forward and extended her hand, which was grasped fondly, pressed slightly, and she heard a lingering farewell." Drake released the clutch, and the Hupmobile was off. Behind it, dealers followed in thirty-two other Hupps. The *Free Press* reporter noted that the dealers would put between 350 and 1,000 miles on their Hupmobiles coming to the send-off and returning home. The most distant Hupp dealer hailed from Rice Lane, Wisconsin, a bone-chilling 760 miles from Chicago. The parade also included another 100 enthusiastic Hupp owners strung out in the farewell procession behind the Little Corporal. "There will be a place in the line for every Hupmobile owner who can spare the time," the morning paper had promised. The local Hupps stopped at the city limits, but the dealers traveled with the Hupp expedition to Chicago.[19] At the Detroit city limits, the cars stopped so that local photographers could take some final pictures. In front of A. G. Grzezinski's real estate office, the Little Corporal was whipped by a stiff wind and its American flag stood straight out in front of the car. Behind it, Hupps were lined up in single file, a coupe the last one in sight; no other vehicular traffic is to be seen on the street save a distant streetcar. In another photograph, a closer view of the three men, they all have looks of grim determination. The departure pictures reflect a bleakness and loneliness that presaged many of their future experiences.

The Little Corporal and its entourage of forty-seven Hupmobiles reached their first stop, Ypsilanti, Michigan, in exactly one hour and twenty-five minutes. That was a far as they went on day one. They drove straight along the old Sauk Trail, trodden for centuries by Native Americans, to get there and reported that although they traveled over "some sandy stretches of road," most of it was "better than expected" and their car made "fair speed." A local Ypsilanti newsman observed that the car's "time [was] better than that of the trolley" between Ypsilanti and Detroit. The town hosted a fête for its visitors—"the biggest event that has taken place here in some time"—in which the Little Corporal "attracted great attention." The entire entourage attended a dinner that evening. Afterwards, "some pushed on to Clinton" (along what is now Route 12), where they intended to spend the night. The Little Corporal's crew and many others, however, decided to call it a day rather than driving in the dark. They promised their hosts that they would start "bright and early" the following morning, "with the world-tourer in the lead."[20]

The crew set out early to rendezvous with the rest of its party in Clinton the next day. The night drivers, however, had passed through Clinton and stopped instead in Adrian, where, a reporter announced, "102 per cent of Adrian's population viewed and admired the latest Hupp product." Drake and his colleagues arrived there about 10:30 A.M., and the reunited caravan headed south, "cheered by as large a crowd as

On a cold, windy, overcast day, a parade of Hupps saw the three men off at Detroit's outskirts. HPA/DJC.

started the party from the Pontchartrain Thursday." The hardy band stopped for a few moments in the small towns dotting the road, Wauseon, Bryan, and Hicksville, Ohio, where "photographers and citizens were out in force." Later, in Indiana, "a party of Fort Wayne enthusiasts" met the cavalcade and escorted the visitors into their city.[21] After enjoying civic festivities and supper that night, the party awoke in the morning to find that it had snowed and was "bitterly cold." Soon after they left Fort Wayne, rain and sleet began falling, producing icy conditions that were responsible for the trip's only accident: a "bad spot in the road" caused the column to stop, and three of the trailing cars collided, "marring their new beauty but causing only damage that can easily be repaired." Headed roughly along today's Route 33, they all stopped at Ligonier and Goshen, where the "cars were given great receptions." Photographers met them everywhere, and a local newspaper proclaimed that "the world touring is attracting no end of attention. Everyone wants to see the machine that is going to make the long trip."[22]

Some of the accompanying Hupps began to leave the procession. A few were delivered to Hupp dealers along the way, and others dropped out as they neared their homes. When the tourers reached Goshen, the local *Daily Democrat* recorded only twenty-six Hupps still in the parade, including the coupe, which garnered a great deal of attention. Enclosed cars were still a novelty, and a Goshen reporter declared it "the first [such] car in history to undertake a test of this kind." The party "took dinner" and then set out for Chicago.[23]

From Goshen, the caravan headed for South Bend, where everyone made another "long stop"—probably more to warm themselves than for the publicity's sake—before heading on to La Porte, Indiana. Arriving in that city of 13,000 at dusk, cold, wet, tired, and hungry, the travelers were informed that between them and Chicago lay a stretch of seven and a half miles of "half-built road." Moreover, after eating, they would have to make the rest of their run to Chicago in the dark, and knowing that "many of the cars are not fitted with headlights," the Little Corporal's crew wisely decided to overnight in La Porte.[24]

On Sunday, November 6, the remaining Hupp celebrants were on the road soon after breakfast, and they crossed Chicago's city limits at noon. Press accounts describe "gaily dressed Chicagoans" who "paused to admire as the cavalcade passed down Grand Boulevard." Reporters were as fascinated by the coupe as they were by the world tourer, noting that "seldom is a heavy closed car allowed to start on such a trip." Chicago marked the end of the official factory-sponsored festivities. The Hupmobilers were already behind schedule. They spent only one night in the Windy City, because they wanted to join the Chicago Automobile Club's 1,000-mile endurance run the next morning and drive with it as far as the Iowa border. From there, they would strike out alone.[25]

The Hupp Company milked every last ounce of publicity from the send-off, parading the round-the-world tourer and its crew before the public and testing the endurance of almost half a hundred other Hupps on the four-day jaunt from Detroit to Chicago. The company's products, even on that short run, were severely tried by bad roads, worse weather, and long hours of operation. To ensure that all the vehicles finished the trial, Hupp sent along an "emergency car" with spare parts and trained mechanics, who, the newspapers announced, "had little work to do." West of Chicago, there would be fewer festivities and more inclement weather, because it was getting late in the transcontinental "season." The Hupmobilists' biggest tests lay just ahead, starting the next day.[26]

THE PREDECESSORS

3

In 1933, the Hupp Company entered a float in Chicago's "A Century of Progress" World's Fair that featured the little 1911 Hupp with Thomas Hanlon seated at its wheel. Surrounded by celebrants bizarrely garbed in American Indian headdresses, Middle Eastern robes, turbans, and African skirts, on the float were signs that proclaimed: "Savages from Darkest Africa, 26th Street"; "Morocco Imperial Government (Exhibit) Julia Taweel and Moroccan Orchestra"; and "Hupmobile Long Life And Dependability Built In Every Car Then And Since. 25 Years Of Glorious Achievement." Atop the float, an enormous disk with a world map painted on it inaccurately showed the route the three men in a Hupp had followed from 1910 to 1912. Lest anyone miss the point, the company had hung a fabric display over the disk proclaiming: "Hupmobile First Car Around the World." On the float's side, another sign read, "The Same Car, The Same Driver, Both Going Strong."[1]

Hanlon might still have been going strong (although there was a good deal more of him than there had been twenty-three years earlier), but the car would have been hard put to complete the parade route on its own. At the time of the parade, Hupp was in perilous financial straits, and the company would exit the automobile business eight years later. And, contrary to its claim, its car was *not* the first to circle the globe, although it may have been the second. An American had already driven around the world before Hanlon, Drake, and Jones left Chicago's cheering crowds behind them. They did drive their Hupp farther, and visited more countries and colonies, than anyone else had done before, and theirs was the first corporate-sponsored global expedition by car. They could also boast that they had accomplished the feat in the smallest vehicle. Long-distance drivers usually preferred the luxury, safety, power, and carrying capacity of bigger cars, which had great advantages in pulling power, speed, road holding, and gasoline and oil capacities but were frequently too heavy for flimsy bridges and hard to extricate from the mud, potholes, and deep ditches that bedeviled drivers everywhere in that era.

Many of the earliest automobile endurance feats were every bit as daring as encircling the planet. In 1900, the Automobile Club of Great Britain and Ireland sponsored a 1,000-mile trial that "took in most of the major cities in England and Scotland" and attracted sixty-five entries, most of which completed it. When Alexander Winton drove one of his cars from his factory in Cleveland, Ohio, 800 miles to New York City in 1897 in only 78 hours and 43 minutes of running time, Americans gasped at both the distance and his daring. Four years later, Dr. H. Nelson Jackson and Sewall K. Crocker pushed, shoveled, towed, and drove their Winton from San Francisco to New York in an amazing 63 days. Right behind them were Tom Fetch, a Packard employee, and Marius C. Krarup, a reporter, who drove a Packard, "Old Pacific," over a different route in only 52 running days.[2]

Motoring across vast areas of the globe became infectious; in 1907, the Paris newspaper *Le Matin* put up a purse for a two-continent race from Peking to Paris. The competition drew twenty-five entries, of which only five started: a huge 40-horsepower Itala; a 15-horsepower Dutch-made Spyker; two 10-horsepower French-built De Dion–Boutons; and a 6-horsepower French Contal tricycle. The race also bestowed on the world one of the finest pieces of early automotive literature, *Pekin to Paris: An Account of Prince Borghese's Journey Across Two Continents in a Motor-Car*, written by Luigi Barzini, an Italian journalist who had traveled in the Itala. Barzini had a fine eye for detail, cultures, geography, personalities, and things mechanical. His book sold hundreds of thousands of copies in its original edition and was reprinted as late as 1973.[3] The race, like the Hupp's expedition, was replete with an unusual cast of characters, at least on the winning Itala. Prince Scipione Borghese hailed from an Italian noble family that counted Pope Paul V (1605–21) and

Chinese laborers pull
Prince Borghese's partially
disassembled Itala along a
deeply rutted road across
the mountains west of
Peking. From Luigi
Barzini, *Pekin to Paris*
(London, 1907).

Napoleon's sister (by marriage) among its relatives, but that had lost much of its fortune. Cool and aloof, the prince was a born adventurer, endowed with an uncomplaining personality and an iron constitution. Ettore Guizzardi, the third man in the Italian entry, was a talented tinkerer who was monomaniacal about maintaining the car. More than once, Barzini found him lying under it memorizing every screw, nut, bolt, spring, and lever.

The cars left Peking on June 10, 1907, and west of China's capital, the crews had to hire locals to pull their vehicles by hand over the mountain tracks. It was backbreaking labor that consumed weeks. Once free of the hills, however, the crews found themselves in the trackless wastes of Mongolia's Gobi Desert. Barzini told of coming to a telegraph outpost at Pong-kiong where he wished to send a dispatch to his newspaper. He handed it to the telegrapher, who after much consultation with his manuals, wrote on the form "#1." It was the first ever sent from the office, which had been open for six years. The Itala crossed the Gobi Desert, skirted south of Lake Baikal to Irkutsk, and then headed across eastern Russia, where peasants had stopped maintaining the roads after the Trans-Siberian Railroad was finished. Luckily, the railway allowed the cars to use its bridges and tracks to cross rivers, streams, and boggy areas. The remainder of the time, they fought the wretched roads.[4]

In the depths of Siberia, the heavy Itala tried to cross a fragile bridge, which gave way under the rear of the car. The vehicle slid backward into the abyss and turned almost a complete somersault with its three riders still in it. They escaped with only minor injuries but covered with hot oil. As happened to them so often in such isolated, trackless spaces, people mysteriously appeared out of nowhere to view the wreckage. Soon, enough had arrived to haul the car out.

In European Russia, Prince Borghese's party found better roads. It coaxed the big Itala up to forty miles an hour and, with no muffler, the giant 7,433 cc, four-cylinder engine emitted a gutsy roar that deafened the riders even as it impressed well-wishers crowded along the roads. The car and its exhausted crew arrived in Paris on August 10, 1907, to the strains of a brass band playing the triumphal march from Verdi's *Aida,* to claim the prize. Eighteen days later, a De Dion straggled into Paris to claim second place; the others failed to finish. Press exposure from the 9,500-mile obstacle course brought Itala increased sales, exactly what Hupp hoped to achieve with its own endurance run.[5]

The Peking-to-Paris race, which had no U.S. entrants, inspired Americans to devise a bigger and more difficult contest to prove their national mettle. In 1907, *Le*

Long-distance travel in remote parts of the world was dangerous. Attempting to cross a flimsy bridge in Siberia, Prince Borghese's Itala broke through it at the rear and almost flipped over on its three crewmen. From Luigi Barzini, *Pekin To Paris* (London, 1907)

Matin and the *New York Times* sponsored a dash "around the world" from New York City to Paris. Actually, it did not encircle the globe, but it came close. Its planned route was from New York to the Pacific Coast, up to Alaska, and across the Bering Strait for a run across snowy Siberia, Russia, and Europe to Paris. The papers' call drew seven entries, six European-made cars and one built in America, the Thomas Flyer.

The seven autos left New York on February 12, 1908, and slogged their way through snow drifts as high as ten to twelve feet until they reached Indiana. A few days later, the famous Iowa mud stuck the cars fast; the French Motobloc team became so disheartened that it put its car on a train and shipped it to San Francisco. The Thomas's crew, however, ramrodded by George Schuster, a hard-driving, inexhaustible man, accompanied by a mechanic, George Miller, and later by the enigmatic and bombastic "Captain" Hans Hansen, who had either quit or been fired by the rival De Dion crew, fought its way across the western wastes. After reaching the Pacific Coast, the men shipped their car to Alaska, where they found the snow so deep and the cold so penetrating that they returned to San Francisco. The other cars, fearing that driving in Alaska would be impossible, bypassed Seward's Folly and shipped their vehicles directly to Japan.

The Thomas's crew followed, landed the huge 70-horsepower car in Vladivostok, and drove it across Russia to Paris, only to find that it was the second car to finish. The race committee, however, charged the winning Germans a thirty-day penalty because they had not gone to Alaska and awarded first place to the American car. The public was captivated by the automobilists' exploits but had little veneration for their machines; the winning Thomas fetched only $200 at auction in 1913. Harrah's Museum in Reno later bought and restored it.[6]

While international transcontinental races garnered the publicity, at least one private American automobile expedition beat the little Hupp around the world, and another was abroad at the same time in 1911–12. What may have been the earliest was led by a singular woman, Harriet White Fisher, who preceded the Hupmobilists by a year. She was followed by the William A. Hall family, who set out when the Hupp was on the last lap of its journey. Fisher traveled in a huge Locomobile touring car, and the Halls in a 1911 Packard. Fisher's book about her adventures, *A Woman's World Tour in a Motor,* was published in 1911, and Melvin Hall's *Journey to the End of an Era* appeared in 1947. Although both drove considerably fewer miles than did the Hupp trio, they visited many of the same places and suffered many of the same discomforts and hardships.[7]

Harriet W. Fisher was a formidable woman, especially when ensconced in her Locomobile, which she drove around the world. Her dog "Honk" is perched on top of the rear seat. From *Around the World with a Camera,* ed. John Sleicher (New York, 1915).

Harriet White Fisher—born in 1869 into a family descended from Peregrine White, who entered the world on board the *Mayflower* while it was anchored off Cape Cod in 1620—was the equal of anything she encountered. She belonged to the Grand Army of the Republic's Red Cross Corps and was one of the first to reach Johnstown, Pennsylvania, after the 1889 flood, where she helped open a hospital, cared for the injured, and stayed to find homes for the orphans. In 1898, she married Clark Fisher, who owned an anvil factory in Trenton, New Jersey, and after he died in 1903, she took over and ran the business. She expanded into automobile repair to keep her eighty-five employees busy in the slack season and became the first female member of the National Association of Manufacturers.[8]

Fisher lived well. She owned a villa on Lake Como in northern Italy, which she kept staffed year round, and she spent her summers luxuriating on the lake's sunny shores hobnobbing with European royalty. In 1909, she hit upon the idea of shipping her car to Europe, driving to her villa for her usual summer, and then proceeding home around the world. For the purpose, she bought a Locomobile and had it fitted with extra-large gas and oil tanks.[9]

She took her nephew as chauffeur, an English servant "who can cook a dinner or write a letter," and her Italian maid (who seems to have spent much of her time ironing clothes so that Fisher could make suitably grand entrances in every town). In photographs of her, Fisher is always formally dressed and behatted; a formidable, buxom woman, she looks every inch the anvil factory owner. She also took her bulldog, "Honk," with her.[10]

Even her domestic trial run was an extensive undertaking. She and her servants drove the big car from Trenton to Washington, D.C., and thence to Pittsburgh, Youngstown, and Cleveland. They returned home via Erie, Buffalo, and the Catskills. Then, on July 17, 1909, she and the car sailed for Cherbourg, whence they motored via Paris to Contrexéville in the Vosges, Nancy, Lucerne, and over the Saint Gotthard Pass to Como. There Fisher embarked on an endless round of parties with her neighbors, all of whom, according to her account, were either titled or intimately related to such blue-blooded folk.[11]

At season's end, Fisher packed the Locomobile with her gowns and retainers and drove to Genoa. She shipped the car to Bombay while she and her crew detoured to Egypt. They rejoined their car in India and drove across the subcontinent; everywhere, Indian royalty, to whom she seems to have had an endless supply of letters of introduction, entertained her lavishly. When not staying in palaces, she and her companions camped out in tents and did their own cooking. The two men hunted to provide food for their table. She complained constantly of high prices, heat, dust, hotels without bedding, bad water, and the never-ending blowouts, but she was entranced by elephants, for she loved animals. On the trip, she adopted an "ape," which perpetually annoyed Honk, two birds, which she hauled around until they escaped from their cage, and a dog she found in Japan. By the time she returned home, her Locomobile was a veritable rolling menagerie.[12]

In March 1910, Fisher arrived in Ceylon, where she drove from one end of the island to the other, marveling at its contrasts. She shipped the car and animals to Japan on April 7, and she and her companions ventured into China, a year before the Hupmobilers arrived there. After exploring Hong Kong and Shanghai, they also visited Singapore. Three weeks later, Fisher rejoined her car and animals and for almost two months coped with Japan's amazingly narrow roads; once she literally had to drive through a family's house "to make connection with the road lying beyond." She motored through Nagasaki, Kobe, Osaka, Kyoto, Yokohama, Tokyo, and back to Yokohama; from there she shipped the car to San Francisco.

After a stop in Honolulu, Fisher arrived in California on June 17, to a great fanfare organized by the Locomobile Company. The firm's mechanics went over her car, tightened the main bearings, ground valves, and cleaned out the carbon-encrusted engine. She left a week later and drove through the Sierras to Lake Tahoe and on to Tonopah and Eli, Nevada, and Ogden and Salt Lake City, Utah, where she encountered the worst roads she faced on the whole trip. Fisher had the rear wheel bearings replaced, retraced her route to Ogden, and followed in reverse the route Hupp's trio would take through Green River, Medicine Bow, Laramie, Cheyenne, and Denver, where she arrived on July 21. Fisher declared "the pleasantest feature of the whole twelve months' tour was the odor of wheat fields and corn," which was much superior "to the heavy sensuous flower fragrance of the foreign lands." East of Denver, she and her crew made good time wheeling the huge Locomobile (the press called it a "great machine") through Omaha, Davenport, Chicago, Toledo, Cleveland, Buffalo, Rochester, and Tarrytown, New York, and finally to Trenton, arriving home on August 17, 1910, just two and one-half months before the little Hupp set out from Detroit.[13]

Fisher embarked on her 20,000-mile trip to escape the humdrum of daily routine and take a peek at the rest of the world. She had little interest in geography and the beauty of the countrysides but was obsessed by the social mores of the upper crust. She symbolized the prevailing notion in the early twentieth century that automobiles were toys of the rich. She was an unalloyed snob, disdainful of most people, whom she persisted in calling "peasants," probably her description of all farmers, and from her oversized symbol of America's industrial might looked down upon the natives as she motored past, leaving them enveloped in billowing dust clouds.[14]

Six months after Fisher completed her world odyssey, Mr. and Mrs. William A. Hall and their son Melvin set out in their 1911 Packard from their Fifth Avenue home to replicate Fisher's journey. They traveled 40,000 miles, wore out 117 tires, burned 5,000 gallons of gasoline, and made what Melvin claimed were only minor repairs to their Packard, using spare parts they carried in their toolbox.[15]

Melvin, a man who would eventually drive around the world four times, drove the entire trip. His father went only as far as Ceylon and then returned home, but his mother soldiered on for the rest of the journey. William Hall was the first to manufacture paper from wood pulp in New England, and his only child, a son of privilege, was bred to a semi-nomadic existence. Born in Bellows Falls, Vermont, in 1895, Melvin was taken to Europe for the first time in 1902, when his father rented a two-cylinder Panhard and hired a chauffeur to drive the family through Belgium, Holland, France, and Germany. Six years later, they drove their own Packard from France to Italy.[16]

Those two jaunts whetted their appetites for further motoring adventures. In the summer of 1911, the Halls shipped a new Packard to Europe to drive to India to attend King George V's Coronation Durbar. That summer, while Hanlon, Drake, and Jones were in Asia, Melvin chauffeured his family across Europe to Warsaw and south "through the land of the Black Mountains—the Montenegrin fastness," where the "sturdy farmers" saluted them with their spades, believing the Halls to be royalty, because only the royal family owned cars. The Halls' route overland to India was blocked by the inconvenience of the Italo-Turkish War, however, so they "brought the car to Bombay" and drove to Delhi.[17]

Melvin was disappointed that the motorcar was replacing the elephant in Indian pageants; although the change "made for a somewhat faster moving procession," he thought it was not as elegant. Not that the scene wanted for pageantry; the Halls found twenty-five square miles of tents on the Delhi Plain with 185 separate camps—"a tented city of a quarter of a million souls." Included were 50,000 soldiers, 48 regimental bands, featuring 3,000 instruments, "the Governor General's orchestra," and seven native bands. The Halls watched rajas pass in silver and gold carriages escorted by footmen carrying golden staves and silver hatchets. They were accompanied by bards who chanted their titles, guards in chain mail, and barefoot tribesmen, some wearing kilts and carrying matchlocks and silver powder horns. Their clothing was even more spectacular; princes wore pink brocade, robes of peacock blue embroidered with gold and pearls, long black gowns with necklaces of diamonds "and ropes and ropes of pearls." The Nizam of Hyderabad sported the Nizami diamond of 277 carats on his black brimless hat. The Maharaja of Indore "wore a dog collar of gigantic pearls and several ropes of emeralds the size of walnuts around his neck." He was outdone only by the Maharaja of Cooch Behar, "the glamour-boy of the lot," in his "peach-colored gown emblazoned with pearls in flowery patterns simulating bunches of grapes." Hall saw rajas sporting pink beards, others with hats made of beaten gold, turbans encrusted with jewels and peacock feathers, and some festooned with what he called "hawsers of emeralds." He was particularly enchanted with the titles, his favorite being that—which he thought "rather like a bird call—of Maharaja Sri Sri Sri Sri Sri Sri Ugyen Wangchuck."[18]

At the festivities' conclusion, the Halls struck out to explore the Indian subcontinent. Traveling under their Durbar authority, which allowed them to affix a special license plate to their Packard, they headed for Jaipur, following "desert trails unknown to motorcars." Over one portion of the road, they had to be towed by a span of bullocks for fourteen and three-quarter miles. Farther on, the roads were clogged with humans, monkeys, horses, donkeys, camels, and all manner of wheeled traffic. Puzzled, the Halls discovered that Hindu pilgrims were on their way to Allahabad to wash in the river Ganga—the Ganges—at its confluence with the Jumna.[19]

The Halls had an affinity for huge celebrations. Arriving in Allahabad, they discovered over two million Indians milling about on the small spit of land that separated the two rivers. The mass of humanity, under the watchful eye of British cannon mounted in a nearby fort, engaged in their rituals. Young Hall was fascinated by the veritable mattresses of hair shaved from hundreds of thousands heads, but not yet thrown into the Ganges to secure the release of the newly bald from ten thousand rebirths. Strangest to the young man were the ascetics who sought godliness through denial, pain, and detachment from the world. He recorded seeing men with withered arms held permanently above their heads, caged, deformed men who had been unable to sit, stand, or lie down in their confined spaces for years, others lying on beds of spikes, a few with clenched fists in which their fingernails had grown out through the backs of their hands, and several hanging upside down, swinging languidly over slowly burning fires.[20]

The portents for violence were great, and, with typical British aforethought, the colonial masters sought to avert it by scheduling the various "sects'" processions to the Ganges at a "prescribed hour." Hall found himself and his car jammed in beside one such parade of about one hundred Nirbanis as they marched, clad only in berry necklaces, to the water. One of them "walked in a line by himself," and Hall noted that "he had the most colossal male organ a human being could very well carry, hanging to his knees, swinging from side to side like the trunk of an elephant." As he passed, barren women ran behind him scooping up and eating the sand upon which he trod.[21]

It took almost a full day before a lull in the parades allowed Hall to extricate himself and his car from the mob. Early the following morning, he and his family took the road to Calcutta. From there, they motored south to Madras and shipped the Packard to Ceylon. They drove 1,200 miles on the island, where Melvin climbed Adam's Peak (Samanala) "with a thousand chanting pilgrims," sailed in an outrigger canoe on the Indian Ocean, and learned to climb coconut trees. He also "learned not to leave a motorcar in the jungle unattended."[22]

The Halls parked their Packard for several hours near Anuradhapura and returned to find an industrious band of "long-tailed monkeys" busily dismantling it. They stole everything that could be twisted, turned, or pulled off, including the control knobs, door handles, tire valves, and even the rubber bulb on the car's horn. They also lifted the Halls' dusters, the Packard's tool-kit, scarves, a watch, an oiler, a canvas bucket, and all the elder Hall's tobacco. To add insult to injury, the thieves hauled their loot into nearby trees and sat holding it while jeering at the Americans. Later, the Halls stopped at a hotel in which crows flew about freely and purloined anything, even food from their plates.[23]

William Hall left Ceylon for the United States, while mother and son continued their peregrinations with the assistance of native guides. They drove through Upper Burma and the length of the Malay Peninsula. From Penang to Johore, they encountered the "most perfect" roads of their trip; they passed through forests of enormous trees, listened to the cries of "myriad" jungle insects, passed dozens of rubber plantations, which made them wonder every time they had to repair another blown tire why American manufacturers did not put more of that rubber in their tires.[24]

Sometime after Fig, their guide-interpreter, left them at Surabaja in Java, mother and son found themselves on a very narrow road. Suddenly, "a mud-caked amorphous mass, like some prehistoric amphibian monster," a "ton and a half or so of ungainly shape," emerged from a rice paddy and stood in the middle of the road blocking their progress. The biggest water buffalo they had ever seen snorted, shuffled its feet, and made ready to charge their Packard. Melvin backed up as fast as possible and sat at a distance waiting for it to wander away. For three hours, he tried various ploys to get around the hulk: he slipped up on it quietly in the car and the beast stood its ground; he ran at it with horn blasting and exhaust cut-out wide open—it charged, narrowly missing the car; at nightfall, he lit his lamps to frighten the animal, but all they did was illuminate its beady eyes. Finally, a very "naked female child" less than three feet tall appeared. She walked up to the buffalo, yelled "woof," and kicked the beast in its stomach; the animal "snorted, wheeled about and shuffled off the road." Years later, Melvin recounted that he had never witnessed such "disproportion between cause and effect."[25] When he and his mother were exploring the Batak Highlands of Sumatra, where motorcars had never been seen, troops of monkeys followed them through the trees, while orangutans sat along the road and ignored them. Sumatran roads featured a series of mudholes, from which the Halls perpetually had to be dug out. They sank so deep in one that Melvin and his mother had barely enough room between the rising mud and the car's top to slither out. Although warned about deadly tigers that infested the area, they saw only one; Melvin tripped over it in the dark just outside his rest house. Luckily, it was dead.[26]

His mother took a side trip to Singapore, while Melvin drove to the Pahang State in eastern Malaya to hunt seladang, a wild bison "that can be among the most un-amiable of jungle beasts." He never saw one, largely because he spent his time keeping a lookout for a herd of rampaging elephants that had been trampling villages. He picked up his mother in Singapore and hired a Chinese guide. He had little to say about touring the "forbidden kingdom," other than that they went to Hong Kong; later they toured portions of Indo-China, where he remembered "such roads as there were did not connect with others nor offer in themselves any great facility for extensive motor touring."[27]

The Halls shipped their car to the Philippines and motored over 2,500 miles on excellent roads there. Melvin deposited his mother, over her protestations, in Baguio, and teamed up with Warwick Green, the American director of public works, for an extensive tour. Green provided directions, gasoline, and a Coast Guard vessel to ferry them from island to island. They left in two cars, but Green's Hupmobile "burned up the first day out" and they continued in the Packard. They drove the length of Luzon to Bangui, where Melvin accidentally drove the car off an escarpment into the river. The locals watched and laughed, but finally offered their water buffalo to pull the car out. The two men demonstrated the car to some Igorots, and Green told of showing the headhunters the first gun they had seen. He had shot a goat, but the tribesmen were totally unimpressed; they would not even look at the gun, regarding it as "an abstruse sort of magic-like a thunderbolt from Zeus." When Green demonstrated a crossbow, however, they wanted to try it; it was a technology they understood.[28]

At the conclusion of his grand Philippine tour, Melvin retrieved his disgruntled mother, and they shipped out to Japan. He drove 1,500 miles on the main island of Honshu over roads he quaintly characterized as "very evidently not designed for tourists." Driving was a test of his nerves. The Packard completely spanned the width of the narrow roads; pedestrians had to dive into adjacent paddies to avoid being hit. The Japanese were partial to 90° turns, and the Packard was so huge, Melvin had to "back and fill with nice precision" to make them.[29]

By the time he departed, he had a reputation as the original "ugly American." Many bridges were too flimsy to support his car, a fact not ascertained until he broke through them. He had trouble getting through most small towns; "in almost every one a tiled overhang would have to be removed," he remembered, or residents had to crop their eaves or take down their shop signs. In one memorable instance, the Halls' car frightened a horse, which ran through the front wall of a paper and bamboo house as its inhabitants fled screaming through the side walls. The animal broke down the dwelling's back wall and a bamboo fence before calming down. Melvin made a "modest offering" toward repairing the damage and breathed a sigh of relief when everyone, save the horse's owner, thought the incident "extremely funny."[30]

Further on, the Halls found themselves followed by an "old woman" on foot. She trailed them for about three miles to a tea house near Fujiyama, where they stopped for the night. The woman burst in on Melvin while he was in his bath, which he recollected "did not perturb her in the least," to return twenty sen, around ten cents, that she had overcharged him. She was Melvin's introduction to Japanese communal bathing rituals; maids at the various inns undressed him, showed him where to lather and rinse the dirt off, and ushered him into hot baths. The first time a "very good-looking Japanese lady" slipped into the tub with him, he was a "little disconcerted." His first impulse was to get out, but he thought "it might be wiser to defer this move." So they "lay there face to face quietly parboiling together" until she emerged, toweled off, bowed, and departed. Melvin admitted he grew fond of the ritual and confessed "on occasion [I] may have even timed my bathing hours accordingly."[31]

They had a memorable ride to Nagoya. As they drove along, the wind grew stronger and began to rock the car. In the city, they found the streets and air filled with curious objects, wooden tubs, long strips of blue and white cloth billowing over them, tin signs threatening to slash them, and roof tiles scattered everywhere. They had motored into the worst typhoon in a half a century. When they arrived at their "European-type" hotel, they found employees bracing its outside walls, barricading doors and windows, and propping up the second story with beams. Melvin and his Chinese guide dragged a roof that had blown off a nearby shed over the Packard and tied it down. "The winds that swept cross-wise with incredible fury" were followed by a six-foot tidal wave. Melvin's iron shutter blew off and took the window with it. He spent the night clutching his drenched bed, which "the wind was bouncing savagely up and down." The hotel stood, barely, but the city was wrecked; it took the Halls three days to make their way out, but even then they were not clear of the devastation. Motoring down the coast to Tokyo, they found the road blocked by a "succession of large junks deposited across it during the tidal wave." They abandoned the coastal route and headed inland, where, Melvin noted, they "fell through a lot more bridges."[32]

They reached Tokyo just in time to observe yet another mass ceremony, Emperor Meiji's funeral. Tradition held that no subject could gaze upon the emperor, dead or alive. All along the route of the funeral procession, the houses were shuttered, and hundreds of thousands of people, holding torches, waited quietly throughout the night for the cortege to arrive. When it finally appeared, the two-wheeled catafalque, drawn by white oxen, was preceded by "long columns of torch-bearers in mediaeval garb" and musicians who played a mournful wail. As the body passed, everyone lowered his head, "like wheat beneath the wind." The dead emperor was followed by hundreds of dignitaries on foot. A space was left in the front row for General Nogi, hero of Port Arthur's capture in the recent Russo-Japanese War, who, with his wife, had committed hara-kiri upon hearing of their emperor's death. Sanded streets muffled sounds, so only the dirges broke the night's silence.[33]

Melvin and his mother accompanied their car from Japan to San Francisco and started out in the middle of the winter of 1912 to drive to New York City. Hall recounted the final leg of his journey in less than a page of his autobiography, and he had nothing but complaints. Stuck in the snow at the Continental Divide, they had to spend a week at a "ranch of sorts," where he was driven to distraction by a "squaw-man" in "an acute stage of the D.T.'s." Years later, he still shuddered at the thought of "the howls of that reptile-tortured spirit."[34]

Across the West, their journey improved little. The thaw had begun on the Plains, and roads were in places "impassable without the help of horses or oxen." They suffered their final indignity a few miles outside Washington, D.C., when "the car sank to the level of its door-handles" in the middle of a muddy road. Melvin concluded, like the Hupp trio, that "in all the countries of our eighteen-month tour the worst roads we encountered, with the exception of China, were in the United States."[35]

Hall did not put up with the lousy American roads long; by the summer in 1913, he was ready for another automobile adventure, one that took him and his family through Scandinavia, north into Lapland until the road ran out. His family was imbued with a particularly virulent enthusiasm for motion and speed, admixed with an intense curiosity about the rest of the world. Their motor incursions into faraway places symbolized America's larger expansionist aims. Behind their Packards came businessmen and troops determined to make the world safe for democracy, free trade, and corporate profits. And the little Hupp was right at the front of that vanguard.[36]

THE AMERICAN WEST

4

C hicago was the expedition's jumping-off place for the West. Despite the public-ity they might have reaped for Hupp by lingering in the city and showing off its car, fears of possible ferocious winter blizzards prompted the three men to push across the continent as soon as possible while relatively mild weather held. Besides, the Chicago reliability run was scheduled to leave Monday, November 7, and it promised the Hupmobile increased visibility and sure routing across the state.

Early that morning, the Little Corporal joined the Chicago Automobile Club's "caravan" as it headed toward Moline on the Iowa border. It was a wonderful day for camaraderie and touring; the jaunty little car reeled off a 215-mile run "in grand style" that put it on the eastern shore of the Mississippi River at sundown. The three men averaged nearly twenty-five miles an hour across Illinois and declared that "on the whole the roads were very good." Such conditions were not the sort of trial com-pany officials wanted to advertise their motorcar's sturdiness, however, so they quickly added "of course there were bad spots and hills but the Hupmobile never hesitated." The firm squeezed the maximum public exposure from the trans-Illinois tour, reporting that the caravan included two other Hupmobiles and that all three "came through with perfect scores."[1]

The *Detroit Free Press* bragged on Hupp's behalf that "the world car came in for more cheering from the thousands who watched the motor parade than any machine in line." It added, however, that "from now on the Around-the-World party will make its way alone and no time will be lost in the rush for the coast." Citizens of America's midwestern towns all seemed to think that people who ventured west of their city limits were entering unknown and frightening regions, best left to savages, beasts, and misanthropes.[2]

The venturesome trio crossed the Mississippi River that evening and spent the night and half of the following day in Davenport, Iowa, where they demonstrated their car and talked to potential dealers. They putted out of town about noon and had driven as far as Iowa City, about seventy-five miles, by dark. They were especially fortunate that Iowa was in a dry spell, for the state's mud was notorious. They did not tarry long in Iowa City but struck out the next morning for Des Moines, another hundred and twenty-five miles due west, where they spent the night. The following day, November 10, they rested from their exertions and, since nobody in town had seen a new Hupmobile touring car, took the opportunity to give "many demonstrations . . . in and around the city."[3]

At dawn, the Hupp crew left for Omaha, about one hundred and forty miles west. They made the run in a single day and stood on the banks of the Missouri River by nightfall. They had made excellent time across the Hawkeye State. Despite stopping frequently at small towns to show off their car and accept the locals' adulation, they crossed the state in about twenty-one driving hours, clipping off an average speed of a little over sixteen miles per hour. Later in the trip, they would think that double-digit average speeds approached the speed of light.

The weather turned decidedly colder as they approached Omaha; temperatures plunged well below the freezing mark. As darkness fell, they stopped to light their headlamps and discovered that the water in their gas generator had "frozen to a solid cake of ice." They drove to a nearby farmhouse and begged a kettle of hot water to pour over it. With their lights finally lit, and swathed in their "sweaters and all other bundling warmers," the three half-frozen adventurers blazed their way into Omaha.[4]

The touring party spent the weekend and half of Monday thawing out. The local paper's warning that "none of the automobile or touring associations is in possession of definite or detailed information as to the routes and roads beyond Omaha" was undoubtedly calculated to foster the idea that the trio's jaunt across America was a great deal more dangerous and unique than it really was. The three travelers were more concerned, however, with promoting Hupp's products and seeking new deal-ers, especially in the rural areas around Omaha. A "large party" of automobilists, led by Omaha's Hupmobile dealer and company representative for Iowa and Nebraska, arranged to escort the globe-girdlers out of the city. The dealer agreed to accompany the trekkers in his runabout as their "pilot and pacemaker" over the next 650 miles to Denver.[5]

The noisy celebrants left Omaha at noon on November 14, but the crowd presently fell away and left the two lonely Hupps to proceed along the "river to river" road from Davenport to Council Bluffs, Iowa, which followed the Union Pacific Railroad's tracks through the most difficult country the three had yet seen. As a re-porter almost gleefully proclaimed, the "going was not so favorable." Nevertheless, the Hupp party ticked off eighty-eight miles that afternoon and arrived in Colum-bus, Nebraska, in time for supper. They covered the distance in only four hours, which included three stops at "agencies"—Hupp dealers—and still averaged 22 miles per hour. The local Columbus paper marveled that the little Hupp climbed "hills that have terrors for Omaha autoists." They put the worst of the gradients be-hind them in the first ten miles out of Omaha; after that "the road was level and fairly good, permitting some speeding."[6]

Barreling across the continent, the Little Corporal's crew were in their element. On Tuesday, November 15, they charged straight west and devoured 250 miles to North Platte in just under eleven hours, averaging almost 23 miles per hour. They re-ported meeting with some "splendid roads" but were also careful to mention that they had traversed "some bad ones" as well. The local newspaper's description of what lay before them, however, was not heartening. It reported that it was "impossi-ble to get lost on western roads, for they usually have just one highway leading to each place, marked in the sand." In other words, the Hupmobilists had reached a part of the country blessed with only unpaved roads, and not many of them.

The campaigners planned to take a short rest in North Platte and leave later the following day. They "discounted" a late start, however, when they read in the local paper that between there and their next planned stop, Sidney, Nebraska, lay "some mighty bad and dangerous roads, with gullies and sharp turns coming freely." In-stead, they rose early, assaulted the deteriorating terrain, and put the 140 miles to Sidney behind them by late afternoon.[7]

"Cheyenne is almost in sight for the Hupmobile world-tourists," the Sidney newspaper exclaimed, and it predicted that they would be there, some 110 miles west, by noon on November 17. Cheyenne's paper the next day, however, told a much different story. Its lead article announced, entirely in the passive voice, that "fairly blown into Cheyenne on a blizzard was the world touring Hupmobile at noon today." The journeymen's luck with the weather ran out west of North Platte when they ran into a snow storm that "wasn't a gentle fall, but a driver that cut." Without windshield or top, the travelers were vulnerable. Worse, old-timers noted that the storm raged across the hills that ringed the city "when all was calm here," which they claimed meant "deep snow farther west."

After fighting the bitter wind-driven snow for 110 miles all day and stopping periodically to adjust their carburetor as they steadily climbed to Cheyenne's 7,000-foot altitude, the Huppers were stunned as they drove up the capital's main street to the cheers of "hundreds of men" decked out "in frock coats and silk hats." Even the local scribe mentioned how odd it was that nobody was dressed in "cowboy outfits." Neither a Stetson nor a pair of cowboy boots was to be seen. The Wyoming Elks were holding their state convention in town and welcomed the world travelers in fine style. It must have been a rare sight.

The frozen excursionists intended to continue on to Greeley, Colorado, to meet a scheduled welcoming party of automobilists to accompany them into Denver at high noon. They were slightly ahead of their schedule, however, and with the driving snow and cold, it took little to persuade them to spend the night and get an early start for Greeley the next day.[8]

As the three men drove south the following morning, a cavalcade of "half a hundred cars," including virtually all the Hupmobiles in Denver, drove north from the city to greet them, led by W. R. Covington of the Krebs-Covington Hupp agency, the company's western distributor. An unidentified newspaper clipping Hanlon saved pointed out that the swell of Hupps had made "splendid time" from Greeley to Denver, "although the roads were hardly up to the standard of previous days." The transcontinentalists hardly noticed the deteriorating roads. They loved driving "through northern Colorado [where] towns are close together" and "the country rather thickly populated." It was a major change for them after their "jaunt through the cattle and sheep country." The party reached Denver early Friday afternoon, November 18, where it enjoyed a "fitting" reception; crowds gathered in the small settlements along the way and in the city to greet the now-famous adventurers. That evening the Krebs-Covington Company laid on a lavish reception for the car's crew and Mile High City notables. The fact that a local paper wrote that William Wreford

The kind of broken country the adventurers confronted across Wyoming. HPA/DJC.

was aboard the Hupp suggests that the company had, in Denver's case at least, neglected to update the promotional boilerplate sent to newspapers to indicate that Jones had replaced Wreford.[9]

On Saturday, the Hupmobilers drove to Overland Park, the local flying field, to display their car. "Globe-Girdler Divides Attention with Sky Pilots at Denver Aviation Meet," a local headline blared. "The globe-girdler attracted great attention at the aviation field," with "thousands crowding around to have a glimpse at the now famous car," the paper gushed. Elsewhere, however, it warned ominously that weather conditions "of the coming week might not be as favorable as they have been heretofore." Snow was falling in Denver while the Hupp was on exhibit at the airfield, and the forecast warned "word from the north is that there is more there." Obviously primed by Hupp's releases, the scribbler reminded his readers of "the way in which the three Hupmobiles made the New York–to–Detroit snow trip last winter." They would understand in light of this why the visiting trio felt "no great dismay." But, he advised, "all three members of the party would not mind a continuation of the good behavior of the weather man." He added that the crew were heartened by the announcement that the Krebs-Covington Company had promised "to furnish a pilot car to the Utah line."[10]

Their next big stop was Ogden, but to get there the motorists had to retrace their steps north to Cheyenne and tackle what the local reporter called "the red desert of Wyoming, the terrible Bitter Creek District, and the Green River Valley, [a] trip to test any automobile, and one that, once taken, does not hold out much inducement for a return engagement." The national automotive press announced that the undaunted crew left Denver on Tuesday, November 22, but they actually motored out the day before, under lowering skies that suggested that incoming reports about snow farther north were correct. The snow held off, however, and the two Hupmobiles reached Cheyenne without undue exertion. From there, they planned to turn west, over a road one scribe termed "a stinker," which roughly paralleled the route that would soon become the state's segment of the Lincoln Highway, along the Union Pacific's tracks. Their immediate destination was Laramie, a town sixty-eight miles away, established as a railway construction camp in 1868.[11]

The next morning, the seasonal meteorological percentages caught up with them. Jones had written home that when the tourers inquired about the forecast, "the oldest residents in the parts of Wyoming passed through, shifted their quids into their left cheeks and declared that the state had never known such a mild fall," and he hoped their "race with the snow has been won." They were not so confident when they awoke on Wednesday morning and looked out at a blizzard. Nevertheless, they bundled up and bumped their way out of town, heading toward Laramie on a road described six years later as "generally level [with] some dirt and gravel." It took them all day "through the Wyoming Desert," where they crossed "much barren country, sage brush being the only thing that thrives as far as one can see." The winds howled around them at sixty miles an hour, and the only other living things they saw to give them comfort "were two sheep herders" and "rabbits, sheep, wild horses, and one herd of antelopes."[12] Not only did they confront trackless wastes, screaming winds, and blowing snow, but they were "climbing all the time across the Laramie plains into the heart of the Rockies." Jones wrote home that "at times an altitude of 9,000 feet was reached; the wind blew some from those snow-capped peaks and through all this sage brush the road was but a trail." The world travelers must have been disheartened to read "the natives says [sic] the worst is yet to come."[13]

The natives were right. On Thanksgiving morning, November 24, the three drove out of Laramie toward Rock Springs, 218 miles away; it took them an excruciating three days to get there. They slogged through the Red Desert Country, which Jones described "as being most desolate," characterized by "light brown adobe soil, dotted only by dusty gray sage brush." Worse was the alkali, which was "so thick that it makes the nostrils and throats raw, makes lips crack and even spoils the drinking water." They never forgot the tortures of this stretch; every account they gave of their trip, even long after, included a recitation of their trials crossing the Wyoming wasteland. Twenty-three years later, Hanlon recalled that all three had bled from their noses and mouths, and that no matter how much they drank, "all the time [we] had a fiendish desire for water [and] the more you drank the worse you got." He thought that this was because when "the alkaline got in our mouth, up our nose, and into our eyes, the water seemed to push it farther inward."[14]

Throughout this leg of the trip, "the grade was continually up" toward the Continental Divide just west of Wamsutter, and they soon discovered that "any down grade simply mean[t] a harder climb just ahead." Worse, they encountered "drifts of sand in the roads, particularly so on hills, making it hard to negotiate the sharp turns which frequently occur." Climbing was particularly difficult, because the Hupp had no fuel pump; it depended upon gravity to carry gasoline from the rear tank to the engine. On steeper grades, when the tank fell below the carburetor, the motor spluttered to a stop. When that happened, they turned the Hupp around and backed up the hill.[15]

Most of the "roads" were just trails, two tracks across a wasteland. Many of them had been worn from the constant cart and wagon traffic, leaving them with "high centers." These humps in the trail caused no end of trouble; the little Hupp was low-slung, and its relatively small clearance frequently caused its undercarriage to scrape. Jones wrote home that "the differential was polished from rubbing" and that at various places along the way they espied "scattered engine pans and other parts of automobiles," although, he bragged, "the Hupmobile has not left so much as a nut in its wake."

The car did not escape unscathed, however. After bouncing down one such rutted road that made a sharp turn, the driver, probably Hanlon, misjudged the ruts' depth, made the hard turn, and when the Hupp rode over the high center and slipped down into the ruts again, its radius rod bumped a protruding rock and snapped. Happily, Jones wrote, "getting into the next town was easy and repairs were made without much delay." That was the only damage to the car the intrepid travelers publicly reported, but in its booklet *Round the World in a Hupmobile: Detroit to*

Coming out of one of the innumerable ravines in the Bitter Creek District of Wyoming. The sparse vegetation did little to hold down the alkali dust that bedeviled the tourers. Hanlon had removed the left front headlamp and mounted it as a spotlight. HPA/DJC.

Manila, published in 1911, the company admitted that the Little Corporal had suffered two "damaged radius rods" and a "broken spring."[16]

The crew was fortunate the car did not sustain more harm from the frequent "gulleys [*sic*] and washouts" that cut across roads throughout western Wyoming. Such depressions were dangerous, time-consuming, and tiring. Jones explained that when "caught in the adobe bottoms of fords, the car needed help from two members of the party, and once or twice the block and tackle had to be brought into use in gullies with almost perpendicular sides." Grumpily, he concluded that "the car stood it better than its passengers."[17]

The trio confronted the mother of all gullies in the Bitter Creek District, about thirty miles west of the Continental Divide. On a pitch-black night when Drake was at the wheel and "couldn't see a yard on either side or ahead of the white splash of light from the gas lamps," they "were going merrily ahead when in a flash Mr. Drake saw a gaping, black drop in the circle of light." He "swerved the car suddenly, all brakes on—and we stopped eighteen inches from the edge of a thirty foot drop into the mouth of a pit"—a pretty good performance for a car with brakes on only two wheels.[18]

Drake might not have seen the pit at all had the three men not changed their car's lighting system. Before they reached Denver, they removed the left-hand headlamp and put it on a swivel attached to a post they mounted on the floorboards against the middle of the dashboard to make a spotlight. It was not an ideal solution; Hanlon had to reroute the gas line up the new pipe, and bouncing down a washboard road on a pitch-black night, the heat from the spotlight must have made it uncomfortable to use. When photographed in Denver, the car had only the spotlight; both its headlamps were missing. A few days later, photographs taken in the Bitter Creek District show that the crew had replaced the right-hand headlamp. They converted the spot back to a headlight in Honolulu, but they later procured another headlamp to mount amidships; photos for the rest of the trip show the car sometimes with all three lights and sometimes with only two.

They had more than their share of troubles driving in daylight, however. When the roads were not "well beaten," they were often deep, sandy tracks that made forward progress difficult up steep grades. The three men encountered a particularly bad sandy stretch east of Rock Springs, in which they could gain no traction. They had to lay canvas strips down in front of the car, drive to the end of them, and repeat the process. They did this for nine miles, thirty feet at a time, fourteen hard hours.

Hanlon remembered that their tempers had *really* frayed when locals charged them an unheard-of $1.00 a gallon for gasoline.[19]

The higher altitudes only added to their trials. The three had to stop constantly to adjust the carburetor as they climbed to over 9,000 feet and then quickly dipped down to as low as 7,500. Jones wrote the factory that the heights were a serious problem, because "in the rare air much of the efficiency of the gas motor is lost," just when they needed all their sixteen horsepower.[20] They reached Medicine Bow, the setting for Owen Wister's famous western novel *The Virginian*, fifty-six miles from Laramie, on the afternoon of Thursday, November 24. The photographs they took in that bleak place, home to 170 hardy souls, show that the snow had stopped. A local news report indicated the travelers were lucky to have been in a car, for "man power would have been unable to make any headway in the teeth of the blizzard which raged all day." Their isolation had been nearly complete: they had encountered only a couple of sheepherders. They sometimes slept outside, in temperatures that remained well below freezing all day. To keep warm, they burrowed under the car, and, as they told a Honolulu reporter, they "were usually tired enough to go to Dreamland without great preparations." It was less cold under the Hupp, but the smell of hot metal and grease and the warm oil that dripped on them made their "dreamlands" a bit nightmarish.[21]

Their next destination, Rawlins, named for Union Civil War General John A. Rawlins, lay fifty-nine excruciating, dry, dusty miles away. They reached Rawlins on Friday, and despite being tired, thirsty, and irritable, they pushed on. Thirty-two miles later, they climbed to the apex of the Continental Divide. There they stopped briefly to memorialize their accomplishment on film. The tombstone of one Frank Yora, deceased on August 14, 1900, is in the foreground of the photograph, with a long rectangular wooden sign marking "the spot of the old roadbed of the Union Pacific" just behind it. There was probably a whopping good story about why Yora was interred there, but even the local county historical society had never heard of him. Except for the car, Hanlon, and probably Jones, there is absolutely nothing else in the picture; no trees, shrubs, or hills. Yora was a lonely man. The photos they took on this leg of the trip, and they seem to have taken more than usual in this hellish region, perhaps because they had to stop so often, feature the men and their car going into gullies, coming out of them, using block and tackle, and struggling up steep hills, or everyone standing around puzzling how to extricate the car from yet another contretemps. Jones never mentioned the pilot car in any of his dispatches, and neither do

the pilot car's drivers appear in any photographs. In a shot taken in Medicine Bow, however, where the world tourers parked their car in front of the Elkhorn Saloon (the town looks entirely deserted), they inadvertently caught the headlamps and front fenders of the accompanying car, tangible evidence that several other men suffered along with them.[22] Both cars and crews finally blew into Rock Springs, known locally for its Killpecker Creek, which flows "through heavy saltpeter deposits," on Saturday, November 26. The three tourers posed for a photograph in their car in front of the "local agency," presumably a Hupp dealership. Jones looks cold and hunched perched on the baggage in the back seat; Hanlon, a cigarette in his mouth, looks defiant and ready for whatever lies ahead; but Drake, for once on the trip, is almost smiling. They all look relieved, no doubt because this patch of their journey was behind them. Even a local reporter marveled at their traversal of the "terrible Bitter creek district," calling it "admittedly the hardest stretch of the transcontinental trip." It took them over three days to cover the 218 miles, an average of only a few more than 70 miles a day of dawn-to-dusk struggles, traveling against a prevailing wind that, the newspaper said, "blows alkali dust and pebbles into the faces of tourists" and where "water has to be carried, for the places where it can be obtained along the road

Civilization did not get much bleaker than in Medicine Bow, Wyoming. Worse, as parched as the three crewmen were, the Elkhorn Saloon appears to have been closed. A pole braces the left side of the saloon against the perpetual winds. The nose of their scout car can be seen on the right. HPA/DJC.

Posing in front of the Hupmobile agency in Rock Springs, Wyoming, the three men seem pleased to have reached civilization. HPA/DJC.

are few." The weary travelers must have wondered why the reporter lived in such a place. The corporate world had reached into that isolated town of fewer than 6,000 souls, however, even if the newspaper copied it wrong. The paper assured its readers "the little Hup has taken sands, silts, and gulches in perfect style and is ready to go on with its task that has proven too much for many heavier cars"—music, no doubt, to Hupp Company executives' ears.[23]

Only tantalizing hints remain of the rest of their trip from Rock Creek to Los Angeles. They were under pressure to get a move on, because they were scheduled to sail from San Francisco on December 13, only seventeen days hence. When Jones mailed a letter to headquarters from "somewhere between Laramie and Ogden," he warned that for the remainder of the transcontinental trip, "it is extremely improbable that news of the party will be telegraphed." They planned to "drive every day from dawn to dark," he said, and he explained that "camp will be established for the night at the end of the run without regard to towns or civilization." Thus, he warned, "there will be no chance to get to a telegraph station until Los Angeles is reached." The company's account simply says, "the trail through Wyoming, Utah and Nevada

was a continuous succession of struggles that proved conclusively that the Hupmobile could withstand any strain that human daring could demand." As proof, Hupp noted that the car and its crew had made it to Los Angeles without further mishap.[24]

When the hard-driving crew reached Ogden, a city of almost 30,000, on December 3, 1910, Jones telegraphed the news to Detroit. With only ten days to make their ship, they pushed immediately southward along the eastern side of the Great Salt Lake toward southern California. It was better than a 700-mile stretch, but across much lower elevations, in milder winter temperatures. Other transcontinental motorists had preferred to take the "southern route" all the way, because it was flatter and the roads better than those across northern California and Wyoming, the "central crossing." The Hupmobile crew followed a route that closely approximates present-day Interstate 15, through Provo, Beaver, St. George, and Las Vegas. Assuming they departed Ogden on December 3, it took them the better part of five days to reach the City of Angels. Their 140 miles a day, at an average speed of about 12 miles per hour of dawn-to-dusk driving, indicates they found the roads in the Southwest tough going. The only time they publicly talked about that portion of the trip, they cryptically noted, "then came the hills and the Great American Desert of Utah, and the sands of Nevada," which guaranteed "that Southern California was most welcome." They did take one photograph in Utah they remembered to label, which

Just west of Rock Springs, the Hupmobilists passed a Wyoming landmark, Castle Rock, at Green River. Just barely visible in the left-middle background are some very active smokestacks. HPA/DJC.

shows the one-eyed Hupp stopped in tracks a foot deep, while the men talk to the driver of a burro team. All are heavily clothed, although eastern newspapers recorded daily high temperatures ranging between 45° and 58°F in Utah and Nevada for those dates.[25]

With close to a half a million citizens, Los Angeles was a shock to the three men after the solitude and loneliness of their last thousand miles. The thirty-six days it took them to cross the West from Detroit must have seemed like half a lifetime as they neared the city. As was becoming a habit, the company's local distributor, one W. M. Mason, with a "party" of automobilists, met them in San Bernardino to escort them into Los Angeles. The entourage swelled as the Little Corporal passed through Pasadena and continued to do so until "the car pulled triumphantly into Los Angeles at the head of a long escorting procession." The city was staging an auto show the following week and wanted the little Hupmobile as the centerpiece of the extravaganza, but the travelers had only five days to get to San Francisco to board their ship. After talking to the tired autoists, a reporter remarked that they would "welcome the change that is to come with the sea voyage."[26]

They stayed less than a day in Los Angeles and then hurriedly drove up the coast, arriving in San Francisco early on Monday, December 12, to a noisy public welcome. One Bay Area newspaper noted that wherever the Little Corporal "had gone crowds have gathered." The trio had little time to enjoy their newfound fame, however. That very afternoon, their car was hoisted into the hold of the SS *Manchuria*. Even its loading became a public spectacle. A large crowd gathered at the dock, and "newspaper photographers were busy snapping their shutters as the car hung suspended over the deck with J. R. Drake sitting at the wheel." His two colleagues were also busy recording the moment.[27]

The *Manchuria* sailed the following morning. Back home, newspapers, coached by the Hupp Company, glorified the car's achievement. They seemed obsessed with the fact that the little Hupp had made it to the coast with all four tires still full of "Detroit air," a tribute to the G. & C. tires made in the Motor City, and about convincing the public that the auto's transcontinental test had been more arduous and longer than others. As a Los Angeles newspaper asserted, certainly with a bit of corporate prompting, "the Hupmobile has a greater mileage of rough American roads to its credit than is usually the case in a transcontinental tour." The reason, the reporter explained, was that it had "made several long detours . . . to include important points." The only "detour," in the true meaning of that word, was its side trip from

Cheyenne to Denver and back, and that was taken only for publicity. The company probably counted cutting southwest from Ogden to Los Angeles as a detour; it was certainly longer than following the central route directly to the coast, but given the season and the Sierra's reputation for massive snowfalls, it was the smartest. No newspaper seems to have known just how far the car had traveled from Detroit to San Francisco, but it was in the vicinity of 3,600 tough miles.[28]

On December 13, 1910, the Little Corporal was at sea on its way to explore the rest of the world, starting with America's newest colony, Hawaii. After the cold, wind, snow, sand, and alkali, the three men, resting their sore muscles in their berths aboard the *Manchuria*, dreamed about a leisurely tour of a tropical paradise.

THE MEN

5

The Hupp Motor Car Company could not have chosen three men who better exemplified the traits Americans believed made them the premier commercial nation on the face of the globe than Hanlon, Drake, and Jones. The crew was every bit as important to the trip's success as the little Hupmobile's durability, rakishness, and quality. The trio packed their specific skills, relative maturity, and congenial personalities to keep the arduous trek from becoming a nightmare.

The three travelers personified the widespread self-conception that Americans were all natural captains of industry, infused with inventive and mechanical skills mated to superb business instincts and madly intent on turning a profit. Such talents, slathered with a patina of verbosity, salesmanship, and infectious collegiality, made American businessmen optimistic, if not cocky. The Hupmobilists not only exhibited all these native attributes but exuded boundless energy and a stubborn stick-to-it-iveness that made their journey successful. Fifteen months on the road in a open car selling to all and sundry was in itself evidence of their dedication and enthusiasm. They suspended their private lives, confronted dangers, battled insects, heat, wind, sand, raging waters, dirt, sleep deprivation, and storms to peddle Hupmobiles. The three were at once unremarkable, representative Americans, and very unusual men.

Their very ordinariness is striking. They hailed from such unremarkable roots that the commonplace details of their private and professional lives were barely noted at the time. Save for their feat of circumnavigating the world by motorcar, they would have slipped off history's pages. That singular achievement marked them as exceptional individuals, however, and made them ambassadors for America's economic foreign policies. In a nation bursting forth from its geographical limits, they gave ammunition to turn-of-the-century observers who believed that America's greatness lay in the superiority of its common citizens.

Nothing in Thomas Matthew Hanlon's background stamped him for distinction. The child of Irish immigrants who had fled that island's woes, he grew up in Detroit's large Irish neighborhood, Corktown. Like many Roman Catholic families, the Hanlons produced a large brood, seven boys and two girls. Tom was born in Detroit on May 10, 1877, and like many immigrants' children, he was forced into the workplace early. He dropped out of school in the eighth grade and worked in a boiler factory during his teenage years.[1]

By the turn of the century, Hanlon had matured into a rather stocky young man, who would become heavier as he aged. Of average height, about five feet eight inches tall, he was topped with a shock of curly blonde hair and had sparkling, friendly blue eyes. His daughter remembered that he was very fair of skin and sunburned easily. Largeness ran in the Hanlon family; Tom's brother, John, better known as "Big Jack," who worked as a conductor on the Fort Wayne & Belle Isle trolley line, tipped the scales at 342 pounds. When he died, his pallbearers had to remove the front windows of his house to get his coffin out.[2]

The Hanlon boys, at least those on record, had an affinity for transportation; another brother, James, was a railway engineer. Tom resisted the family impulse to run machines on rails, however, and instead was fascinated by automobiles. By 1902, he was working for the newly formed Cadillac Automobile Company, a firm created by Henry M. Leland, who had been associated with Henry Ford and who in 1920 founded the Lincoln Motor Company, and Charles Hastings, who would be so important to Hanlon's later career. A scratchy photo, probably taken November 2, 1902, shows a group of "testers for Cadillac" posed in front of twelve Model A, single-cylinder Cadillacs. Standing at the rear is a smiling, already thickening Tom Hanlon.

The three intrepid travelers sit for their portrait before leaving Detroit. From left to right, Thomas Hanlon, Joseph Drake, Thomas Jones. HPA/DJC.

Clad in a leather coat and necktie, a well-smoked cigar gripped between the fingers of his heavy driving gloves, and topped off with a chauffeur's hat and a pair of goggles, he looks pleased with his lot in life.[3]

Hanlon was born to drive; the longer the distance and the faster the pace, the happier he was. After Hupp laid him off when it temporarily closed its doors in 1936 during the Depression, Hanlon could no longer afford a car. His daughter thought "it was the worst thing to happen to him . . . [he had to] take the streetcar everywhere." He stayed with Cadillac at least through 1906, when his driving mastery catapulted him into the local newspaper under the cutline "Made Long Auto Trip in Creditable Time." The fuzzy photograph shows Hanlon sitting behind the wheel of what the paper identified as a "four cylinder machine," but that looks very much like a 1906 single-cylinder Cadillac. Whatever the car, Hanlon drove 346 miles from Detroit to Joliet, Illinois, in sixteen hours and forty-three minutes, maintaining an overall average speed of almost 21 miles per hour.[4]

Testers for Cadillac posed on November 2, 1902. Hanlon is third from the left in the back row with cigar and necktie. HPA/DJC.

In August 1906, instead of taking the train to his summer place on the Hudson River at Larchmont, New York, as he usually did, the former Michigan senator Thomas W. Palmer went most of the way by car, accompanied by his valet and driven by his chauffeur, Hanlon. The three took a steamboat from Detroit to Buffalo, New York, where "the machine was awaiting them." Hanlon drove the traditional route across upstate New York, stopping in Rochester, Syracuse, Fort Blaine, and Poughkeepsie, before reaching Palmer's summer home. It took him four and a half days of steady driving to cover the 490 miles over what Palmer characterized as "bad roads." On the return trip, Hanlon beat his earlier time; he made the run in one day less.[5]

Hanlon was an expert chauffeur in the early days of motoring. He was adept at wheeling fragile, poorly balanced, underpowered machines over the rutted and pitted trails that passed for roads and could also repair the cars, a highly desirable talent, given how often they broke down. His daughter described him as a "great tinkerer" who could "fix everything"; she thought him a "genius in that regard." He could visualize the juxtaposition of mechanical parts and how they should work and was endowed with the natural mental and physical dexterity to conjure up remedies. Numerous photos taken after he returned from going around the world show Hanlon deep in some Hupmobile's innards, grease up to his elbows, cigar clenched between his teeth, and a broad smile on his face; he was in his element.[6]

Hanlon was the crew's "mechanician/driver," responsible for the Little Corporal's maintenance. In the evening, after a long day on the road, he lubricated the car, checked its oil drip frequency, which lubricated the motor's upper parts, and oil level, and made whatever adjustments might be needed, vital at higher elevations. He did most of the driving, although Drake was also photographed at the wheel—he often took over in cities to show his colors as the group's leader. Most photos snapped in the boondocks, however, where the going was rough and the driving hours tallied in the double digits, show Hanlon wrestling the car through swamps, across rivers and creeks, and up and down mountains and arroyos. He did the heavy driving.

Hanlon's personality was as important as his mechanical aptitude, for personal affinities held the team together. In some respects, he was a stereotypical happy-go-lucky Irishman. Infected with a contagious sense of humor, he was a genuinely funny man. He slipped much of his humor into storytelling; he loved to unwind long, colorful yarns, and a half century later, his daughter still remembered him as "full of blarney." She had always assumed he was pulling her leg with his tales. One of his favorite stories was about how he had suffered through a blizzard on May 10. Years later, Mariann happened upon an old issue of the *Detroit Free Press* that reported that a surprise snow storm had hit Detroit that day. It made her a believer in at least some of her father's tales, such as the one he told about the night the three slept under the Hupmobile in the West to keep warm and awoke with a rattlesnake for company. Or his descriptions of New Zealand Maoris as "swashbucklers and pirates" who "wore large knives." Or his stories about the "not nice" cannibals he had encountered in the Philippine wilds. His trip armed him with a lifetime of seemingly outrageous tales.

An easygoing fellow, Hanlon liked his beer. He was also renowned for presiding over memorable wakes. When his brother Bob died, he sat him up in the casket, plopped a top hat on his head, and drank to Bob's success in the afterlife. He was an inveterate smoker, and photos frequently show him smoking cigarettes (always Camels) and cigars; he must have taken a huge supply with him, for he gave them

away liberally, along with pencils, which probably featured a mention of Hupp on them, to locals who came out to ogle the adventurers, especially in remote areas, where the crowds sometimes looked threatening.

Hanlon would eat anything that was put in front of him, a predilection that aided his digestion in some of the lands he visited. He favored pickled pigs' feet at home and liked hot, spicy food. He was a particular fan of the raw fish he ate in the Philip-pines and of what he termed "the strange foods" he ingested in China.

For a man who lived almost all of his life in Detroit, Hanlon was partial to warm climates; he enjoyed heat and humidity. He was especially taken with Hawaii, the Philippines, Fiji, India, and Egypt. His all-time favorite place, however, was Japan, with its flowers and mountains. Of course, he was there in late spring, the perfect sea-son.

Hanlon was also an inveterate gambler and sports enthusiast. Every Saturday night, he, his wife, and his in-laws settled in with their beer for a furious game of pinochle. His daughter Mariann mirthfully claimed that they were placed in "their

Hanlon with two Japanese friends. HPA/DJC.

drawers in the mausoleum like they are still playing pinochle." Hanlon was an avid Tigers' fan, and a half a century later Mariann retained fond memories of her father listening to Tigers' games on the radio, drinking beer and smoking Camels.

He was the only married man in the crew and had a son, Wilfred, who was born around July 1907. But Hanlon always had an eye for pretty young women. Several photographs show him with his arms draped over women's shoulders and a happy grin on his face. He was especially fond of Japanese women; perhaps like Melvin Hall, he enjoyed their bathing rituals. Among his few remaining papers, Hanlon left a note to the effect that Japanese women's genitals ran crosswise instead of front to back. This from a man who, around his daughter at least, never told an off-color story and indeed was hesitant to mention sex at all. She recalled that when she became pregnant, Hanlon sidled up to her and asked, "Daughter, are you in a family way?"

Despite his easygoing nature, however, Hanlon had his serious side. He was de-

Hanlon entertaining a business contact. HPA/DJC.

voted to the Hupp Motor Car Company and spent the rest of his career with it. His job was not just a paycheck; it was his very identity. He talked Hupps, owned only Hupps, took his family photos in, on, and around Hupps, and believed that they were the best cars on the road. He hated Fords and Chevrolets and compared them unfavorably to Hupps at every chance he got. After his journey, he was promoted to head Hupp's service department, a very respectable position in Detroit automobiledom. While on the trip, he carried a business card that identified him as "T. M. Hanlon, Engineer Dept" at Hupp. The company's closure was the worst thing that ever happened to Hanlon; it left him adrift.[7]

The bluff, outgoing Irishman was teamed with two very different men for the journey, yet there is no hint of the discord often found on arduous trips. The impression Hanlon left with his daughter was that "he and Jones were buddies and loved what they were doing. Drake was rich." Hanlon and Jones did have more in common with each other than they did with the more serious, less jocular Drake. Even the photographs hint of the Jones-Hanlon friendship; they are often smiling as if they share a common secret or joke, while Drake often looks as if his world is about to crash down around him. And when Drake got sick and the other two drove on without him through New Zealand and Tasmania, Jones's write-ups exude a lightness of tone missing in his other recountings, which tend to be a great deal more factual and businesslike.[8]

Less is known of Thomas Owen Jones, because he committed the cardinal sins of peaking early in his career, moving about all the time, never marrying, leaving no issue, and dying young. He did not even carry the same name as the rest of his family. He was born in Utica, New York, on September 28, 1887, which made him only twenty-three years old when he joined Hanlon and Drake. He was raised by Mr. and Mrs. George Owens of New Hartford, New York, a village just south of Utica. Mrs. Owens had been married previously, and Tom was the issue of that union. His siblings, two brothers and a sister, were born of her subsequent marriage to Owens.[9]

Unlike Hanlon, Jones was well-educated. He graduated from New Hartford High School and attended Ohio State University, where he graduated in 1909. Fresh out of college, he took a job with the *Grand Rapids Herald,* but he stayed there less than a year, leaving to go to the *Detroit Free Press,* where he "was connected with the sporting department." While he was there, his colleague Will B. Wreford was tapped to join the Hupp team. When he pulled out, Jones was named to take his place.[10]

The press never failed to mention that "Jones was always a sportsman" and "was possessed of a fine physique and much interested in athletics." Undoubtedly, he and Hanlon closely followed domestic and foreign sporting events. They played baseball together aboard ship on their way to Hawaii and probably enjoyed the informal banter characteristic of sports enthusiasts.[11]

Like Hanlon, Jones had an engaging personality. His obituary mentioned that he was "well-known and admired." The *Detroit Free Press* declared he had "many friends in Masonic circles," while the trade press noted that he "leaves a long line of friends through long connection with the industry." Like many men of his generation, Jones was a congenital joiner. During his short stint in Grand Rapids, he became an Elk. In Detroit he was a member of the Palestine Lodge, F. & A. M., and when he lived in Indianapolis, he again gravitated to the Elks. He obviously sought and enjoyed male fellowship in traditional societies. However, he probably found more male companionship than he needed on his fifteen-month jaunt around the world with Hanlon and Drake.[12]

Jones was a handsome fellow, perhaps five feet nine inches tall. Unlike Hanlon, he was slim. He probably enjoyed a drink with the older Irish American, and, being single, he doubtless had an eye for any pretty lass who crossed his path. With his dark hair, thick eyebrows, and full lips, he must have had few problems attracting women. A Tasmanian newspaper reporter who recounted his travels with the two Americans wrote that they were a boisterous, fun-loving pair who thoroughly enjoyed what they were doing.

Jones was brought aboard the Hupp because of his writing skills and his newspaper connections. Hupp hired him to be the team's "chronicler," responsible for keeping Hupp's home office informed and sending the *Detroit Free Press*, his former employer, periodic updates on the more interesting aspects of their trek. His job was made easier early in the trip because local newspapers along the trio's route sent copies of their articles to the *Free Press*. The farther the travelers drove from their home base, however, the fewer mentions they received in their hometown papers. When they were abroad, the Detroit news reports were usually ascribed to letters Jones wrote to Wreford, cables he sent to the *Free Press*, or releases from Hupp's front office. There were not very many of them in 1911, perhaps one a month. It is not clear whether Jones wrote less often, his letters took forever to get back to Detroit, or he and his colleagues drove beyond the end of the telegraph cable. Whatever the reason, news of Hanlon, Drake, and Jones declined as they circled the far side of the globe. Nor did information flow more freely when the trio dashed across Europe. Unlike their predecessors Melvin Hall and Harriet Fisher, Jones never published an article or a book about their adventures. He may have been the trip's "chronicler," but he was not its historian.

More is known about the trio's third member, the brother of Hupp's president, J. Walter Drake. Although affiliated with the firm since its very beginning and later its vice president, Joseph Drake never attained his younger sibling's national stature. The death of his first wife before the trip instilled something of Hanlon's wanderlust deep into Drake's psyche; once, when reminiscing with another widower, he noted, "I did not have the mental balance you have, so started wandering about, trying to get away from myself." Another time, he wrote a friend, "You understand how it is with a person who is never anywhere, which is my case, but sometime I am going to make a tremendous effort to get somewhere." That "somewhere" was evidently not Detroit, for he spent as little time as possible in the Motor City.[13]

Born in 1873, he was two years older than his more famous brother, and there is no evidence Joseph attended college, unlike J. Walter. Nor was he a lawyer. His obituaries give the impression that he did little of note between 1873 and 1908, although he was a jeweler in New York City just before he joined Hupp. As secretary of the Hupp Motor Car Company, he was tapped by his brother, who had a reputation as "a leader in advancing the automobile abroad," to take charge of the trip's arrangements and accompany the car. He was to contact and solicit foreign distributors and dealers and hustle orders for new Hupps.[14]

Drake looked like an accountant; he lacked Hanlon's brashness and Jones's beguiling good looks. A photo of Drake, Hanlon, and Wreford, taken when the latter was still expected to make the trek, shows Drake seated and the other two standing, a typical pose for the age, when the father was often photographed seated with his dependents arrayed around him. With his thick, dark, hair, already receding on the sides, clean, rather sharp facial features, and just the hint of a smile, Drake has something of an innocent air. His bow tie and perhaps the angle of the shot give the impression that his head was a bit small for his frame; other photos, however, indicate that this was not the case. His picture exudes the sense that he was a dependable man, comfortable with his responsibilities.[15]

He was not without a rather dry sense of humor. After the trip, he wrote Hupp's London agent that "for some time I have been troubled with shortness of breath, spots before the eyes, falling out of bed, loud ringing in the ears, etc., and have been in a quandary to learn the cause of it." Then he explained: "I had forgotten all about the ten shillings you owe me but already begin to feel better having had it called to my mind that it is due me. . . . I think it will effect a permanent and complete cure." He could even laugh about his dental problems. He was missing some or all of his teeth, and upon returning home, he ordered new dentures from a dentist in New York City. When they arrived, Drake thanked the good doctor for "putting me in shape again so I can enjoy my meals, social evenings, and one thing and another, without feeling that I have to desecrate the Sabbath and other days by not having any teeth."[16]

Each spring, with or without his teeth, Drake joined friends and fished for a few days in New York State. In February 1912, barely a month after his return, he wrote one of the group, "You can bank on my being up to the Beaver Kill this spring if I have to sell out my motor stock to get there." He admonished his fishing buddy not to "get up there first and dig out all the big trout, as I think I am entitled to one or two after my absence last spring." He was also a bit of a gambler, although evidently not a lucky one. After one bad run, he wrote a London associate, "Yesterday one of my dear brothers trimmed me to the tune of six pounds, and this morning I signed the pledge to wear the white ribbon and have sworn off on all betting." From the few political references in his surviving letters, it appears that Drake supported William Howard Taft, the father of "dollar diplomacy," in the hard-fought three-way 1912 presidential election. He wrote his London dealer: "You might introduce a man called T. Roosevelt, who is at present causing quite a disturbance here, and try and place him somewhere by all means"—in other words, yank Teddy and his Bull Moosers out of the United States.[17]

Drake's abilities helped make the world tour a success. He dealt with a mind-boggling welter of details: expenses, visas, car licenses, spare parts, clothing for four seasons, shipping schedules, bewildering currencies, political connections, hotels and meals, arrangements for gala welcomes, business relations with prominent locals, publicity in foreign lands, distributorships, agencies, direct sales, and routing the car.

Hupp's secretary had only about ninety days to pull the whole journey together. Without accurate U.S. road maps, and with only the haziest notion of what roads were like in the rest of the world, Drake plotted a course to ensure the little Hupp maximum exposure by including the largest cities wherever possible. Being unable to see to all the details himself, he sent Hupp's export manager, C. H. Dunlap, to Europe to make arrangements there and to New York City to see to the Hupp's display at the 1912 auto show. It was Drake who dispatched Hanlon and Jones to check with the AAA in New York on the best routes across the United States. John Baker was delegated to correspond with U.S. consuls in countries on the itinerary. Consuls were responsible for connecting American businessmen with foreigners who could best advance sales in their colonies and countries. Hupp's overseas agents and dealers also helped Drake. He and Baker were especially successful in persuading them to turn out Hupp owners in their sales territories for grand welcoming parades. Often the dealers assigned an employee and a Hupmobile to scout for the Little Corporal and arranged for interpreters to accompany the travelers along "stretches of the route." Drake's careful preparations paid off; almost every town and city greeted the adventurers with pomp and victuals. In return, the trio drove local dignitaries around to demonstrate their car and enable the worthies to be seen. Dozens of photographs show the latter seated in the car displaying unusually broad smiles.[18]

Ensuring adequate supplies for the trip caused Drake many sleepless nights. Gasoline was not much of a problem; it, or something close, was available in most areas. In more remote territories, several cans of extra petrol lashed to the running boards sufficed. For general supplies, he organized something of a progressive sys-

Drake preparing to leave New York City on his way back to Detroit in January 1912. HPA/DJC.

tem. Drake shipped spare parts, fresh clothing, trinkets, cigarettes, cigars, and other necessaries ahead to their next port of call. While they were slogging across the American West, for example, he sent everything on to Hawaii. From there, the supplies accompanied them on board ship to Australia and New Zealand, where he used what they needed and stored the rest at a local Hupp distributor. Anywhere the company already had dealers, the crew enjoyed a local source of parts, even if they had to be taken off a new car; in the more remote areas, Drake's organization courted risk by driving for periods with no available help. Only in Japan did his system break down; he had already shipped his spares off the island when the Hupp's rear axle snapped.

Three weeks before the Little Corporal left Detroit, Drake still had only the sketchiest idea of its route. Reading between the lines of his October 16, 1910, press release in which he announced the trip and presented details, it appears he was only certain of traveling to San Francisco, sailing to Hawaii, and on to Asia. The trio visited most of the countries and colonies he mentioned in the newspaper article, but not always in the order he announced. Drake had only the haziest notion of what their route would be west of China, but he confidently predicted that the Hupmobile would be shipped to South Africa from Egypt to drive the length of the African continent from Cape to Cairo. The itinerary's uncertainties made it impossible for Drake to schedule space on a ship in advance; luckily, however, the worldwide shipping glut and the proliferation of scheduled shipping lines made it possible for him to wait until the last minute to secure passage. The ships occasionally took the three men to ports they had not expected to visit, but such detours only added spice and color to their journey. It helped that Hupp advertised that its world tourers were not in a race; they had the leisure to alter their destinations and itinerary depending on local conditions and shipping schedules.[19]

Drake was in many respects an ideal trail boss. Serious, with a streak of humor, well organized, and invested with high corporate authority, he easily assumed responsibility for the daily details that did not interest Hanlon and Jones. Although not as ebullient as his two cohorts, he was sociable enough, liked people, and got on well with them. He was gregarious, if more restrained than his younger colleagues, and was a more typical Detroit auto executive; he belonged to numerous golf and country clubs, and at his death, he still held memberships in a club in Brisbane, Australia, two in Santa Barbara, California, and one in Detroit. They were the kinds of places where he could mix business and pleasure at a social level somewhat above that of the Elks. Given Hupp's foreign sales increases, Drake successfully worked his more restrained magic with well-heeled businessmen around the globe. He was a salesman who generally coped well with Hupp's corporate restraints and foreign institutional and cultural differences. He was a self-starter.[20]

The three men made an ideal team. Their ability to see humor in the oddest events and places, and to deal with vastly different people from themselves, carried them through many uncomfortable and dangerous moments. With their outgoing personalities, businesslike attitudes, and mechanical skills, they embodied the salient characteristics of American capitalism. Combining their quest to expand the Hupp Motor Car Company's international market with scenic tourism, they pressed on behind the little silk American flag fluttering on the Little Corporal's radiator cap, committed to finishing their journey and driving home under their own power.

THE PACIFIC

6

On December 13, 1910, the Little Corporal and its crew steamed out to conquer Oceania, in an island-hopping expedition that would take them from San Francisco to Hawaii, Fiji, Australia, New Zealand, Tasmania, New Guinea, and the Philippines. Their itinerary was strenuous and exciting; they knew little about the cultures they would find on the islands and nothing about their roads. For the moment, however, the three men were happy to be at sea, free to clean up, rest, eat robustly, and enjoy themselves on their six-day ocean journey. The 3,000-ton *Manchuria* was fairly new, having been launched in 1906, but it would have a short life span; it was torpedoed in World War I.

Once at sea, a baseball game was organized on the boat deck. Declaring themselves "world's champions," the nine participants chose two female passengers as their "mascots." Jones played first base; Hanlon, shortstop. Drake was not on the team, not even one of its three substitutes; perhaps he looked after the mascots.

On board, the trio met T. J. O'Brien, U.S. ambassador to Japan, who was returning to his post after a two-month vacation at home in Grand Rapids, Michigan. O'Brien gave them valuable information about Japan and warned them that "roads in the interior are very narrow and not ideal for touring." He said, however, that America's "trade relations with Japan will continue to grow immensely" and that the "American automobile has a firm hold in that country." Hupp was quick to pass on to American newspapers O'Brien's observation that "Hupmobiles are to be seen in every place where there are automobiles, for their popularity is well established."[1]

The world tourers arrived at Honolulu on December 19 to a "very enthusiastic" greeting. They replayed the San Francisco loading of the car in reverse; the crane lifted the little Hupp out of the cargo hold with an almost cheerful, waving Drake at the wheel. "Several Hupmobile owners in Honolulu . . . were at the landing" waiting to escort the Little Corporal to the Vann-Hamm-Young Company, Hupp's local distributors. The newspaper noted that "the reception was typically American and similar to those experienced by the world-touring party throughout the various cities on their transcontinental trip." The reporter added that while "one or two other cars have made globe girdling trips," all "have been following as straight a line as possible" and "none has touched at Honolulu." Moreover, "of all the cars that have ever essayed the world trip, the Hupmobile is by far the smallest."[2]

The three men were fortunate that the diphtheria epidemic that had swept across the island of Maui, just to the southeast, was finally under control and doubly lucky to have left the islands before cholera swept through Honolulu in early March. They were also pleased that the island's roads were not clogged with horseless carriages. There were 630 other automobiles registered with Honolulu police headquarters, as well as new car owners awaiting the "passing . . . upon their qualifications as Chauffeurs."[3]

Almost ninety years later, Hanlon's daughter recalled that he had loved Hawaii and had often told stories of its salubrious climate and tropical foliage. After the bitter cold and high winds they endured in western Wyoming, Honolulu's 76-degree temperatures must have seemed like heaven. Photographs show the Hupmobilists in typical tourist poses, sporting clean clothes, at the Hawaiian state house, watching "surf boats" off the city's harbor, driving along smooth, though unpaved, roads flanked by lush vegetation, which frequently overhangs their car. A particularly nice snap shows Hanlon and Drake, obviously happy, sitting in the car on a high-crowned road, surrounded by palm trees. They had reinstalled the left headlight, but it was not properly aligned; at night it must have given Hanlon a good view of the islands' exotic birds perched in trees. The Hupp Company turned some of the photos into postcards, which it distributed to prospective buyers for them to send to the factory to ask for the "1911 Hupmobile Illustrated Catalogue."

Hanlon and Drake enjoyed Hawaii's tropical foliage and smooth avenues. HPA/DJC.

The "official" company version of their Hawaiian stay recounted that the explorers drove on "various islands," but "by far the most interesting performance of the world-touring Hupmobile was a thrilling climb to the crater of Kilauea, one of the largest active volcanoes in the world." Located on the southeast side of the island of Hawaii in what is now the Hawaii Volcanoes National Park, Kilauea's top towers 4,090 feet above sea level. The company explained that "near the center of this great hole in the earth is a smaller pit, approximately 1000 feet in diameter, that fills with lava at irregular intervals and forms a lake of fire from 15 to 20 acres in extent."[4]

The fun was in getting there. The crew had to drive thirty-eight miles and up four thousand feet, "an ascent," Hupp declared, "that will test the merits of any car," and, it boasted, "the Hupmobile is the only car of its size that has ever made the climb." A photograph the men took on the way up shows that they drove on a roadbed that seems to consist of lava granules; only rocks and lava outcrops appear in the bleak background. They drove to within 100 feet of the smoking crater, where a crevasse blocked their further progress. They walked to the very precipice, where they remained long enough to pose for a photo warming their hands before they "were driven back by the fumes of sulphur." They said "it looks like a mighty slow moving river[,] the crater is ¾ of a mile in circumference and 400 feet deep and flows underground into the sea."[5]

The Hupp party did not remain in the islands long. On January 3, 1911, a little over two weeks after they arrived, they hoisted the Little Corporal aboard the SS *Moanna* and sailed for Brisbane, Australia, via Fiji. They cabled their home office when their ship crossed the 180th meridian on January 15, 1911, noting that they had lost a day "that can never be recalled." The following day, they reached Fiji, where the waters were so shallow that the ship had to anchor a quarter of a mile from the dock. Hanlon remembered that we "were met by . . . a small barge which carried the Hupmobile to shore." The little motorcar caused quite a sensation, because, Hanlon claimed, it "was the first car to land and be driven in those islands." He fondly recollected that "there were crowds coming from great distances to see this new invention." They liked what they saw, and Drake signed up a dealer and took orders for a dozen new Hupmobiles, a number the tourers thought excessive, because only twenty-seven whites lived on the island.[6]

Hanlon later said that he had passed through Fiji four months afterwards, which

Hanlon entitled this shot, "a good road runs up to the crater (Kilauea)." Hanlon had moved the spotlight back to the car's left front side. HPA/DJC.

If the trio took pictures of their car on Fiji, they have not survived, are unlabeled, or were mislabeled. This photo of a fruit seller on the island, however, proves that they were there. HPA/DJC.

would have been possible only if his steamship took a most circuitous route, and told a story of leaning over the rail next to an Englishman as they approached the island. His friend spotted a car in the distance and asked Hanlon what kind it was. When Hanlon immediately replied "a Hupmobile," the Englishman questioned how he could tell from that distance and bet a dinner that it was not one. Hanlon always finished the story with the quip, "I dined free." He knew the new Hupps had been delivered.[7] The *Moanna* lingered off Fiji one day, just enough time for the men to drive around and take a few pictures. The remainder of their voyage to Australia, however, was much less serene. A stubborn fire broke out on the ship, probably in a coal bunker, and burned for eight days, though the passengers were not told until just before they docked. They were aware, however, that a woman aboard had died of the plague—perhaps an early case of the cholera that ravaged Hawaii—four days before they reached port and had been buried at sea.[8]

At the rate misfortune dogged the *Moanna*, the Hupmobilists must have been happy to see Brisbane on January 23. "The first world touring car that had ever passed through Australia" was met by the usual company representatives and gawkers, who trailed it into town, where the trio made their obligatory stop at the local Hupp dealership. After a few days in Brisbane, the men drove 800 miles down the coast to Sydney, home to almost a quarter of Australia's 4.4 million people, where they were an instant sensation. "Wherever the car stopped in the down-town districts during the week's stay in Sydney," the company bragged, "crowds gathered and often police had to pave the way for the car and keep the walks and streets clear." The city was providentially endowed with numerous hills, which, Hupp said, provided a good opportunity to demonstrate the climbing qualities of the car. The Hupmobilists liked the city and its citizens and spent much time snapping photos of the cliffs and British warships in the harbor.[9]

The Little Corporal in front of the Houses of Parliament in Sydney. HPA/DJC.

The Hupmobilists loved Sydney, with its smooth roads and vistas of the water. They memorialized these attributes in this snapshot on the city's Harbor Road. HPA/DJC.

"Our North Island Escort," shown in Auckland, where Drake recuperated while Hanlon and Jones toured New Zealand and Tasmania. HPA/DJC.

They would have liked to linger longer, for the weather was perfect, in the low to mid seventies, but they had a deadline to board a ship sailing from Melbourne, another 500 miles south. Behind schedule, they drove partly at night, when they "were pestered by kangaroos and rabbits attracted by our lights," so many of them that they "made it almost impossible to drive." They "had to stop and turn out [their] lights at times in order to go on." Ever after, Hanlon was convinced that the millions of rabbits, which competed with horses for the sparse grazing, would help them sell Hupps.[10]

The Hupp travelers had arrived in the midst of a drought; it had not rained in southeastern Australia for eight months, and "cattle were dying by the thousands." Australians were proud of their merino sheep, one of the continent's economic mainstays, but they too were dying and could be purchased for as little as twenty-four cents each. Worse, the motorists had difficulty finding water; they observed peevishly that in "three different instances, we had to pay fifty cents for water for our radiator."[11]

Early in the week of February 6, they reached Melbourne, Australia's second-largest metropolis, which they described as "a beautiful city with many old buildings and botanical gardens." They marveled at the quality of the roads, built with convict labor. Back home, many supporters of the good roads movement were also calling for using prisoners on a vigorous road-building program.[12]

The men remained in Melbourne only a few days before they sailed for Auckland, New Zealand. They steamed through the Hauraki Gulf to the growing city of 102,000 souls, arriving before February 15. There Drake suffered an undisclosed ailment or accident that required surgery and an almost three-week convalescence. Hanlon and Jones drove across both islands and Tasmania (to which they took ship from Dunedin on New Zealand's South Island) without Drake, who, when he had mended, returned to Sydney, where he rejoined his colleagues.[13]

After demonstrating the Hupp's merits in Auckland for four days, Hanlon and Jones headed south, inland through the hills they called "the Alps of the South Seas" (not, however, to be confused with the Southern Alps, on New Zealand's South Island), where the slopes were some of the worst they encountered on their trip, with "short pitches of about 30 per cent grade to long steady climbs of from three to twelve miles." The *Detroit Free Press* noted that the famous automobile tourer Charles Glidden, who had driven all over the globe, was said to have characterized New Zealand's mountains as "the worst in the world."[14]

The Hupmobilists' first day out was a long, difficult run, at least after the first forty miles, when the Little Corporal hit a "stretch of deep pitch holes." The road was deceptive; sand filled the holes, giving the appearance of an even, smooth surface, but "the awakening came when the car dropped a foot or so at the end of a firm stretch." A few miles further on, the "rain fell in torrents." They were on a road cut out of the side of a hill, and the pelting downpour turned it into "a mass of sticky clay; the residents declared it impassable." Nevertheless, the Hupmobile and the pilot cars plugged through, making but one stop before reaching Rotorua, 162 miles from Auckland, by late afternoon.[15]

Rotorua was Maori country. The indigenous people had fiercely resisted white colonization of their islands, postponing New Zealand's settlement almost a half a century after eastern Australia's. They were, as a geography text of the period explained, "a hardy, warlike race, living in protected villages, in the midst of cultivated fields." That was exactly how Jones and Hanlon found them. They photographed the Maoris' distinctive houses and, although both believed and reported home that the natives were a "canabalistic [*sic*] people," they appeared friendly as they swarmed

The hills outside Auckland were formidable, prompting the Hupp motorists to stop and take this photo atop Mt. Eden. HPA/DJC.

over the Little Corporal, symbol of yet another wave of colonization, to have their pictures taken.[16]

That night the presumed cannibals amused their two guests with a *haka*, the warriors' traditional dance. Jones cabled home that they had been "greatly entertained" and were enthralled with the "curious customs of this race." They were just as intrigued by the nearby thermal springs, "where geysers shoot intermittently and boiling pools of water abound," in which the Maori cooked their food (and conceivably their victims). Jones was especially amused that he could catch trout in a nearby cold stream and flip the fish over to a boiling thermal vat without taking it off his line.[17]

The party left at noon the next day and drove through the thermal district to Wairakei, just north of Lake Taupo, where the "really hilly district" commenced. Most of these "hills" peaked at about 3,500 feet and Hanlon spent the afternoon prodding the little Hupp up them, through deep sand and along roads built on cliffs, "full of short turns just wide enough to permit the car to pass." The duo reached Tarawera that night and pushed on sixty miles to Napier, on the coast, the following morning. The Hupp had "conquered" the "largest and most picturesque" of the hills, Tibiokura, "the supreme test for cars on the North Island," they boasted, a trial that

Hanlon was in his element as Maori women swarmed over him and his Hupp. HPA/DJC.

included four miles of climbing on a road whose "surface [was] none too good, with many sharp grades."[18]

To see as much of the island as possible, Hanlon and Jones cut west to what they called Wanganni, probably modern-day Wanganui, in a very long day's run, during which they detoured to look at the "magnificent Manewatua gorge, where the road hangs over the side of a cliff, the river roaring 200 feet below." At "Wanganni," they reported, local citizens raised such a clamor to buy the pace cars that their escorts sold them on the spot, "and they were being driven by new owners before noon." The Americans thus drove the final leg of their itinerary on the North Island alone, 137 miles to Wellington, which they covered in only five and a half hours, rocketing along at twenty-five miles an hour. Jones wryly noted that they made better time than "the railroad express through the hills" and pointed out that they would have been faster had they not climbed Paikakariki for three miles.[19]

From Wellington, New Zealand's capital (although smaller than Auckland), Hanlon and Jones took a ferry to Lyttelton on the South Island, from where they drove the few miles north to Christchurch on Sunday, February 19. The 80,000 citizens of the South Island's capital greeted them effusively. A newspaper informed

Jones and Hanlon took Hupp's Christchurch agents for a spin in the world tourer. HPA/DJC.

Christchurchians that "two unpretentious American citizens" had arrived in "their absurdly small but apparently thoroughly reliable car." Hanlon and Jones pronounced their trip a "chug around the earth" and, in a good public relations ploy, congratulated New Zealanders on their roads, which beat those "over home by dizzy miles for evenness." In fact, they got carried away, telling the reporter, "we are quite happy," because "your roads are boulevards compared with our high-crown horrors." Not only were the Kiwis' thoroughfares wonderful, Hanlon said, but "your towns are neat and your climate is always up on deck." If that were not enough to please the locals, he continued, "Say, you call this 'God's Own Country,' too, don't you? Well, we aren't a bit jealous, but you sure are entitled to."[20] Hanlon explained that they had already covered 6,089 miles on their "chug"; "the car behaved splendidly all the way, and so far nothing has been done in the way of repairs."[21]

Three days later, the two men drove their car the few miles to Sumner, over "another tremendous hill—the Zig-Zag," a road that "twists around the hill in the sharpest kind of hairpin bends—not one, but half a dozen of them." They later declared that "around these it is almost impossible to drive unless one knows the road," complaining, "the turns usually come on the steepest part of the hill—rises that nearly stand the car on end." Afterwards, one of their South Island pilot party, obviously with a warped sense of humor or an exaggerated sense of corporate fealty, told Hanlon and Jones, "We could have taken you 10 miles further and avoided the hills, but we wanted you to come over the Zig-Zag to show the people." Jones did not enjoy the detour; he told the Christchurch reporter that it was "almost as tough a strain as biting the prongs off a hay-rake."[22] On February 22, the two men left for Timaru, down the island's east coast. The scenery was beautiful, and they were pleased to find no hills, but not so happy at having to ford 200 "water races" used for irrigation. The following day, they raced 140 miles to Dunedin, taking a six-mile detour up Mt. Cargill, where they stopped to photograph the car next to a 200 foot drop-off into a valley. With nothing scheduled for the two days before their ship to Tasmania was due in Dunedin, the two men decided to drive another 139 miles to Invercargill, the southernmost city in the world. They made the trip easily in one day and took numerous photographs of themselves and their car in the little town of 15,000. The next day they motored back to Dunedin to meet their steamship.[23]

Parked outside the trio's Christchurch hotel, the little Hupp drew a curious crowd. HPA/DJC.

Hanlon and Jones in In-
vercargill, New Zealand,
the country's southernmost
town. HPA/DJC.

They scattered their corporate spores everywhere in their whirlwind tour of the
islands; soon thereafter, Hupp named three new distributors in Australia and New
Zealand and announced that it had shipped 500 cars to Australasia in the prior
twelve-month period. Hupmobiles were a "hit" in the Antipodes, and the company
forecast increased future sales, saying that "even with duty and transportation costs
added," Hupps were still cheaper than European imports.[24]

On February 27, the world tourers sailed with the Little Corporal on the *Utimaroa*
from Dunedin bound for Hobart, Tasmania, the capital of the island, which they
reached three days later. They stayed only a couple of days in Hobart, whose population was then about 27,000, but a local reporter, styling himself "Spark," accompanied
the two Americans around Tasmania and left a detailed account of his adventures.
With Spark as a guide, they set off for Launceston, 125 miles to the north. They started
"at rather a late hour for a long journey," and even the newsman admitted that "traffic
in Hobart is badly regulated . . . right side, left side, any side, or centre seems to suit vehicles." Hanlon, who was behind the wheel, became somewhat exercised at the melee,
which kept him "busy with horn, voice, and brakes and [he] called forth some terse remarks on Hobart traffic-handling methods." As they sped across the Bridgewater
causeway through Brighton and "over the plains to Bagdad," they bowled along, "with

exhaust cut-out open, the little Hupp slapping along at a steady 40," enjoying the orchards alongside the road. They stopped to take pictures and buy some fruit and motored on to Oatlands, where they remained for an hour to take tea. Nightfall was approaching, and when they lighted their lamps, they found one of the burners was faulty and Hanlon had to replace it. They took off with both lamps blazing, but within a mile or two, the lights "played mean" on them. Spark recounted: "We coaxed, probed, screwed, used every wile and artifice known to motorists, but nary a good flame could we get." They had wasted valuable time and natural light and hoped the cars scheduled out of Launceston to meet them would reach them before it turned completely dark. The Little Corporal limped into small towns "with only one burner going at half power," but Spark knew the road, so they "were able to 'Hupp' along at a good clip." After a few cars finally straggled out for the meet, Hanlon got "the little car going a million" and "kept the engines [*sic*] running at 1750 [r.]p.m. and held the trail as though he had done nothing else but drive between Launceston and Hobart for the last five years."[25]

A well-dressed Hanlon with "the world's southernmost gas lamp." HPA/DJC.

Outside of Launceston, "a call for lubrication was duly attended to and, whilst [Hanlon was] pouring it in (without a funnel), an alarm of 'Fire!' caused us to . . . transform the Hupp into a fire engine pro tem." They arrived at a burning cottage only to find the "inmates" had brought it under control. The three reached Launce-

Above: Along the Launceston road Hanlon, Jones, and Spark met what Hanlon labeled a "group of Americans," obviously proud of their Hupps.

Right: Jones looked back as Hanlon chugged down what he characterized as "Boulevard across Tasmania built 100 years ago." It was a far cry from roads in Iowa and Wyoming. HPA/DJC.

ston just as the post office bell rang 11 P.M. Even at that late hour, Spark noted, "a couple of motorists were around awaiting our arrival, and extended the boys a cordial welcome."[26]

The next day, Hanlon and Jones booked their berths and made arrangements to ship the car back to Australia. Later, they were entertained by the Tourist Association, which gave them literature and Tasmanian souvenirs, including a deck of playing cards, in which "the joker (a Tasmanian devil) . . . tickl[ed] Mr. Hanlon's fancy immensely." They drove out to the Hobart power station, where they took the grand tour and looked out over Cataract Gorge, which they described as "a spot to delight the eye and what was more practical, to give us a chance to show the Tasmanians what we could do in the line of hill climbing." The power plant's chief engineer offered the Americans a ride across it "on the wire," an aerial cage the generating plant used to haul heavy materials across the chasm. Halfway across, Hanlon exclaimed that "he wouldn't have missed the experience for 25 dollars."[27]

On the way back to Launceston, coming down Denison Hill, the travelers suffered their first serious mishap since leaving Detroit. A tire blew out when Hanlon was going close to forty miles an hour. He could not stop the car, and the tire worked itself off its rim while rounding a turn, which, Spark observed, "would have spelt disaster for any but the most experienced of drivers. Tom F. Hanlon [sic]," he noted with relief, had, however, "served his driving apprenticeship in racing cars, and took his M.A. degree in the Rocky Mountains trails and the gorges of New Zealand." Thanks to Hanlon's ability to keep the car on the road, "the Hupp is . . . still registering mileage and not a heap of twisted scrap down at the bottom of the gorge."[28]

They limped back into Launceston to prepare the car for their departure that night. Spark was sorry to see "the adventurous and charmingly interesting couple" leave and promised to follow their future "movements." He believed the Hupp's motor was good for 50,000 miles, because Hanlon "knows Hupp engines and parts better than anyone" and "the supply of duplicate parts carried on the car is sufficient to see them well through." Moreover, he averred, "[Detroit Mayor] Breitmeyer will have a valuable souvenir in the small silk flag," which had "accompanied the car everywhere."[29]

On March 4, Jones and Hanlon boarded the SS *Grantala* for the day's run between Launceston and Melbourne. They "had thoroughly demonstrated the going qualities of the Hupmobile to all New Zealand," they cabled home. They lingered for three days in Melbourne before retracing their 800-mile route north to Sydney, where

The Hupmobilists did not take their car off the ship at New Guinea, but they disembarked to look over the island. This "scene at "Frederichs Willielms-hafen," as Hanlon spelled it, was the only known photograph they took on the island. HPA/DJC.

they found Drake waiting for them, "entirely recovered." On March 10 or 11, they sailed for Manila on the SS *Prince Waldemore*.[30]

The ship stopped at German New Guinea, also known as Kaiser Wilhelm's Land. The island of New Guinea, which shared aboriginal and animal life with Australia, was occupied by Dutch, British, and German overlords. The Germans had a penal colony in their territory, and the three Hupmobilists were surprised to learn that the guards provided their prisoners with guns to hunt "tropical birds of paradise" for their feathers, which tourists valued. If the prisoners did not return by 6 P.M., they were locked out for the night, presumably a greater punishment than being locked in. The *Prince Waldemore* could not get closer to shore than about half a mile, and the motorists were astounded to watch sailors deliver cattle by pushing them off the ship's deck, forcing them to swim ashore.[31]

The exact dates on which the trio arrived at and departed Manila remain confusing. The *Prince Waldemore* stopped at every port for which it had freight and was not the fastest vessel afloat. The Hupp Company later claimed that it had received a wire announcing its car and crew arrived in Manila on March 27. Earlier, it had told the

Detroit Free Press that the voyagers had reached Manila's docks on April 5. Hanlon labeled a photograph of the ship's captain, "Manila Harbor, April 1, 1911," however, indicating that the Americans had arrived by that date. When the Detroit newspaper published a lengthy article on the Hupmobilists' adventures in the Luzon highlands, it said that they had driven out of Manila on April 6. Hanlon, Jones, and Drake may have arrived on March 27 and spent over a week in the Philippine capital and then headed into the hinterland, except that several accounts take pains to explain that the three men left Manila the day after they arrived in the islands.[32]

Whether they reached the Philippines in late March or early April, they were greeted with "the typical American reception" of "a regular parade of Hupmobile owners, a band, greetings by the consul, and a general gala day among the American colonists." The well-scripted celebration was organized and led by the local Hupmobile dealer, who, when he later visited Detroit, told a newsman that he had met the Huppers at the dock with a slogan-emblazoned truck, the band, and "a squad of Hupmobile owners."[33]

The three men had reached the outer edges of the new American empire. The

"Arrival at Manila" featured the Hupp dealer's hired "slogan emblazoned" truck with a band, which greeted the Little Corporal at the pier. HPA/DJC.

United States had taken the 3,000-plus Philippine islands after defeating Spain in the 1898 war. During that conflict, Americans had returned the insurrectionist leader Emilio Aguinaldo to the islands to raise an indigenous allied army against the Spaniards. In the midst of the war, on June 12, 1898, Aguinaldo formed a provisional government and proclaimed the islands' freedom from Spain. General Aguinaldo assumed that the United States supported Philippine independence, and when he discovered that the 1899 Treaty of Paris gave the islands to the North Americans, he revolted against his former ally. The United States sent 70,000 troops into the Philippines, and by late 1899, the conflict had turned into a nasty guerrilla war. Americans captured Aguinaldo through trickery in 1901, but sporadic outbreaks of fighting continued until all the islands were pacified in 1906. President Theodore Roosevelt appointed William Howard Taft the islands' first military governor.

The Manila Hupp dealer hinted at the rapid rate of Americanization, saying, "nobody walks if he can help it in Manila," where "the people . . . have the automobile fever badly and . . . are particularly enthusiastic over American cars." The capital's citizens, he averred, especially liked the Hupmobile, "a little car built on aristocratic lines," which was not too heavy and did not consume as much expensive gasoline as non-American, "foreign cars."[34]

Their enforced idleness aboard ship quickened the Huppers' "scent for adventure." Eager to get back on the road, they left the next day without waiting for a guide and interpreter and headed up 200 miles into the highlands to the summer capital at Baguio, a noted hill resort. They also professed an interest in driving up Mt. Taal, northeast of Manila, "in order to reach the smoking grounds of the recent earthquake." The three had a penchant for thermal pools, geysers, volcanoes—preferably still active—and anything high that could prove their little car's hill-climbing abilities.[35]

The first few miles of road out of Manila were in wonderful shape and the Little Corporal hummed along. The good road soon petered out, however, and they entered a 150-mile stretch that made their "going laborious every mile of the way." Bridges built under Spanish rule had crumbled, and "the disused roads were overgrown with grass." Fallen bridges "forced dashes across untracked country—through rice fields, across the innumerable fords and in some cases floating across on rafts." In the middle of one of those rice fields, they happened upon an imposing monument erected to the memory of Colonel John M. Stotsenburg, an American soldier killed in a skirmish against Aguinaldo's insurrectionists in 1899. The three cor-

porate adventurers were lucky they were there before the summer wet season made the roads impassable, but even so, reporters alleged, "it was not uncommon to have mud and water come up above the running board."[36]

By afternoon, Jones reported, they had reached what he called the Penaranda River, probably the Pampanga River, the second-longest on Luzon, which flowed 120 miles from the mountains into Manila Bay. Their only means of crossing it was over a railway bridge. Its ties, however, were eighteen inches apart, too far to enable the Hupp to bounce along the tracks. The Americans solved the problem by hiring locals to lay planks across the ties, which allowed them to proceed about ten feet at a time. After about an hour and a half, they finally made it across, only to confront several more railroad trestles forty feet high and too narrow for the workers to pick up the planks and carry them to the front of the car. They were stuck, but the Filipino laborers lifted the car and turned it around—and then they had to recross the first bridge by laying the boards down again. Exhausted, the Hupmobilists quit for the day and spent the night with an American schoolteacher.[37]

Hanlon labeled Colonel John Stotsenburg's lonely grave simply "here's grave among rice fields." HPA/DJC.

Above: Philippine ferries, as this one on the way to Baguio, were not substantial craft, but strong enough to keep the Hupmobile afloat. *Right:* The only way over the Pampanga River was on the railroad bridge where the ties were spaced too far apart. Philippine workmen laid planks across the ties for the Hupmobile. The next railway bridge was narrower. HPA/DJC.

Left: Sometimes there were no ferries or bridges at all, in which case the little Hupp plunged right into the water. Hanlon described this scene as "disturbing the peace of a Caribou Wallow."

Below: Of all the mud-holes Hanlon mucked through on the trip, he remembered this one encountered on his way to Baguio, where goo oozed over his front tires, as his worst. HPA/DJC.

They recrossed the Pampanga the next day at San Isldio on a raft made of bamboo poles. It was so light and unsteady that "natives" had to swim along its sides and hold it up to keep it from sinking. Once ashore, they fought their way along overgrown paths for the rest of the morning until they came to the Cabanatnan River, where they found a bridge that they swore was made out of bamboo and grass. An American engineer working nearby doubted whether the bridge would hold the Hupp, but they chanced it and made it over without mishap. They chugged along without benefit of road for the rest of the day, bumping "across open fields and through caraboo wallows" and soon discovered that they had no idea where they were. For three days, they bumbled around the countryside, eating raw fish and rice, unable to talk with the locals, and fearing the dreaded headhunters who reportedly lived in the area.[38]

In Manila, the Hupmobile dealer worried because he had heard nothing from his guests. After two days, he "sent a scouting party out after them." He also wired the Hupp Company "World car lost in Igorrote [sic] country. Searching party out." The three intrepid explorers, with "little food and no protection against the cold, the poisonous insects, and reptiles or attacks of wild beasts," decided to "keep on," and they "forded mountain torrents, cut logs to 'jack' the car through mudholes and labored through thickets." Their renditions of how they were finally "saved" varied with their audiences. For official publication, they either did not speak of their misadventure or said they had simply chanced upon the main road again and continued without incident to Baguio, mentioning only that when they arrived, they met the car sent out to find them. "Did a big steak look good! after a detachment of [American] soldiers found us and brought us to Bagio [sic]," their incomplete typescript of the story exclaims.[39]

American engineers had rebuilt the forty miles of road south of Baguio down to the railhead, but it was too narrow for cars to pass on it. They operated it on the "block system"; vehicles were held "at one of the camps until all approaching in the opposite direction have passed." The Americans also operated a "stage line of eight-cylinder automobiles . . . between the end of the railroad and Baguio."[40]

The embarrassed Huppers followed the buses up to the capital but found the route difficult. For twenty-two miles, they steadily climbed over "the Benguet Road," and they then faced . . . the "Zig-Zag," a 1,600 foot ascent in seven miles, where, they noted, "the road winds around and around the mountain until in some places seven different stretches of it may be seen below." The Manila Hupp dealer described it as

"a winding detour averaging about 10 per cent grade all the way—some climbing for an automobile."[41]

The twisting Zig-Zag road up to Baguio tested both men and machine. HPA/DJC.

The Hupmobilists finally reached their destination, 4,000 feet above Manila, and entered the town "amid cheers and congratulations from numerous American friends." It was not their fellow Americans, however, whom they had motored all that way to see; they were more interested in the natives, among the most exotic people they encountered on their tour. They "spent one week there among the Egrote [Igorots] or head hunters" before they returned to Manila.[42]

The Philippines' American masters estimated that approximately six-sevenths of the islands' eight million inhabitants were "civilized" in 1911. The new colony was a melting pot. The "aboriginals," or *negritos,* were increasingly being pushed into the hinterland by the Malays, whom Americans considered "more powerful and intelligent." Sprinkled among these two groups were "half breeds," Chinese, Spaniards, and a growing number of North Americans.[43]

The Benguet Igorots, who lived around Baguio, numbered about 28,000, and a *National Geographic* writer found them "a robust and vigorous people, . . . short,

The Igorots were as fascinated by the Hupmobile as the Americans were with them. Once the Hupmobilists' fears that they were headhunters had been allayed, they posed easily with one another. HPA/DJC.

heavily built, and strongly muscled." They were in a transitional stage between their historical culture and customs and those of their several conquerors. By the time Hanlon, Drake, and Jones arrived, for example, they had started to adopt Western dress; the men wore "clouts" and, when they could get them, shirts, pants, and coats, many of them army castoffs. The women wore numerous skirts and bound their hair in towels. A few years earlier, they had begun covering their breasts in public, but they frequently went about topless when working in their houses and rice fields. Both sexes adorned their bodies with jewelry and tattoos. They were monogamous, "although the men sometimes kept concubines."[44]

These Igorots were a peaceful, settled people, "industrious agriculturists." Despite what the Huppers believed, they had never been headhunters, even though a Detroit newspaper, while they were away, featured an article on the tribes that maintained "no head, no wife has hitherto been the rule among the Igorot." Not far away, however, the Bontoc Igorots were known for removing their enemies' heads and as late as 1911 proudly ushered visitors into a special communal room where they kept their skull collection. Numerous other tribes also had a history of head-hunting, and their new American overseers planned to do "away with this mischief almost entirely" by building roads to connect the tribal villages to increase their "social acquaintance." The Hupmobilists could not tell the various tribes apart, however.[45]

The three men were fascinated by the Igorots' custom of eating dogs. Every Sunday morning, lowlanders brought packs of hounds into the highlands to sell to the hungry Igorots at a dog market in Baguio, which, the *National Geographic* reported, "presents a unique spectacle." The Detroit explorers attended such a selling frenzy, parked their car in the midst of it, and photographed the natives and their dogs swarming around and over their machine. Igorots filled the little car and faced the camera proudly as though they had run the mechanical beast to earth. The Americans must have been struck by the dogs' scrawniness; none appeared healthy enough to provide decent sustenance.[46]

Understandably, Hanlon, Drake, and Jones were in no hurry to retrace their route out of the hills. At the end of a week in Baguio, however, they drove down to the railhead, where they loaded their auto onto a flatcar to ship it back to the capital city, where they lingered "for a good two weeks rest." While there, they sought out Aguinaldo, who had retired to spend the rest of his many days farming his ancestral

Hanlon, with cigar, looks bemused by the Igorots at their Sunday dog market. "Starvey stuff and roast," he scribbled at the side of this photo HPA/DJC.

While in Manila, the Hupp Company representatives gave rides to nearby village worthies. Here, Hanlon demonstrates his car's load limits to members of the "Cabanatuan Council," who seem particularly pleased. HPA/DJC.

lands. "A hard man to find," he had become something of a recluse, rarely seen, and even less frequently speaking for attribution. The American travelers were told he had two "estates" and was reluctant to meet anyone from the United States. They drove to one of his homes anyway, located on the shore of Manila Bay near Cavite, and found he was out. Just as they were leaving, however, Aguinaldo and his children arrived. The three men presented a letter of introduction, and, surprisingly, he invited them inside for lunch. He told them he was "happy and contented" and thought "our people are happy and contented." He had a high opinion of Taft, who, he asserted, had "won the hearts of the Filipinos when he was governor-general. He came into close touch with us," the former ex-rebel said, "he learned to know us." Despite his friendliness, Aguinaldo hesitated to affirm his support for American colonialism, saying, "We are well satisfied under the dominion of the United States—so long as the generous attitude of the present administration is maintained," a qualified endorsement of Taft's "dollar diplomacy."[47]

The Hupmobilists characterized Aguinaldo as the George Washington of the Philippines, a man who had fought America "not because he has the soul of a war-

Left: Aguinaldo, the former Philippine insurrectionist leader, sat with his two children for the Americans' camera after lunch. *Below:* After the Hupmobilists assured him that his picture would not be published in the islands, Aguinaldo agreed to ride in the little Hupp and be photographed in front of his (former?) headquarters with Hanlon at the wheel. HPA/DJC.

rior, but because his people's appeal to him to lead them to freedom was too urgent for him to resist." They found him dressed in the "linen suit, high mountain boots and pith helmet of the prosperous Filipino farmer." He permitted them to photograph him and his two children, but when they invited him to sit in the car for another picture, he refused "absolutely." After much cajoling, however, he agreed, as long as they promised not to use the picture in the Philippines. They took at least two snaps of him in it, one with Drake and Hanlon, in which he appears anxious to disembark from the infernal machine as soon as possible, and another with Hanlon alone, in which he seems more comfortable. They may have even taken Aguinaldo for a spin around Manila.

They did not have long to entertain Aguinaldo, however, because they had to catch a ship to Japan, via Hong Kong and Shanghai. They arrived in Hong Kong on April 28 aboard what they called the *Prince Edle Frederick,* actually the Norddeutscher Lloyd Line's *Prinz Eitel Friedrich,* a large, almost 9,000-ton vessel, that made the regular run between Yokohama, Japan, and Hong Kong. Their future itinerary, however, was still subject to change. About the time they left Manila, Hupp published *Round the World in a Hupmobile,* a twenty-four-page pamphlet, which predicted that "before this book is off the press they will have visited Shanghai and Tokio." "From there," the company promised, "they will skirt the sea-ports of India; then they sail to South Africa, where they are scheduled to make the run from 'Cape to Cairo,' most of it over unbeaten trails." All Hanlon, Drake, and Jones could be absolutely certain of as they sailed out of Manila Bay that April day in 1911, bound for the British colony of Hong Kong, was that they were heading deeper into the heart of Asia.[48]

THE CAR

7

The sturdy little Hupp Model 20 that circumchugged the globe, although built in 1910, was a 1911 model. Before the 1920s, when Alfred P. Sloan introduced the uniquely American concept of "planned obsolescence" at General Motors, car manufacturers introduced improvements whenever convenient, anytime during the "model year." Packard, for example, did away with yearly designations entirely, preferring to identify its cars by a series number, which until 1953 never hinted at the year of manufacture. Not until just before World War II did the auto producers settle upon late summer or early fall to announce their new models. They did so in part to schedule their changeovers to coincide with the vacation season, in order to guarantee their workers, many of whom were joining the CIO, steady employment.

Hupp brought its 1911 offerings out in early November 1910 and manufactured them into the initial months of 1912. The Little Corporal, which sold for $900 f.o.b. Detroit, and was advertised as "the lowest priced touring car ever offered in this country," was one of the very first of the new models off the production line, and Hanlon, Drake, and Jones had no time to fine-tune it. Mechanically, however, it was essentially identical to the tried-and-true runabout; only its frame and body were

The little Hupp's chassis was a conventional ladder design with three cross members. With three semi-elliptical springs and friction shock absorbers on the front, it offered a stiff ride. *Hupmobile, the Four Cylinder 20 H.P. Car Extraordinary* (Detroit, 1910).

new. The company was so confident that its new car was utterly reliable that it offered purchasers a *lifetime* guarantee against defective materials and workmanship, at a time when the industry's standard warranty ranged between ninety days and one year.[1]

The chief differences between the Little Corporal and its forebears were its body style and stretched chassis. Hupp increased the tourer's wheel base from 86 inches on previous models to 110 inches, just over nine feet. The additional length and new body added 400 pounds to the car, bringing its weight to 1,600 pounds. The chassis was of the traditional "ladder" design, with three crossbeams, located at the front, back, and just behind the motor, to strengthen its side members. Hupp advertised that its new car had rebound, friction shock absorbers, when many other makes still had leather straps on their springs to dampen jolts. The Little Corporal had two pairs of semi-elliptical springs in the front and a transverse one in the back behind the rear axle at the very end of the chassis.

The car rode on traditional wooden-spoked wheels. Curiously, the lighter models were equipped with twelve-spoke wheels, but the world tourer featured ten-spoke wheels on the front and a more conventional twelve-spoke arrangement on the rear. Despite the axle-busting terrain the car navigated, it never suffered from any wheel problems. By contrast, in the 1908 Peking-to-Paris race, the winning Itala, a much heavier car with much thicker wooden-spoked wheels, was bedeviled with

THREE MEN IN A HUPP

problems when the constant soaking and drying loosened the spokes from the rim. Once, the crew were forced to hire an illiterate Siberian carpenter, who measured everything with his thumb and whose only tool was an ax, to build an entirely new wheel for them. The result was aesthetically upsetting but sturdy enough to enable them to finish the race. For the 1911 season, Hupp did increase the size of its rear tires to 31" x 3½" from its earlier 30" x 3" to accommodate the car's increased weight. Some tourers were fitted with the narrower front tires, while others came with the half-inch-wider tire.

The Little Corporal's heart was its four-cylinder, 112-cubic-inch, water-cooled engine, which was a model of reliability, if not of power. Like most, it was a "long stroke" design; its stroke was longer than the diameter of its bore. It was quite close to being "square," however, having equal bore and stroke dimensions, with a bore of 3¼" and a 3⅜" stroke. Like many engines in 1910, the cylinders were cast in pairs, two sharing a single casting. Hupp claimed superiority for its motors thanks to their Parson's white bronze bearings, offset, heat-treated, ground-steel 1¼"–diameter crankshaft, and "noiseless cam shaft."[2]

The company boasted that its little engine produced a "full 20 horse power" and patiently explained to its customers that this was "all the power you will ever want or need," more than sufficient to "pull you over the hills and up the grades." Hupp's

The Little Corporal's heart was a sturdy, four-cylinder power plant that pumped out 16.9 horsepower for 47,000 miles through every imaginable terrain and weather condition. There was nothing sophisticated about it; it was simply well made, sturdy, and dependable. *Hupmobile, the Four Cylinder 20 H.P. Car Extraordinary* (Detroit, 1910).

horsepower claim was an exaggeration; the power plant actually produced a rated 16.9 horses, 15 percent less than advertised. With a ratio of 95 pounds to one horsepower, the car was no rocket.[3]

The engine was not easy to take apart to fix. The top and bottom halves of the motor were separate castings, and the engine had no removable head. It was difficult to change the rings, for they had to be inserted from the bottom of the top casting. Complicating the task, the three eccentric, bevel-split packing rings, made of close-grained iron, which fitted into a spiral groove on the pistons, were troublesome to compress for insertion into the cylinders. They were only there to maintain sufficient compression, not to keep oil out of the combustion chamber. Just the opposite, in fact; they were designed to allow oil to reach the top of the motor for lubrication. Many shade-tree mechanics worked new rings into the block by twisting piano wire around each and snipping it off just as the upper part of the ring slid into the bore, a tedious and complex job.

The valves were on the left side of the engine and both inlet and exhaust valves were 1½" in diameter. Valve heads were made of nickel-steel and welded to carbon stems before each was ground at the factory. Spark plugs were located directly over the inlet valves. Gasoline reached the combustion chambers via a Breeze updraft carburetor. The car featured a cleverly designed intake manifold that included a "chamber" extending from the carburetor to the exhaust header that prevented condensation and warmed the fuel-air mixture before it reached the combustion chambers, an idea that came into vogue in the 1920s.[4]

A Bosch high-tension magneto, mounted on the side of the engine, supplied the spark for the combustion. Stealing a French idea, Hupp set the magneto slightly in advance to create a hotter spark at higher engine speeds, which eliminated the need to set the spark manually with a lever on the steering column, a fixture on most early cars. The company claimed its fixed setting and offset crankshaft, "which positioned the connecting rod throw already on its down-stroke when the piston was top-dead-center," eliminated the dangers involved in cranking; there was no risk the crank would snap back and break an arm. The whole arrangement, Hupp claimed, was safe enough to allow a child to start the motor. Owners agreed that the car was easy to crank; compression was low enough to make it possible to turn the crank 360° with little effort. Five wires connected the magneto to the four spark plugs and an ignition switch, "the only operative device on the dash."[5]

The Hupp's clutch was a multiple disk, with "nine plates of saw-blade steel" en-

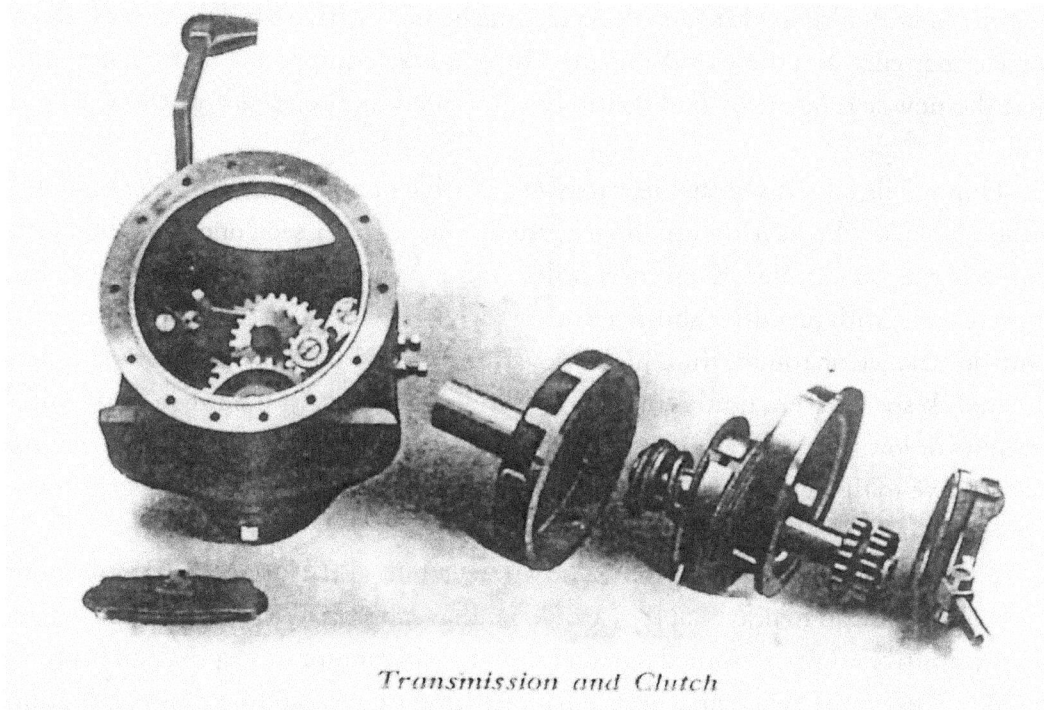

Transmission and Clutch

The Hupp's clutch and transmission assembly lacked sophisticated complexity. But it gave the car two forward speeds and a reverse and was simple enough for Hanlon to make roadside repairs should it prove troublesome. *Hupmobile, the Four Cylinder 20 H.P. Car Extraordinary* (Detroit, 1910).

cased in oil. The sliding gear transmission had only two forward speeds and a reverse. The lower gear ratio was 2.7 to 1, while the higher one was a direct drive, or 1 to 1. Power from the transmission was delivered through a drive shaft affixed with "dust proof" joints to the differential. The rear axles were 1⅛" "cold-drawn piston-rod steel, journaled on Hyatt bearings at the wheels," with ball bearings at the differential case with shim adjustments. While this arrangement was sufficient for "normal" driving, the Hupp suffered catastrophic failure in Japan when the "cold-drawn, piston-rod steel" axle broke and there was no replacement on hand.[6]

The Little Corporal avoided engine overheating, the most common problem early motors endured. The spectacle of "horseless carriages" stopped alongside roads, surrounded by motorists garbed in dusters looking angrily at a fierce column of steam ascending from their radiators, was too common to bear much notice. Hupp cooled its engines using the common "thermo-syphon" system, which worked on the principle that hot water rises. The car had no water pump, and its cooling system's capacity was about three gallons. Hupp had experienced overheating problems with its earlier models, but for the 1911 season, it widened its radiator, increased the number of its vertical cooling tubes from four to five, and enlarged "the intermediate" holding tank. It also made available a fan, attached to the flywheel, for cars destined for warmer climates; the world-touring Hupp was so equipped. The firm declared that the new arrangement had "entirely eliminated any tendency of the water to boil."[7]

Hupmobile advertised that its cars were capable of reaching fifty miles an hour, although those who have driven them agree they have never seen one going that fast, unless it was on a trailer. Even forty miles an hour was a shattering experience for most drivers; with primitive shock absorbers, wooden wheels guaranteed never to be quite in balance or round, thin, high-pressure tires, and the car's light weight, such breakneck speeds were unnerving. A more sedate velocity, in the range of the high twenties or low thirties, was more tolerable. At lower speeds, owners reported getting twenty-five to thirty miles per gallon of eleven-cent gas, right about the world-touring Hupp's average gasoline consumption.[8]

Fearless motorists who did charge down steep hills at fifty miles an hour or more in their Hupps had to pray that they would not have to stop. Early automobile brakes were primitive affairs, designed to halt a slow-moving motor—eventually. Hupp offered brakes on the two rear wheels only, featuring two expanding brake linings on each wheel designed to rub against a drum 10" in diameter. Activating the brakes was no simple task. The operating manual advised the driver to brake gradually, for if he applied the brakes suddenly, there was "danger of stripping the tires from the wheels . . . doing them considerable damage," or "otherwise straining the car." Facing catastrophe, the operator was counseled to judge just how quickly he needed to cease motion. Given enough time, he needed only to depress the brake pedal slowly. If some more drastic threat loomed, the company recommended depressing the brake pedal while engaging the outside emergency brake at the same time. Two brake shoes were operated by the pedal and the other two by the emergency brake. Both systems were mechanical, but, when in good adjustment, their action could be just as quick as later hydraulic types.[9]

Steering was rack-and-pinion, controlled by a wooden steering wheel 15" in diameter, set at what the company advertised was a "rakish slant," connected to the column by a four-spoke aluminum spider and located on the right-hand side of the car, as was common in 1911. Hupps were sold with a number of standard features: two side lamps and one rear lamp that burned oil, not to illuminate the road but to warn others of the car's location; a "dragon horn" mounted outside, just ahead of the dash, and operated by compressing a rubber bulb; a complete set of repair tools; and a tire pump.[10]

Hupp bragged that its fit and finish were the very best, tufted leather upholstery, stuffed with horsehair, the dash "a beautiful specimen of the Cabinet Makers Art," finished in "highly polished circassian walnut," and the running boards pressed steel. There was a "snap and beauty in every line," the company said. It was particularly proud of the "long, clean sweep of the fenders" and of "how completely the body of the car is guarded against splashing water and mud." And Hupp's admen understood the commercial uses of pride and envy; "wherever the Hupmobile appears on the streets, its dashing appearance instantly draws the attention of motorists and pedestrians alike," they promised. Certainly, the globe-trotting Hupp drew more than its share of oglers, especially when it turned up in remote areas of the world where no one had ever seen a car before.[11]

To paraphrase Henry Ford, the 1911 Hupp came in any color the buyer desired so long as it was blue. Earlier Hupps had been painted red, but for 1911, the company changed its color to a deep blue, accented with white stripes and gray wheels. It painted its global explorer shiny black, however, perhaps to emphasize its "specialness" or, more probably, because it was thought that black would hide dirt, grime, and mud more effectively.[12]

This side shot of Hanlon taking Auckland, New Zealand, citizens on a demonstration ride shows off the Hupp's clean lines, accentuated by the fenders' sweep, the car's low profile, and simplicity of design. HPA/DJC.

The Hupp Company offered its customers several options at extra cost. For $40 more, a buyer could purchase a top that offered minimal protection from rain, sleet, and snow. Such comfort-loving motorists also usually opted for a "glass wind shield" at $30 to keep the bugs out of their teeth. The hearty trio who circumnavigated the planet enjoyed neither option. And for those motorists who wanted to see where they were driving in the dark, the company obliged with an offer of two "gas lamps, with brackets and connections attached to the car" for another $20 and a "Prest-O-Lite Tank" that held compressed acetylene to operate the headlights for only $18.[13]

Lighting on early automobiles was not for the uninitiated. The 1911 Hupp came equipped with a carbide generator that produced acetylene by mixing water with calcium carbide. It was mechanically simple, but when the water froze in the generator, a problem the Hupp explorers encountered in the wickedly cold nighttime temperatures of the American West, the process became a nightmare. While on the road, Hanlon stopped at dusk, got out of the car, and lighted both headlamps. Acetylene gave off a very harsh light, too glaring for many oncoming motorists, and he frequently had to stop to readjust his lights. Some towns and cities had passed ordinances forbidding drivers to turn their lights all the way up, which demanded that the law-abiding motorist pay attention to his luminosity. When turned on fully, however, even on the blackest night, the headlamps threw amazing beams of light "several hundred yards in length." Auto enthusiasts claimed that someone three or four hundred feet from such headlamps could read a newspaper at night with perfect ease. Headlight adjustment was also a problem on horseless carriages. With bumpy roads, stiff suspensions, and constant onboard vibration, the lamps were difficult to keep aligned. They tended to either slip toward one another and focus on some point on the road about a dozen feet in front of the radiator; tilt down, illuminating the car's crank handle; or tilt back, aimed skyward.

By 1911, however, engineers were experimenting with easier lighting systems. Some cars carried acetylene tanks, doing away with the need for the carbide generator; such tanks could hold from thirty to fifty hours of gas. Elsewhere, particularly in towns and cities, car makers experimented with electric lamps powered by a storage battery replenished by a generator. Such lights were not as bright as acetylene lamps, and their operating systems were more complex, necessitating dash lighting and a dial to make certain the generator was keeping the battery charged, but they had the great advantage of being operable from inside the car.[14]

The little 1911 Hupp was the essence of simplicity. Well-engineered, built from

the best materials available, and finished to the finest standards, it was a basic driving machine. Its lack of mechanical sophistication meant, however, that Hanlon had to work harder to drive it and keep it in good repair. To the uninitiated, the car was a mechanical maze, full of idiosyncrasies, creative beyond belief in its ability to break down. Many early car owners, cursed with mechanical ineptitude or a lack of interest, bypassed the technical perplexities by hiring chauffeurs, if they could afford to do so, which not only had instant snob appeal but took care of maintaining and repairing the vehicle. Many auto companies sponsored courses in which they trained both chauffeurs and owner-drivers alike in the arcane minutiae of automobiling. Moreover, specialized auto journals carried articles on proper driving methods, and many newspapers started auto sections that regularly purveyed similar information.

Hanlon had to follow a relatively complicated procedure just to start the little Hupp. His factory recommended that before he touched the crank handle, he look in the gas tank to be sure he had enough gasoline, check the radiator and the oilers in the engine compartment, which replenished oil the motor burned, and fill the grease cups on the suspension joints. He was also warned to measure tire pressure and in-

This frontal view of Hanlon, cigar securely champed in his teeth, illustrates the vehicle's lighting system. Next to Hanlon's left foot is the carbide tank on the running board that supplied the acetylene to the three lamps, one of which was slightly elevated. A side lamp is also visible. HPA/DJC.

spect the brakes. That done, he moved the "change speed lever," later called the gearshift, located outside the Hupp, to the neutral position, "just opposite the notch in the quadrant" where he put it when he stopped the car. While still outside the car, he reached in and turned "the switch plug" on the dash to the center, which completed the circuit to the magneto, and adjusted the hand throttle under the steering wheel about a quarter of a turn.[15]

With the car in "neutral" to ensure that it would not run over him when he cranked the engine and the magneto turned "on," Hanlon engaged the crank at its lowest point and gave it "a quick pull over compression." If the engine did not respond after two or three tries, Hanlon opened the throttle wider, manually primed the carburetor using the small lever on top of its float chamber, and cranked again. After the engine started, he quickly slowed it down with the manual throttle to prevent undue bearing wear.

Only then could he climb inside the car. To start moving, he pressed the left pedal, the clutch, to the floor "as far as it will go," and moved the shift lever all the way back in its quadrant, which was the "low speed position." He eased out the clutch while increasing the engine speed either manually with the lever beneath the steering wheel or by pressing down on the accelerator pedal, located between the clutch and brake. That was the easy part. To shift gears, he was required to "double clutch," an art requiring physical agility, an ear for engine rpms, an ability to estimate the car's speed, and an appreciation of the engine's temperature, since it heated both the transmission and clutch oil. He first pressed the clutch pedal down, threw the shift lever forward into neutral, released the clutch, revved up the motor so that its speed approximated the transmission's speed, then again depressed the clutch and pushed the shift lever all the way forward, listening for the tell-tale clashing in the gearbox that signified a discordance in rpms. If he heard nothing, or only a low gnashing, he slowly released the clutch while increasing the engine's revolutions and was off in high gear.

When Hanlon wanted to reverse the Hupp, he pushed in the clutch pedal, moved the shift lever to the reverse notch in the middle of the quadrant, and released the clutch slowly. The lack of syncromesh gears sometimes made it difficult, however, to get the shift lever into reverse; he then had to repeat his double-clutching maneuver to slip it in. Downshifting while climbing steep hills was especially tricky. He had to "double clutch" back into low gear before the car came to a stop or started rolling backwards down the hill. Even then, he had to pause, because "oil prevented fast-action of [the] clutch plates," before he punched the accelerator.[16]

Hanlon's maintenance duties were equally complex. The factory issued very specific instructions for owners to keep their machines "perfectly oiled," which required more than just checking a dipstick. The Hupp used a splash system of motor lubrication that made it critical to maintain a specific oil level. Every morning, Hanlon opened two petcocks located on the bottom half of the crankcase. If oil ran out, he kept them open until it stopped; if no oil flowed, he added some through the "vent tubes" until it did and then immediately closed the petcocks. He also had to check the speed of the oil drip into the crankcase while the engine was running. The factory set the "oiler" for 16 drops per minute, a rate calculated to replenish the crankcase oil burned when the motor was operated at top speed. If the motor used more than that, Hanlon reset the rate accordingly.[17]

The Hupp Company recommended that owners change oil every thousand miles, a procedure Hanlon followed about forty-seven times on the trip. To do this he unscrewed the petcocks in the bottom of the crankcase, drained the old oil, and flushed out the sludge and dirt by running kerosene through the engine. When it ran out clean, he closed the cocks and refilled the crankcase with fresh oil. He did the

The Hupmobilists took very few pictures of the car while it was moving. This one, shot in Ontario in January 1912, shows the oil smoke, perhaps mixed with condensation, that trailed the Hupp everywhere. HPA/DJC.

same with the transmission fluid, which he replaced at the same time. He renewed the differential fluids every week, because transmission grease tended to run "through the propeller shaft tube" into the differential, which became overfull and forced oil out the wheel seals onto the brake linings. Hanlon filled the universal joint with grease once a week, remembering, as the factory manual reminded him, "to replace the plug." He oiled the chassis through twelve holes twice a week. He gave the two grease cups on the rear spring box a turn each day to squeeze in fresh lubrication. To complete his preparations, he oiled the brake-rod connections and gear-shifter mechanism.[18]

Hanlon checked the radiator's level every day, and in anticipation of freezing nighttime temperatures, he had two choices. He could drain the system in the evening and refill it the next morning, being careful to leave the petcock open all night, or he could replace the water with a recommended anti-freeze mixture of "15% wood alcohol, 15% glycerin and 70% water." That was good enough for "average" winter temperatures; for below zero readings, Hupp advised increasing the alcohol to 25 percent and lowering the water to 60 percent. The difficulty with this recipe was that the wood alcohol evaporated when heated and had to be replaced, which changed the mixture's proportions.[19]

Even the gas tank was not maintenance-free. Early automobilists were plagued by condensation in their tanks, and Hupp engineers recommended that owners periodically drain the tank to get rid of the accumulated water. Furthermore, gasoline contained the detritus of refining, transportation, and storage in dirty tanks. The company advised straining the gas through a chamois when filling the tank. One also had to be wary of buying gasoline already tainted with water; in the dead of winter, the water collected in the fuel line to the carburetor and froze. When water, debris, or ice clogged the line, Hanlon had to detach it from the carburetor and drain it. When all the water had run out, he filtered the gasoline into a bucket through a strainer to catch any stray contaminants.

After reattaching his gas line, Hanlon checked the carburetor to ensure that his fuel mixture was not overly rich. The factory preset the carburetor "at a point where it will give the greatest efficiency," explaining that with its hot-air connection to the exhaust, an even temperature was maintained in the intake manifold that "will require very little adjustment." But, factory advisors warned, if the adjustment spring weakened or if the outside temperature changed, some fiddling was necessary, and they recommended specific hot- and cold-weather settings for the "air valve." For the

Power Plant Unit, Showing Carburetor and Magneto

The left side of the Hupp's engine featured the carburetor on the lower left and the Bosch magneto above it and to the right. *Hupmobile, the Four Cylinder 20 H.P. Car Extraordinary* (Detroit, 1910).

owner's convenience, the needle valve had the settings marked on it, but once the valve was screwed all the way in, it formed a "small shoulder" on the seat that upset all the calibrations.[20]

Ideally, Hanlon wanted his motor to run "lean," burning a smaller proportion of gasoline to air in the combustion mixture, so as to increase his mileage per gallon and retard the formation of carbon deposits. Faced with a steep hill or terrain that would tax the little engine, Hanlon stopped, opened the hood, and adjusted for a richer mixture for additional pulling power. Often he had to do that when the engine was cold, run it richer until it warmed, and then reset for a leaner optimum. If the engine backfired through the carburetor, he knew his mixture was too lean; when the motor heated up more than usual and spewed a black, smoky mixture with a heavy gasoline odor through its exhaust pipe, Hanlon knew the mixture was too rich. On very hot days, the factory suggested removing the plug in the warm air cavity that surrounded the intake manifold to admit outside air directly onto the exhaust manifold.[21]

The company assumed that the average motorist would perform heavy repairs on his machine. The twenty-three-page operating instruction manual that accompanied each car contained specific directions on how to disassemble and repair even the most complex components. If Hanlon's clutch began to slip, for example, the booklet explained how to remove the entire clutch assembly, replace its defective parts, and align the clutch drum with the crankshaft when putting it back together. It contained

Side Cover Removed, Showing Cam Shaft, Tappets and Magneto

The crankcase side cover unbolted to pull out the camshaft, tappets, and magneto. It was tricky to reinstall, however. *Hupmobile, the Four Cylinder 20 H.P. Car Extraordinary* (Detroit, 1910).

helpful hints to avoid such time-consuming repairs as well; should "a grinding rattle develop in the transmission," it advised that the culprit would probably be a dragging reverse pinion, which Hanlon could adjust without pulling the entire unit.[22]

Should the engine manifest "knocks or unusual noises," factory engineers suggested Hanlon place a crowbar to his ear and touch the other end to various parts of the motor to pinpoint the sound's location. Most knocks, they promised, indicated a loose connecting rod, caused by a bearing that had "become too free at the crank shaft end." This was not a repair to be made on the side of the road, unless, of course, it happened on some godforsaken remote trail in a tropical colony. Then he had to pull the crankcase side cover, remove the cap from the connecting rod, and file the bearing caps down enough to take up the slack. If he overfiled the shims, he had to scrape the bearing. That was the easy part; putting it back together, he had to reset the timing, which involved aligning two separate sets of punch-marked gears and being certain that all the valves were against their tappets before he bolted the cover back on.[23]

If the engine still ran unevenly or had a dead cylinder, the handbook advised Hanlon to grind his valves. They could be removed without disassembling the entire motor, although extraction of the pin, ring, and spring required a delicate touch. Once they had been taken out, he scraped off carbon flakes that had built up on the beveled underside of the valve head. When it was tolerably clean, Hanlon smeared a mixture of Emery flour and lubricating oil on the valve seat and the underside of the valve head. The valve had two indentations on its top, and after he had inserted it in its seat, he took a forked tool that caught those indentations and twisted the valve around. Hanlon could also use a hand drill to twirl the fork, reversing direction every three turns or so, always making certain the paste was spread around the seat.

If the valve's underside was badly pitted, Hanlon resorted to more drastic grinding measures, using Emery alone to grind out the pits and finishing it with the flour. If the valves were in very bad shape, he bought ground glass at a hardware store, mixed it with kerosene to form a thin paste for an initial abrasive, and then finished the polishing with Emery flour, taking care that none of the glop found its way into the cylinder, where it would be equally abrasive. To test whether the valve was properly seated, he cleaned off all of the abrasive and twirled the cleaned valve in its seat. If the fit was proper, both would show "a bright ring clear around" where they had rubbed. If, after he put the valve assembly back together, the engine still misfired, the chances were that he had a spark plug problem, which was much easier to remedy. Hanlon simply pulled the offending plug, scraped off the carbon deposits, and used the recommended "thin dime" to regap it to $^1/_{32}$" before replacing it.[24]

In a world where dealerships were scattered and factory-trained mechanics rare, Hupp owners had to assume responsibility for maintenance and repair of their autos. The company had faith in their mechanical aptitude and abilities. Nowhere was this more obvious than in its recommendation that the easiest way for an owner to make "serious" repairs was "to remove the engine and transmission unit from the frame." It was not that difficult, the repair manual promised. Disconnect the hoses, remove the radiator, unbolt the dust pan, take off the exhaust pipe and gas feeder line, disconnect the throttle connections and the magneto wire, free the transmission case from the two radius rods, disconnect the clutch mechanism, unbolt the engine and transmission from the frame, and the engine was ready to be hoisted with a block and tackle into the nearest tree.[25]

Curiously, Hupp's maintenance and driving instructions ranged from suggestions that assumed the motorist had great mechanical skills to others that implied drivers were all muddleheads. Alongside instructions on how to check the compression in cylinders, the company's list of thirty-one pointers included admonitions not to fill the gas tank by lamplight or drive on flat tires. Many recommendations embodied implicit corporate assumptions about its cars and customers. Hupp advised, for example, that drivers not turn the engine crank more than a couple of times before checking to find out what was wrong. It assumed its product would start quickly and easily. In cold weather, engineers suggested, motorists should inject gasoline directly into each of the cylinders through priming cups attached for that purpose. They cautioned against driving Hupps at full speed, warning they would wear out faster if one did. It was much smarter to drive at a "moderate" speed, because it would "gain for you the reputation of being a careful operator."[26]

Hupp linked good driving habits and regular maintenance to its drivers' overall reputation for intelligence and good character. Letting the engine race, it advised, was not a good idea, because among other things, "it is a sign of bad judgment." Driving fast around corners, it warned, also "indicates poor judgment." In the years when the rules of the road were mostly unwritten, survival depended upon a goodly dollop of common sense. Before drivers' license exams were mandatory, the company assumed an obligation to proffer advice on proper driving procedures, explaining basic rules such as "always pass to the left" and "keep on your side of the road to avoid trouble." A very practical piece of advice in a land crisscrossed by dirt roads recommended that the new driver "be considerate in the matter of raising great clouds of dust as you pass others on the road." Perhaps its best advice to Hupp owners was to "be calm and patient when things go wrong." The company laid the blame for most breakdowns on the owner, however, warning "that almost every usual cause of trouble is, as a rule, the result of negligence, carelessness or inexperience." But, the firm promised, almost any trouble "can quickly be remedied if the rules are followed," as outlined in its handbook. Eventually, the motorist would learn how to fix his car and would not have to refer to the handbook, a tacit admission that driving Hupps was fraught with mishaps. "Learn your car and learn to be reasonable with it," and you would "find that it will stand for lots of your own shortcomings." In short, Hupp thought its cars were more dependable than their owners.[27]

Given the complexity of maintaining and operating the 1911 Model 20, the company's managers were correct in assessing the blame for most of their cars' breakdowns. But American roads, arguably the worst in the world, dusty in the dry seasons and quagmires after rain, also took their toll on the new machines. When company engineers compiled a list of the most "common sources of trouble," they put "inadequate lubrication" at the head of it. Like all other horseless carriages, Hupps had numerous friction points open to the elements; lubricants attracted dust, mud, and dung particles, which increased friction at these vulnerable junctions. Moreover,

the United States was a land of great meteorological and geographical contrasts. Hupps were expected to perform flawlessly in temperatures from −60° to 120°F and from below sea level to over 10,000 feet in altitude. And so were their drivers, exposed to the elements and often so heavily bundled up that they were barely able to move, much less drive with finesse.[28]

The beatings that climate, terrain, and human ineptitude inflicted on cars were so great that motorists expected them to wear out after only 10,000 or 20,000 miles. The world-touring Hupp's 47,000 miles was an astonishing total, which the company featured in its advertising for years. When Hupp introduced its "long stroke" model 32 in 1912, it headlined its ad with a reminder that the "Globe-girdling Hupmobile . . . Pays Striking Tribute to the Staunchness of its Splendid Successor." Like thoroughbred racehorses, "staunch" cars begat superior offspring. In a time when most Americans still depended upon horses, the illusion was a powerful one. In 1911, most autos were used for local trips; only the most adventuresome embarked on a trek of a thousand miles or more. Early autos rolled up mileage readings slowly, and most

The Hupmobile was designed to plow through the deepest snows on the coldest days, such as this slog through Canada in the dead of winter with the temperatures hovering around zero. HPA/DJC.

car owners assumed that their motors would never amass the numbers Hanlon and his colleagues put on theirs. The company agreed; in a testimonial for its Model 20, for example, Hupp quoted an owner who professed amazement that he had driven his Hupp 4,000 miles "and have not as yet spent a cent for repairing" it.[29]

Hupp gambled when it sent its little car off with so much fanfare, but the company hedged its bets by sending Hanlon along. With his experience and inborn mechanical aptitude, he was the perfect man to keep the Hupp tended and in good repair. He knew not to beat the machine to death, overload it, or race about at breakneck speeds. He respected things mechanical and had faith in Hupp's products. But the Little Corporal was, as advertised, extremely sturdy, and, in good fettle, equal to its "globe-girdling" task.

THE FAR SIDE OF
THE GLOBE

8

As the *Prinz Eitel Friedrich* steamed through the spring sunshine ferrying Han-lon, Drake, and Jones to China in April 1911, the three men relaxed and looked forward to their forthcoming adventures. They appeared unaware of the political changes convulsing China, where bloody revolts were rapidly spreading across the countryside. The adventurers avoided the growing chaos, however, thanks to China's impossible roads, which prevented them from venturing out of Hong Kong and Canton into the arms of the revolutionaries.

China had been in decline for centuries, and its defeat in the Sino-Japanese War of 1894–95 exposed the technological and military backwardness of the Celestial Empire. Japan seized Taiwan, and European imperial nations demanded concessions from the Manchu Dynasty, carving out "leaseholds," mainland territorial possessions that they governed as colonies. Many younger Chinese, inflamed by nationalist passions, pressured the Manchus to modernize and armed themselves to expel foreigners from their soil. When a movement calling itself the Righteous Harmonious Fists, whom Westerners dubbed the Boxers, surrounded the foreign legations in Pekin (Beijing) in June 1900, an international army, including 2,500 U.S. troops, freed them.

The Boxers' defeat did not quell the internal unrest—it turned toward replacing the dynasty with a republic. When the Hupp Motor Car Company's diplomats disembarked in Hong Kong and showed their corporate and American flags there on April 28, 1911, a bloody civil war raged.[1]

The world tourers blithely drove into the middle of the melee to sell Hupps. Luckily, they discovered that Hong Kong and, the next day, Canton, were "absolutely unsuited to motor car traffic owing to the narrow streets, in most cases from four to six feet wide, with innumerable sharp turns." Worse, "occasionally" they confronted "a series of steps which have to be mounted in passing through the thoroughfare." Melvin Hall and his mother, on their world tour, voiced the same complaints about Hong Kong's roads. They too attempted to drive to Canton, which confirmed their opinion that "China, as a country for touring, doesn't exist on the motoring map." The evening after the Hupmobilers arrived in Hong Kong, they ferried their car to Canton, where they discovered that "there is none of roads [sic], they are too narrow, [and] good for rickshaw travel only." They departed the following evening, "only two hours before a Revolution at Canton started."[2]

Hanlon and his fellow travelers just missed the carnage. While they were there, thirty thousand Chinese troops of doubtful loyalty were besieged in Canton by followers of a rebel, Wu Sum, described as "a Chinese who was educated in Japan and wears European clothes." Canton's viceroy had fled to a nearby gunboat after several rebel leaders and their armies converged outside the city. Wu Sum was allied with a warlord, Luk of Shuntak, whose rag-tag fighters cared little for republicanism but were excited by the opportunities for rape and pillage. Correspondents inside Canton on April 30, the day after the Hupmobilists departed, reported "bodies of slain are in the streets. . . . Famine prices are asked for foodstuffs. . . . there have been few attempts to bury the dead, and the stench from the decomposed bodies fills the air."[3]

Hupp's salesmen quickly perceived that Hong Kong and Canton were not promising markets, and they immediately shipped out of Hong Kong for Shanghai's more peaceful environs, which they reached safely on May 2, 1911. Hupp had an agency there, which a Detroit paper bragged had "already made the Hupmobile the popular small car of that city."[4]

They found Shanghai's driving conditions much better. Jones wired home that "in the international district of the city at least the streets are wide and the inhabitants more accustomed to automobiles," which he said numbered about 400 machines. The three men were shocked, however, by all the "native beggars [who] infest the roads

Left: The first thing the tourers did on arrival in Shanghai was to pose the Little Corporal in front of the local Hupp dealership. In this particularly fine photo, the locals try out the Model 20. Behind it are a Hupp Torpedo and a shiny, new coupe. *Below:* Driving in Shanghai was much easier than in Canton, but it was still a tight fit for the Hupmobile on side streets. HPA/DJC.

The little Hupp drew a crowd, many of whom were beggars, wherever it went in Shanghai. Hanlon looks a bit nonplussed by the size of the crowd. HPA/DJC.

leading to the places of interest" and "will risk being bowled over to gain a copper or two." The Americans took the gamble and the Shanghai newspaper rewarded their daring by reporting the Little Corporal "was the centre of attraction wherever it appear [*sic*] in the business section." Like many newsmen, the local scribe tried to make the trio's trip an even greater feat than it was. He noted that the car's odometer already registered 8,000 miles and estimated that by the time the trek was over, it would show 80,000. Add in "the sea voyage," the Shanghai *Celestial Empire* continued, and it "will bring the total distance to 100,000 miles." After listening to the Hupmobilists' plans to drive the length of Africa, the reporter predicted that they would not get back to Detroit until August 1912.[5]

The wayfarers "encountered a most thrilling adventure," when they attempted to enter Shanghai's Walled City, which was said to be closed to all Christians. They boldly drove right up to the "very gates," where "they were attacked by the deadly Chinese mob." The newspaper reported "the police, coolies and the populace generally rushed forward from all sides and by gesticulations, shouting, and blocking the way prevented further progress by the party." Drake, Jones, and Hanlon "were only extricated from their perilous position by the timely arrival of the native police." The Chinese made it very clear to them that American commercial interests did not have free rein everywhere; the sojourners had pushed up against the limits of dollar diplomacy.[6]

Otherwise, Shanghai was an agreeable city and the adventurers lingered there until about May 12, then boarded the 5,224-ton Norddeutscher Lloyd steamer *Bülow* for Yokohama, where they landed two days later. The cherry trees were in full bloom, a sight Hanlon never forgot. He repeatedly told his daughter how stunning all Japan's flowers were.[7]

The Hupmobilists were apprehensive when they landed in Yokohama. Although "on our way to Japan we heard nothing but sensational war talk," they wrote home, "contrary to all advice, an American flag was carried." The United States's relations with Japan were anything but friendly in the early part of the century. Japan and Russia had divided up the Chinese province of Mongolia, which challenged the

The adventurers at the tomb of the Chinese statesman and general Li Hung-chang (1823–1901) in Shanghai, dressed in their best business garb. HPA/DJC.

The Hupp representatives stopped long enough to record a "typical turn in the raising district" to show the narrow Japanese roads, with houses built right to the edge. HPA/ DJC.

American "Open Door" policy in China. Moreover, under the 1907 "Gentlemen's Agreement," the United States and Japan had agreed to halt further emigration of Japanese to America. The two countries were also arguing over the depletion of the Alaskan seal herd, and American diplomats were anxious about the Anglo-Japanese Alliance, which signaled Great Britain's withdrawal from the Far East and recognized Japan's ascendancy in the region. Despite their strained diplomatic relations, however, the two nations were never close to war in 1911. The three men discovered that their fears were groundless when they drove through the islands, their American flag whipping in the breeze, and "everywhere . . . were greeted with the welcome of 'Banzai,'" a patriotic shout of cheer.[8] More threatening were Japan's deplorable roads; even the Japanese admitted they were horrible. A Tokyo importer of Paige-Detroit cars visiting Detroit told reporters that due to "the character of the country," only "light, small cars" could be driven there. The hills, mountains, and the "very narrow precipitous roads" put long-wheel-base cars at a great disadvantage. Furthermore, he said, "the streets of the cities are very narrow, the bridges are light, and the turns are very abrupt." He added that "it is frequently necessary in traversing some parts of the mountains and some of the villages . . . [to] lift the car around bodily and to send someone ahead to clear the way." The big cities were not much better.

"Japanese bazaars and stores in a great many instances occupy what in America we would call the sidewalk with merchandise," he explained, which "makes it difficult for large wheel-based cars or cars with large fenders to get through."[9]

The driving difficulties did not dampen the ardor of the Japanese for automobiles, however. Although the nation of fifty million people had only about 200 cars in 1911, and 150 of these were in the Yokohama and Tokyo areas, citizens snapped up all available cars for sale. Because Japan did not manufacture any automobiles, Henry Ford believed that it was "one of the most energetic foreign boosters of the American motor car." While the Huppers were touring Japan, a Ford dealer wrote the factory predicting "a fair road is now open for motor cars" on the islands, although he admitted that "with its crowded cities [it] was a difficult market." British cars were the most popular there; in 1910, Great Britain exported a grand total of 28 to Japan.[10]

Hupp officials had high hopes for Japanese sales. Even before their world-touring car arrived, the company had contracted with the Tokyo Motor Car Company to distribute its automobiles and had shipped at least one runabout to its manager, T. K. Oguri. In late 1910, Oguri decided to advertise "the advent of the lightweight Hupmobile" and prove Japan need not always be "the despair of the touring motorist." He set out on a 5,000-mile jaunt that took him "the entire length of Japan." He started in Tokyo and drove to Yokohama and on from there to the Korea Strait. He then worked his way up the west coast to Aomori, at the very northern tip of the main island, and returned to the capital down the east coast. Hupp's publicity blurb admitted that the journey was not easy. "Hundreds of miles had to be traversed along the rough ties of the narrow railroad," Oguri recalled, and "in many cases the Hupmobile had actually to make its own roadway." The roads, he averred, "test[ed] out the driver's skill and the endurance of the car to the very utmost."[11]

Despite the paucity of cars, roads, and tourists, however, the Japanese were far ahead of Americans in laying down "auto rules." Police had the right to stop, inspect, and require repairs on any car they thought a danger. The national speed limit was set at eight miles per hour, probably unattainable on most roads, and six miles an hour in the cities. When a motorist wished to pass or approach another car or carriage, he was required to "go in special slow speed" or come to a complete stop. And in a land known for its pageants, the government required motorists to halt until any "procession, festival, funeral, fire brigade, carriages, etc." had passed; either that or the driver "must go the other way." Failure to obey such rules resulted in "detention or monetary penalty."[12]

The Hupmobilists posing for their obligatory photograph in front of their local distributor, the Tokyo Motor Car Company. HPA/DJC.

Amid the fragrant spring blossoms of this idyllic, almost pre-motorcar world, Hanlon, Drake, and Jones were determined to demonstrate and sell Hupps. Oguri met them at the dock and escorted them to Yokohama's Grand Hotel, where the management thoughtfully supplied each with two geishas. They drove around the city streets where, Jones reported, their car "created a stir in Japanese motoring circles." They left the next day for nearby Tokyo, where they checked into the Imperial Hotel.[13]

The three Americans were candid when they told the *Japan Times* that their trip had been organized "to get in closer touch with the [Hupp] agents everywhere, to size up business conditions and to observe the progress in road improvements in all parts of the world." They had come to do business. Drake's diplomatic spadework and good luck helped. Thomas J. O'Brien, the American ambassador to Japan, whom they had met on their way to Hawaii in January, invited them to the U.S. embassy. According to a Detroit lawyer who visited the ambassador in Tokyo about the same time as Hanlon, Drake, and Jones, O'Brien "seems to come to the nearest of one not an Oriental to understanding the Oriental character." O'Brien talked about Japanese business conditions with the lawyer and probably with the Hupmobilists. "There was a disposition to look on [the Japanese] as treacherous," but they were not, he told the lawyer. "It is true that the trading class is considered unreliable," he said, but he explained that until a few years earlier, "trade was left to the lowest classes as an occupation menial and degrading." Now, he disclosed, "men of the highest class are . . . in commerce and there is a different idea of the binding force of contracts."[14]

The Hupmobile's crew remained over two weeks in Tokyo, luxuriating at the Imperial Hotel, which also provided each with two geishas; Hanlon made certain he was photographed with his. The high point of their visit to the city was an invitation, probably arranged by O'Brien, to visit Count Hijikata, an eighty-one-year-old "retired minister of the imperial household." The Hupp company announced that Hijikata had "received the world tourists at his beautiful home in a most hospitable manner and through an interpreter heard the story of the world tour." By all accounts, the count was "an enthusiastic motorist" and was especially fascinated by things American. Jones wrote that Hijikata had "visited the United States about 20 years ago" and "never tires of telling the wonders he saw then."[15] On May 31, Hanlon steered the Little Corporal north out of Tokyo, accompanied by Oguri, driving his own new Hupp. "Although they had been advised repeatedly not to attempt" to tour the country "because of the narrow roads, mountain ranges, and bridges," after they got out of the city, they "became convinced at once the trip would be well worth while from the standpoint of scenery"; they felt they had discovered the "real" Japan.[16]

Drake and Hanlon in Tokyo with Count Hijikata, on the left, and Mr. Takata, who would later become Hupmobile's Japanese distributor. HPA/DJC.

Right: Hanlon and Jones in front of the Imperial Hotel in Tokyo on May 31, 1911, before driving off to brave Japan's roads. *Below:* The trio traversed an eighty-mile stretch of nearly impassable road to receive an enthusiastic welcome when they arrived in Shidzoka. HPA/DJC.

The Japanese ferry at Nikko was a primitive arrangement of cross timbers laid across a small barge and a larger boat. Hanlon looks pleased to be afloat but at the same time apprehensive that he may not be for long. HPA/DJC.

Happily, the roads were not as deplorable as claimed: "We found the information as to narrow roads to be correct, but there was no place at which we could not pass other vehicles." The only horrible roads they encountered were on an eighty-mile stretch near Shidzoka and anywhere the Japanese were doing roadwork. They were elated to find "there was no bridge that we could not cross," which meant they "were forced to ferry but once."[17]

They were also surprised at the locals' reaction to them. "Much of their route lay through country where a motor car had never before been seen," they reported, and many of the horses they encountered "reared and plunged, while drivers hung on." Instead "of getting angry," the Hupmobilists were astonished to find, the Japanese "took it all as a joke." Even when "a farmer's wagon turned over completely when his horse bolted," Jones recounted, the owner "apologized for blocking the road and did his best to make the highway clear." Melvin Hall, on his tour of the "island empire," found the Japanese were as "frightened" as their horses at his auto's approach, which made motoring "rather a gamble and a succession of risks."[18]

The Americans were amazed at the human congestion on the roads. They were

The American automobilists attempt to help a Japanese farmer revive his horse, which bolted at the sight of their Hupp. Hanlon described this scene as "the second cart that came to grief." HPA/DJC.

full of people, walking, standing, and gossiping; they were used as public space. The tourers' biggest problem was that there was "no telling how many children will be in the narrow road around a turn, or where they are coming from on a straightaway." The worst spots were in the cities, although they noted that Tokyo's main streets were "wide enough to allow dodgings but side streets—never." The road from Yokohama to the capital was particularly dangerous, Jones said, because it "is 20 miles of nearly continuous house-lined street." Melvin Hall discovered the same difficulties shortly afterwards; the road was so narrow and the buildings so close to the thoroughfare that he had to keep his top down, and in a few places he had to remove it and his windshield to snake through the physical constrictions.[19]

The Hupmobilists were initially puzzled when some "natives ran away screaming as the car approached." They later learned that the panicked people thought "that the gates and emblems spanning the road at the edge of every town, erected there to prevent the entrance of the devil, had failed to function," and that the beast had finally arrived in the guise of a black Hupp full of Occidental evil spirits.[20]

The three evil ones found many sights along their route beguiling. Years later

This Japanese village scene illustrated Jones's wariness of overcrowded, narrow streets. HPA/DJC.

one of them typed a short summary of his journey and noted "it was a common sight in our travel through the interior, to see thousands of nude women working in the rice fields from the age of 12 years and up to aged women." Hanlon never tired of describing these beguiling, bucolic scenes; his daughter remarked that she finally understood why the three men had spent so much time in Japan.[21]

Hanlon told her Japan was his favorite place, he loved its people, mountains, scenery, flowers, and music. He was captivated by the music everywhere he went, but was especially fond of the Japanese variety. He also fancied the traditional Japanese hotels they frequented in the countryside, buildings built of bamboo with paper partitions inside. They followed rural customs, remembered to take their shoes off before entering, slept on beds of silk quilts, and sat on the floors to eat at tables they swore were only six inches high.[22]

The Hupp party drove from Tokyo to Mt. Fuji, where they met up with a Mr. Ishi of the Tokyo Automobile Company, who had gone on ahead. The *Japan Times* announced that the three American visitors "have conceived a unique idea of scaling Mt.

Surrounded by Japanese flags and a milling throng, the car accompanying the Hupmobilists' prepares to assault Mount Fuji. HPA/DJC.

Fuji in their powerful car." Ishi, driver of Oguri's Hupp, agreed to offer it and his services as a guide for the attempt. If Hanlon, Jones, and Drake concocted the scheme, they did so before they saw the 11,932-foot mountain. There was no road, Fuji was "still capped with snow," and the ascent was almost straight up. The adventurers spent the night of June 1, 1911, at an inn on the mountain's north side, where they laid plans for their assault. The innkeeper hired forty workers to clear a road "as much as possible." Ten "stout men" were sent up "armed with mattocks," while another group carried "provisions and other necessaries." A smaller party went up "to help lower the machines in the steep descent." The Japanese and American motorists prepared the guide car by wrapping its tires "with strong hemp-palm ropes to prevent their being cut by jagged stones." At 9 A.M. on June 2, "the party was given a grand send-off by hundreds of local people"; the weather was perfect, and "not a speck of cloud was seen on the mountain top." The following day, the *Japan Times* announced that "no news has yet been heard from the touring autoists as to their success." Four days later, the paper ran a two-inch notice to the effect that "the attempt to motor up Mt. Fuji seems to have been given up owing to the unexpected difficulty of the venture," adding "it will be cruel to recall in this connection the story of the tower of Babel."[23]

After their failed attempt to scale Mt. Fuji, Oguri took the scout car back to Tokyo. Hanlon turned north into the mountainous terrain leading to Nikko, "the great showplace of Japan . . . famous for its sacred bridge and temples where shoguns worshipped and were buried in days gone by." Jones wrote home that although "in Nikko one gets the first view of Japanese mountain scenery," it also required "a car of hill-climbing ability to make the grades about the town." He sent back descriptions of "high peaks, rushing torrents and beautiful lakes" that made "a fitting setting and justify the Japanese enthusiasm over the town." While visiting the shrines, the three also demonstrated their motorcar's abilities to Japanese infantrymen.[24]

The Detroiters worked their way southward over the twisting mountain roads to the coastal town of Kamakura, south of Yokohama, where they went to see the great statue of Buddha known as the Daibutsu. The huge bronze casting, "lacking five inches of being 50 feet in height," with a face eight feet long and eyes "said to be of pure gold and silver," was a leading tourist attraction. Regulations at the "squatting figure," as the *Detroit Free Press* irreverently and wrongly labeled it, were strict. Tourists were allowed near the Buddha, but only an approved photographer, "the eye of whose camera never sees ought that it should not see, as a tourist's camera might," could take their pictures. The autoists did not object to using the official photographer but insisted they position their Hupp right in front of the Buddha for the picture. When they "drove into the grounds which surround the statue," the Detroit news release explained, "they were met with protestations from the attendants, and it was only after much argument, discussion and explanation that the car was allowed to continue and pose before the huge bronze figure." The arguments must have been a veritable drama, complete with gesticulations and raised voices in at least two languages.[25]

The world travelers suffered their most serious mechanical breakdown in Kamakura—their rear axle broke. They were in dire straits, because "we carried no spare axle and all of our small parts and most of our tools had been shipped on ahead to India," Hanlon recalled many years later. The closest parts depot was in Yokohama, "a long, long trip by ox team." "We were just about licked," Hanlon remembered, until he spotted a potter's shop, which gave him an idea. The Americans purchased a *jinrikisha* (rickshaw), removed its axle, and negotiated with the potter to borrow his wheel to use as a lathe. He did not understand what they wanted, so he *sold* them the shop for twelve yen, about six dollars. Hanlon went to work using all the tools he had, a screwdriver, chisel, file, hammer, pliers, and the little foot-pow-

Flying the Rising Sun alongside the Stars and Stripes, the Americans drove into Nagoya past Japanese cavalry drilling below the old castle walls. HPA/DJC.

ered potter's wheel. Over eight days, he fashioned his chisel into ten different tools "to shape and taper the axle" and "saved the file for the last and most important job, cutting the threads on the finished axle." While he labored, townsfolk, including a swarm of beggars to whom the trio threw hatfuls of coins, jammed the shop to watch. When Hanlon had finished, for the grand total of $44 that he had spent on the shop and the *jinrikisha,* he had fashioned an axle that not only fitted but carried them the rest of the way around the world. In 1930, Hanlon "wondered what became of the remains of that jinricksha and the little pottery shop—and whether they have passed out of existence."[26] With their makeshift axle, the automobilists headed west to visit Nagoya and then drove to "Kioto," Japan's ancient capital, a sacred city. There, they reported, "the Geisha girls were extremely interested" in their "diodoso," or motorcar. They posed their Hupp in front of a shrine of the Buddha and filled it with admiring women, who "donned their brightest kimonos and prettiest ornaments" for the photo and ride. The *Detroit Free Press* published the picture to show how the legendary geishas appreciated Detroit's products.[27]

144   THREE MEN IN A HUPP

The Hupmobilists offered contradictory versions of the rest of their Japanese tour. When the company published a short account in 1930, it claimed they had driven to Nagasaki, at the very tip of the island chain. In their more informal renderings, they failed to mention their long drive there, and said they drove to Kobe, or Kaba, as they sometimes called it, where they rested a few days before sailing back to China.[28]

Hupp issued a press release claiming that from "Hawaii [to] . . . Japan, in fact, from every port where the world tourists have stopped, additional orders to the regular schedule have come in from our agents in those countries." The company's export manager was especially proud of an order from his Sydney, Australia, dealer for twenty-three Hupps, "said to be the largest single shipment of motor cars ever sent to that country." Just before they left Japan, one of the Hupmobilists told a Singapore reporter that "when the novelty of motor cars wears off and horses forget to be frightened, motoring in Japan will be a recreation hard to excel with the splendid scenery and friendliness of the inhabitants as added inducement."[29]

Hanlon, with a half a dozen pretty geishas, photographed in front of an apparently disapproving Buddha. HPA/DJC.

Above: The Americans did not record their exact itinerary through Japan, but this photo shows the crowd they drew in Nagoya. Hanlon identified the man with the motorcycle as J. D. Lawrie.
Right: The crowded conditions on Japan's horse-drawn transport were a powerful incentive to buy cars. HPA/DJC.

This is the most enigmatic photo in Hanlon's collection. He captioned it "Goodman and Alias 'Dr. Sun Yat Sen,' Singapore," but Sun Yat-sen was reportedly in the United States from February until Christmas 1911. HPA/DJC.

The trio paused in Kobe until about June 21, when they embarked for Shanghai. In at least one of their informal accounts, they confused their May visit to that city with their return after they had explored Japan. One later wrote that after Kobe, they explored Shanghai and Canton, and then "visited Pekin, China—touring thru to Hong Kong, China, glad to leave China and its poverty behind." Beijing was over five hundred miles from Shanghai, and Hong Kong was even farther. The drive would have taken a great deal of time, and the few known exact dates for their Asian journey suggest that they could not have made the side trip to Beijing. Drake did tell the Detroit press, however, that "in China we had the pleasure of an interesting chat with Dr. Sun Yat-sen, the leader of the revolutionists." Neither of his two companions mentioned the meeting nor did any newspaper publish accounts of it.[30]

From Shanghai, they sailed to Singapore, where they arrived before July 7, according to a date Hanlon scratched on a postcard he never mailed. From there, they toured nearby islands, starting with "Sabuan-Borneo." Only Hanlon had anything to say about the island, which he dismissed as "just another oriental port." From Borneo, they crossed the Java Sea to the island of Java. Hanlon liked Java and his next stop, Sumatra; he remarked that the former was "a wonderful country," which boasted of "plenty of plantations, coffee, tea, and rice." He was more impressed, however, by the "good looking women, half cast and what have [you]."[31]

The Hupp tourists in a coconut grove in Java.
HPA/DJC.

"Calling on the Natives in
Java." HPA/DJC.

When Melvin Hall and his mother motored across Java only a few months later, he was also enthusiastic about the countryside. He "found many miles of splendid roads, and put 2,000 miles of touring to our credit." Like the Hupmobilists, the Halls were adventurous. Hall recounted, "if we went to a place and were told that there was a road that led perhaps fifty miles but didn't go anywhere and wasn't particularly interesting in point of scenery, that didn't deter us. We took it anyway, and frequently were well rewarded for our trip." Of course, when the road was as advertised—uninteresting—he admitted, "we might have to back down half the way that we came up before we could find a place to turn around in."[32]

From Sumatra, the three men took their car back to Singapore, where they arrived in late July or early August. The *Detroit Journal* announced at that time that they had "practically completed their conquests of the Orient." The rival *Free Press,* which had long supported the better-roads movement in the United States, was more interested in the port city's streets; "Singapore has over 100 miles of highway that will compare favorably with any roads in the world," the tourers wrote. "The roads have a rock foundation with a top dressing of lava, which is easily crushed and at the same time is porous enough to absorb a large quantity of water," a real advantage, they claimed, because "within a few minutes after a heavy tropical rain the road is in perfect condition."[33]

Hupp considered Singapore "one of the leading motor cities in the Orient." The car maker asserted that when its global adventurers arrived, their "Hupmobile was immediately compared to the heavier cars of foreign make." Drake went to work and "an agency was closed with the leading motor concern of the city and a large order placed for the opening wedge of the Hupmobile invasion of the Malay Peninsula."[34]

Hupp was not the only company competing for Singapore's automobile market. Henry Ford's secretary, James Couzens, had called attention to the growing Chinese market and to Singapore's importance as an entrepôt to satisfy the teeming mainland's demand in a speech to a Detroit businessmen's club several months earlier. He cited a case in which a Singapore car dealer had special-ordered a Model T that he had sold "to the Mongol pope or Buddha in Urga Mongolia." To illustrate the dealer's enterprise, Couzens explained that the agent had had to go to "the end of the Peking-Kalgan railway and . . . cross the desert of Gobi" to deliver the car. The secretary claimed that "the demand for cars in China grows in larger proportion than right in our own country" because "the wealthy Chinese are a progressive people and are quick to understand the advantages to be gained from having your own individual transportation

"Taking the Sultan of Sulu for a ride" in Singapore. HPA/DJC.

THREE MEN IN A HUPP

line." Joseph R. Drake and Hupp agreed and applauded the United States's insistence on the Chinese Open Door and sympathy for the revolution as the necessary foreign policy underpinnings for continued American penetration of Asia's largest market.[35]

Drake's pretrip planning with the State Department bore fruit in Singapore. The acting U.S. consul general arranged an audience for the venturesome trio with the visiting sultan of Sulu. The Hoosier humorist George Ade had made the sultan famous with his 1902 comic opera about America's Philippine adventure, *The Sultan of Sulu*. The real sultan was the leader of the Moros, a large, highly cultivated tribe that inhabited the Sulu Archipelago, an island group in the southwestern Philippines. Jones wrote a Detroit newspaper that the sultan "showed a keen delight at having the opportunity to take a ride in the famous car" and was "as enthusiastic as a child over his spin through the streets of the city in the sturdy little Hupmobile." Car companies competed to attract famous personalities to their marques, an association, no matter how brief or fleeting, that attracted lesser mortals to their products.[36]

The sultan's motoring friends left Singapore in late August and steamed to Rangoon,

The tourers parked in front of the ornate entrance to the Shew Dagon Pagoda in Rangoon, Burma. HPA/DJC.

Burma, a city of a quarter of a million. While there, the Hupmobilists admired a huge Buddhist shrine that featured the Shew Dagon Pagoda, an enormous turret-topped building that could be seen above the trees miles away. They circled it on the city's smooth roads and photographed it from every angle. The three men were also fascinated by the hordes of "coolies" they saw everywhere. They recorded perhaps a hundred of them who gathered near the port every afternoon and remembered watching about two dozen of them hauling a huge cannon on railway tracks through Rangoon's streets.[37]

The Little Corporal drew crowds in Calcutta's thoroughfares. HPA/DJC.

After exhausting Rangoon's scenic possibilities, Hupp's ambassadors shipped out for Calcutta, then home to over a million of India's 295,000,000 citizens. Located at the mouth of the Ganges River, Calcutta, despite its rather poor port, was an important transshipment point for the river valley's agricultural produce. There the Americans toured the city's temples and architectural delights and were especially taken by the Jani Temple, with its multitude of decorated spires and statue of the sacred elephant. They also took time to walk through Calcutta's botanical gardens and to pose in front of the largest tree in the world, although its presumed immensity is lost in the photo's dark background. More interesting is the British colonial dress the Huppmen adopted; they looked every bit the commercial imperialists they hoped to become.[38]

Their itinerary after Calcutta remains unclear. The numerical sequence of their photographs indicates that they took a steamer down the east coast of India to

Madras. If so, they later retraced their route to Calcutta and then drove across the Indian subcontinent. Their numbering system, however, is anything but conclusive proof of their itinerary. The men had at least two cameras, many photos have two sets of numbers, and others have none. The pictures they took on their run from Calcutta to Bombay, via Delhi, remain unnumbered, as were those they shot on Ceylon. The map the Hupmobile Company displayed in the 1933 Chicago parade, while wrong in some instances—they did not drive the width of Australia and the length of China—showed they drove from Calcutta to Bombay and then went down India's west coast to the Gulf of Mannar, across from Ceylon. The most sensible route, assuming they were not forced to detour because of shipping schedules, was for them to have driven from Calcutta to Bombay and embarked there for Ceylon and on to Madras, from where they left for Egypt.

Whatever their precise route, they talked and wrote little about driving all the way across India. The photographs Hanlon pasted in his scrapbook constitute the only evidence for their extended India tour. Like Hall, they discovered that although India was crisscrossed with "trunk lines, stretching straightaway across the country" that were "far from bad roads," in "the rainy season no one can travel, and in the dry season it is easy to lose the direct road." Hall found India's driving conditions similar to Japan's: "motoring in India isn't any solitary performance, as one might imagine," he wrote, "the trunk roads [are] crowded day and night with pedestrians, bullock trains, wagons and what not." Worse, he complained, "this is traffic driving with a vengeance and requires caution at all times."[39]

The monsoon season over, they set off from the Calcutta viceroy's residence, suitably attired in white suits and pith helmets, and drove Hall's and Fisher's routes in reverse. They chugged northwest up through Allahabad, where Hall, a few months later, was trapped by the hundreds of thousands bathing in the holy waters, stopping at Ambah, which Hanlon persisted in calling "Amber." There, the three men took a much-photographed elephant ride out to a deserted city that featured a huge ruin, the palace of Ambah. They drove the short distance to Agra, where they took pictures of the Taj Mahal, the magnificent white marble mausoleum built in the seventeenth century by the Mogul emperor Shah Jahan for his favorite wife. They took turns photographing one another standing alongside its reflecting pool.[40]

Leaving Agra, they motored over dusty roads and through numerous tollgates to Delhi, the capital, where they arrived two months before the scheduled Durbar. One of the crew took a picture of the city from a high elevation and another of a man

Hanlon and Jones perched atop their elephant ready to depart for the deserted city of Ambah. HPA/DJC.

jumping off the roof of a domed structure five stories down into a pool, under which Hanlon wrote "fool jump into Ancient Pool near Delhi." Jones also snapped a picture of the "street to Temple Delhi," which was so narrow the tourists could not have shoehorned their Hupp down its crooked path.[41]

They turned very nearly due south from Delhi to Jaipur, where they lingered long enough to thoroughly tour the city and take numerous souvenir photos. They motored out to the maharajah's palace, a huge, magnificently decorated pile at least seven stories high, and in his park kept a respectful distance as groundsmen "teased the alligators." The Hupmobilists also looked over Jaipur's fighting bull, took pictures of the ornately decorated gates into the old walled part of the city, and snapped vignettes of city street life, particularly its two-wheeled carts.[42]

After Jaipur, the trio aimed their Hupp southward down the roads to Bombay. Ford was also testing the Indian market and had already established a dealership in Bombay, the major western port city, which then had just under a million inhabitants. Ford's agents, both Americans, drove a Model T around India checking out the driving conditions. They reported that a common sight everywhere was "the old-fashioned toll gate." "Dressed in his native costume," they reported, the toll keeper "waves a flag for the motor car to stop." The "native," they claimed, was "on to the

speeding pranks of the automobilist and is on a continuous lookout that no motor car shall pass by without paying his small toll." They found the roads particularly good around Bombay, where "the well-to-do natives have been interested in the motor car."[43]

Despite Bombay's fine roads, large population, and pockets of wealth, the Regal Motor Car Company's local dealer estimated that there were only about 1,000 cars in the city, 80 of them American. Most of these were cabs. The Hupmobilists wrote that everywhere they went in Calcutta and Bombay, they encountered "fleets of European taxis" and warned that "one has to step quite as lively to avoid being jolted by motor cars as in a crowded American city; in fact, even more so, as there is no pretense of a speed limit there." In New York, the three told a reporter that the fleets of European taxicabs in India presented "an interesting incongruity of western and oriental civilization."[44]

Everywhere across India to Bombay, Hanlon took time to soak up the local culture. Long afterwards, he mentioned that "there were beautiful temples and house[s] of worship, [and that] these temples were built of gold." His practical eye fixed upon architectural "trimming [which was] a mason['s] work," he thought, "a real lost art today." The tourists' photographs indicate that they were curious about the "natives" as well; they bought numerous postcards that showed Indians going about their daily business. Two of their strangest depict a scene in an opium shop and a prepubescent girl labeled "Young Hindoo," who wears only a few strings of artfully placed beads. They also bought cards showing dhobis washing clothes in a river, a mass immersion at Chowpali in Bombay, and the docks and boats at Apollo Bunder in Bombay.[45]

They remained in Bombay long enough to sign a contract with a Hupp distributor for India and left there by ship, probably the *Afghanistan*, sometime in October, bound for Ceylon and Madras. Their stop in the land of tea must have been very short, for they did not offload the little Hupp. Instead, they took a train from Colombo up into the island's central highlands, where they snapped numerous pictures of the tracks snaking through the mountains. After their rail excursion, they steamed up India's east coast to Madras, where they took their car and thoroughly explored the city of a half million souls. Madras had wide, smooth streets, and they photographed a local temple, Cornwallis's Well, the city's harbor, and its downtown streets full of two-wheeled bullock carts and two- and four-wheeled rickshaws pulled by "coolies."[46]

They were just three weeks shy of having been on the road for a whole year and were eager to return home. From Madras, they circled the remainder of the earth, starting in Egypt, in just ten weeks. The travelers had a January date at the New York City auto extravaganza, where they promised to be a featured attraction. But they still had work to do on the other half of the globe.[47]

THE CORPORATE
HOME FRONT

9

The managers responsible for steering the Hupp Motor Car Company around threatening potholes on the other side of the globe operated at the outer margins of their financial capabilities, fought for public recognition amid the babble and boasts of scores of other fledgling auto manufacturers, and tried to scare up sales even before they had the manufacturing capacity to fill the orders. Led by headstrong, independent personalities teased by the Model 20's early successes, the firm strained to keep up. Even as the three corporate salesmen worked on the far side of the world, the tensions led to squabbling inside Hupp's front offices. The infighting forced the firm's namesake out in a nasty public lawsuit that negated some of the favorable publicity generated by the world tour and culminated in the formation of at least two new motor car companies. While none of this acrimony directly affected Hanlon, Drake, and Jones, internal corporate problems diverted company executives' attention from their around-the-world venture.

Hupp's internal bickering cost the company valuable press attention. Just as the company's illustrated pamphlet detailing its tourers' adventures through their trials in the Philippines appeared, corporate quarreling intensified, and the firm never published a sequel describing the rest of their trip. Worse, the Hupmobilists almost became corporate orphans; while they frequently kept in touch with headquarters, the men in Detroit responsible for releasing tantalizing snippets about their exploits to the press did so less frequently. They even remained uncertain about the Little Corporal's route, publicly continuing to claim, for example, their car was going to undertake a Cape-to-Cairo run.

None of this confusion marred the firm's first years. Hupp thought of the expedition as an international corporate sales promotion, a more effective exercise than simply sending company executives abroad to sign up dealers, as Hupp had hitherto been doing. In 1910, Hupp had sent its "export manager," C. H. Dunlap, on a five-month tour of Europe "promoting agencies" there. Just after the three globe-girdlers left Detroit, Hupp sent Baker and Nelson to the Paris automobile show to "study" foreign cars and identify "such features as may be adaptable to the Hupmobile." On their way back, they met with Hupp's "representatives and distributors" in England. Upon landing in New York City, they made arrangements for Hupp's display at the Madison Square Garden automobile exhibit and assured local reporters that their London agents would "dispose of all the cars that we can ship to them," because European cars were also small and lightweight, although "none of them are as light in weight or as low in first cost" as the Hupp. The two officials prophesied that Europe would become a "splendid market."[1]

The company was eyeing more than Europe, however. A month after Baker and Nelson departed for Paris, Hupp announced that its manager responsible for the "antipodes" had just returned from an eight-month tour of Australia, Tasmania, and New Zealand, where he had demonstrated a new Hupp, recruited sales agents, and returned with orders for sixty-four new cars. "It seems that the combination of an American car and an American representative worked well," Robert Hupp ruminated. Hupp also energetically pushed sales in the Canadian market. In April 1911, the company purchased a factory at Windsor to build cars. Hupp promised the firm would buy many parts from Canadian sources and manufacture others at the local factory, which was designed to assemble five to seven cars per day. The Windsor plant enabled Hupp to avoid the high Canadian import duties.[2]

Even as Robert Hupp pushed for expanded overseas sales and struggled to get cars out of his factory, he was busy building a corporate empire of his own. Perhaps taking a cue from Durant's attempts to make General Motors an automotive colossus, Hupp founded several supplier businesses and bought control of another car

Hupp's Windsor factory,
where cars were assembled
using Canadian and
American components.
Hupp Herald, Fall 1997.

company. His overall plan remains unknown, but by early 1911, his personal companies, which did business with the Hupp Motor Car Company, presented him with conflicts of interest and divided loyalties.

Hupp began branching out into other automotive businesses early in 1910. He had become dissatisfied with the quality of some suppliers' products and decided he could manufacture better parts. Following the same procedures he had used to establish the Hupp Motor Car Company, he allied with other Detroit capitalists to finance several small businesses. He formed the Hupp-James-Geyman Foundry Company to create a supply of gray iron, built a new plant, and hired 150 men. To improve the quality of the Model 20's forgings, he organized another private firm, Hupp-Johnson Forge Company, with 75 workers. He also went into the machine shop business with the Hupp-Turner Machine Company, which within a year employed 200 hands.[3]

Concurrently, in the spring of 1910, he became interested in electric cars, advertised as the answer to city driving woes. They were quiet and especially suited to women, who had difficulty cranking large motors. Hupp believed that electrics did not have to be tall and top-heavy; he thought that automobiles' center of gravity should be as low as possible. He formed the Hupp-Yeats Electric Car Company to build a lower, more stable electric car, and that winter he tested one "on the hills in and around Los Angeles," where, he reported, "I drove a Hupp-Yeats over the streets and roads without driving chains and experienced no skidding or side-slippings." He was proudest of the fact that he had "covered roads that even the gasoline car owners in Los Angeles would not attempt under prevailing conditions."[4]

Globe-girdling *Hupmobile* completes tour

Pays Striking Tribute to the Staunchness of its Splendid Successor

HUPMOBILE LONG STROKE "32" FIVE-PASSENGER TOURING CAR, $900

F.O.B. Detroit, including equipment of windshield, gas lamps and generator, oil lamps, tools and horn. Three speeds forward and reverse; sliding gears. Four-cylinder motor, 3¾-inch bore x 5½-inch stroke. Bosch magneto. 106-inch wheelbase, 32x3½-inch tires. Color, Standard Hupmobile Blue. Roadster, $900.

STANDARD 20 H.P. RUNABOUT, $750

F.O.B. Detroit, with same power plant that took the World-Touring car around the world. Four cylinders, 20 H.P., sliding gears, Bosch magneto. Equipped with top, windshield, gas lamps and generator, oil lamps, tools and horn. Roadster, $850. Coupe, $1100.

NEW York's eyes were opened during Show Week to the splendid "staying powers" of Hupmobile construction by the triumphant return of the World-Touring car.

The amazing achievements of this car, in its 40,000-mile trip, conferred additional distinction upon the new Hupmobile Long-Stroke "32"—first publicly shown at New York—because both are the fruits of the same skilled organization and the engineering leadership of E. A. Nelson.

Hupmobile sturdiness so strikingly exemplified in the World-Touring car, receives new and more impressive expression in the Long-Stroke "32," with its distinctive features of construction and its generous power—found heretofore only in cars costing a great deal more than $900.

HUPP MOTOR CAR COMPANY
1281 Jefferson Avenue, Detroit, Mich.

The accompanying views are reproduced from photographs taken during the Hupmobile's World-Tour

Hupp advertisement comparing the new, more expensive 1912 Model 32 Hupp with the old Model 20. The decision to abandon the low-price field drove Robert C. Hupp from the company he had founded. WRHS.

In May 1911, Robert Hupp consolidated his five privately owned companies—he had also created the R.C. Hupp Sales Company to sell the Hupp-Yeats at nine locations and operate "a large number of electric car garages" where drivers could recharge their batteries—into a new entity, the Hupp Corporation. The new company was capitalized at $700,000, with $400,000 paid in. Its constituent parts shared property overlooking Lake St. Clair, "forming a little industrial city" on its sixty acres. Hupp promised each would "retain its own organization," but all five would "be operated with one selling, purchasing, accounting and financial department."[5]

This was Hupp's company; he created, organized, and ran it. Given his ambition and driving personality, he must have chafed at not running the motor car company that bore his name; he was only a vice president there, even if he did manage its daily operations. He left no doubts about who was in charge of the new company, however; Hupp plastered his name on all five separate units and on the combined firm, of which he was president. Charles Hastings, who worked for him at the Hupp Motor Car Company, was vice president of the new Hupp Corporation. Hupp's brother, Louis G. Hupp, rounded out the list of officers as secretary and treasurer.[6]

Hupp was careful to announce that his new firm was "entirely distinct and independent of" the Hupp Motor Car Company. He also touted the new corporation's "co-operative system," in which "a large number of employees [have] a financial interest in the company which employs them," ensuring that they "were giving of their best efforts to assure increasing and profitable business." Slightly over two months later, the Hupp Corporation reported that it had sold 250 Hupp-Yeats cars in its first six months, which officials believed "exceed[ed] anything done heretofore in the same length of time by a newcomer in the electric car field."[7]

Exactly what J. Walter Drake, Denby, Nelson, and other executives of the Hupp Motor Car Company thought about the Hupps' extracurricular activities is unclear, but they could not have been enthusiastic about them as they struggled to meet the demands for their Model 20 in a plant that was already too small. The auto company was hardly a settled operation, although it was profitable enough to build two entirely new factories in just three years.

In the midst of their efforts to manufacture cars, Hupp officials debated the configuration of their next offering. Most managers, including President Drake, argued that Hupp should scrap the Model 20 and build larger, more expensive cars in the mid-price range. Robert Hupp adamantly opposed that idea but failed to persuade his colleagues. In August 1911, the executives agreed to introduce "a car of entirely different design, at a higher price." Afterwards, Hupp said that "owing to this decision," he had "concluded to withdraw entirely from the Hupp Motor Car Company," because he could not "conscientiously adhere to the policy decided upon." Charles Hastings elected not to follow Hupp out of the firm and was promoted to fill his vacated position within a month.[8]

Less than six weeks after leaving, Robert Hupp announced that he was going to manufacture a gasoline-powered car, the "R.C.H." He had worked on a prototype before his resignation and he had a photograph of the new car, the Model F, later called the Model 25, out to the newspapers by September 10. His new car updated the Model 20, which by mid 1911 lagged technologically behind its competition. The R.C.H. was powered by a more modern four-cylinder, "long stroke" motor, "productive of great pulling power," generating 22 horsepower. Five weeks later, while the three world travelers were dashing across Europe, Hupp was ready to produce his "25," which he modestly claimed was "one of the greatest automotive propositions ever offered." He explained that he could deliver so much value for only $700 because he had devised the "most thorough cost and production system that the industry has ever seen." The car was a quality machine and had its steering wheel on the left side, "with center control—something very unusual in this type of car." It was a good-looking two-seat roadster with doors, sporting an "English type" body. His early advertisements were emblazoned with "R.C. Hupp, Manufacturer" in bold print and, in much smaller type, "(Distinct from and having no connection whatever with the Hupp Motor Car Company)."[9]

Hupp Motor Car Company officials were not amused. On September 21, 1911, they filed a bill of complaint in circuit court asking for an injunction to restrain Hupp from using his name "in connection with the manufacture of gasoline motor car" or in any way that would injure the Hupp Motor Car Company. The claimants pointed out that Robert Hupp had asked his former company to adopt his name and predicted that two Hupp companies would be "a source of confusion and embarrassment." Drake told the press that he had sought the injunction because he was sure "the impression is almost certain to be conveyed that the formation of the Hupp Corporation implies a break in the organization which has been responsible for the remarkable success of the Hupmobile." Claiming that he had no "desire to take any action which will militate against [Hupp's] possible success," he worried that the R.C.H. "in the hands of unscrupulous dealers ... might be palmed off as a product of the Hupp Motor Car Company, as a new model of Hupmobile." The next day, in a newspaper interview, Robert Hupp disingenuously argued that his new company was named for his brother Louis. He denied that he was trying to trade illegally upon his name and severed his last connection with his former firm when he notified the Hupp Motor Car Company that he would "be unable to manufacture any more parts for their cars after November 1."[10]

Robert Hupp was in no hurry to resolve the suit; his attorney waited almost five weeks before going into court to answer the filing. By the time the judge signed a consent decree in February 1912, the globe-girdling Huppers had arrived home to find a very different corporation from the one they had left. The court found for the original firm and ordered Robert Hupp to change the name of his firm to the R.C.H. Company. The Hupp brothers were enjoined from using their names in the automobile business, although they could use them to identify themselves as R.C.H. officers in advertisements. In return, the Hupp Motor Car Company agreed to give Robert Hupp $49,021, a second installment of "part of the purchase price agreed upon" to buy out his interest in the firm. By 1911, the original company was capitalized at $500,000, and if the two payments were equal, Robert Hupp had owned approximately 20 percent of the Hupp Motor Car Company.[11]

Hupp lost no time in promoting his new firm. He told the trade press that the R.C.H. Company had raised its capitalization from $800,000 to $1,000,000 and promised to produce 10,000 R.C.H.s in 1912. His new car, however, never caught on the way his Model 20 had. When Joseph Drake visited the London automobile show in the late fall of 1912, he wrote home that "with all the advertising and fuss the R.C.H. made about their enormous contract for Europe and shipping over four cars for the Olympia Show, they have one very ordinary car tucked off on the end of somebody's stand." He concluded: "That's all there is of the R.C.H. It is creating no comment and attracting no people." J. Walter watched R.C.H. as well and took some pleasure in its difficulties. In late November 1912, in a note penned to his brother, who was traveling to India, he told him: "This enterprising concern [R.C.H.] is in about the same condition as when you left with prospects no better." J. Walter was prescient; the R.C.H. never attracted the public's fancy; nevertheless, Robert Hupp soldiered on with the car for several more years.[12]

The Hupp Motor Car Company's history was typical of many U.S. automobile firms. With few assets, its founders dreamed of saturating world markets with their little car and risked public ridicule to attract national recognition by sending their Model 20s through Arctic conditions to New York City and on a marathon worldwide excursion. In 1911, the firm's managers, save Robert Hupp and perhaps Hastings, wanted to manufacture cars they would be proud to drive to the Detroit Athletic Club. The transition to the mid-price range was natural for most companies, but not Hupp. It drove Robert Hupp out; ironically, he later tried to manufacture and sell more expensive cars of the type he had earlier voted against building.[13]

The six or eight months of corporate dissension diverted the company's attention from its world travelers and cost it much favorable publicity. Moreover, the firm's announcement of its new higher-priced automobiles negated the principal message it had been sending to domestic and foreign buyers. While the Hupmobilists advertised the trailworthiness of their small, light, durable machine, adaptable to all climes and conditions, their company proclaimed that it was going to build the very kind of car that it had trumpeted was inferior to its little Hupp.

Hupp's product decision did not, however, totally negate the tourers' corporate usefulness. Wherever they went, their easy personalities, access to the local press, introductions to men of importance, and contacts in foreign business communities spread the gospel according to Hupp. The public's perception of the little Hupp's durability helped sell later models. The belief that Hupmobile built quality cars, at whatever price, became an article of faith to many people around the globe. And, if nothing else, the world tour manifested a corporate élan, a tangible example of Americans' assumptions about the inevitability of their corporate domination of the world's markets, even those of continental Europe, the next stop for Hanlon, Drake, and Jones.

THE CONTINENT

By mid October 1911, Hanlon, Drake, and Jones had been on the road over eleven months but still had 45 percent of the globe to circle and only ninety days to do it if they were to appear at the 1912 New York auto show. They therefore stepped up their pace. "[T]he world tourists expect to skirt the Mediterranean Coast. . . . [and] wind up their long journey with a hurried visit to the principal continental cities and to reach New York in time for the automobile shows," the *Detroit Free Press* noted.[1]

Europe was not as exotic as many of the lands they had already visited and generated less dramatic headlines in the United States, where Hupmobile sold 80 percent of its output. Moreover, dozens of other American auto companies had dispatched their representatives to Europe to establish agencies; newspapers were full of articles about their expectations. Hupp too had been active in the continental market and had contracted with prominent businessmen in the larger European cities to demonstrate, sell, and repair its cars. Drake's task in Europe was to keep these agents updated on company policies and products, transmit their complaints home to his brother J. Walter, and glad-hand salesmen, mechanics, and prospective purchasers. Thanks to the

A dredge at work in the Suez Canal when Hanlon, Jones, and Drake steamed through to Egypt. HPA/DJC.

company's extensive spadework, the global wanderers needed to make only a "hurried visit" there.

En route, however, Egypt offered Hupp its last chance to feature its car in an exotic locale. After visiting Ceylon and Madras, Hanlon, Drake, and Jones embarked in October 1911, probably at Bombay, and steamed across the Indian Ocean to the Red Sea. It was a pleasant fall passage, with just the kind of weather Hanlon loved. As they glided through the Suez Canal, they photographed a dredger working to keep the channel open. When they reached Port Said at the waterway's northern end, they off-loaded the Little Corporal and drove to Cairo. The *Detroit Free Press* reported on November 12 that the trio had arrived "a few days ago," but it was wrong by at least two weeks. The intrepid adventurers had visited the Sphinx and pyramids on November 3; they were in the land of the Pharaohs by the end of October.[2]

Almost twenty years later, Hanlon reminisced that the "convict labor on the highways was always apparent in that part of Egypt." Likewise, he never forgot that Egypt "was one of the most trying places on the entire world tour because of the high temperatures." He delighted in telling his listeners that "at Cairo 140 degrees Fahrenheit was not unusual—much to our discomfort."[3]

The excessive heat did not prevent the American tourists from photographing their car in front of Egypt's most famous relics. Many of the figures in their pictures cast long shadows, showing that they beat the worst of the heat by leaving Cairo early in the morning to drive out to visit the Great Pyramid and the Sphinx. Jones reported that they wanted to get the car close enough to photograph it right in front of the monuments. A good road led out of Cairo "to these interesting objects," he wrote, and "a winding highway has been built up the hill on which the great pyramid stands." The roadway ended there, unfortunately, and Jones commented that "even travelers who come up in horse drawn vehicles get out and go the rest of the way on foot, donkey, or camel."[4]

Not the indomitable Hupmobile, however; Hupp's global envoys were deter-

The Little Corporal "plugged" through the sand in Egypt. HPA/DJC.

The road to Egypt's antiquities was relatively smooth until the Hupmobilists drove closer to the pyramids. The little Hupp spooked the donkey right behind it. HPA/DJC.

Above: This was as close as the Hupp tourists could get to the Sphinx. The two men in the middle of the picture are standing in a declivity caused by wind scouring sand around the Sphinx's shoulders.
Right: Hupmobile with guides at the pyramids. HPA/DJC.

mined to be the first to drive a motorcar up to the Sphinx and the Pyramids. Despite the fact that "motorists in Cairo advised against" driving so close and that "none of the garages in Cairo will permit its cars to attempt the trip," the Hupp's crew, garbed in dark suits, ties, and hats, forged on in a businesslike manner. Jones bragged that "performing unusual feats has become a Hupmobile habit." Determined to drive to the Sphinx's ear, "the car bucked into the sand in which a person walking would sink to his ankles and came to a halt on the brink of the pit in which the wonderful old sphinx is located." There, a Detroit newspaper allowed, they "posed for several pictures from many angles."[5]

Years later, Hanlon told his daughter that he was "really impressed with the pyramids" and that he had liked Egypt because there were so few tourists; his photographs show almost no visitors at all. November 3, 1911, a Friday, must have been a slow day. The Hupmobile made its much photographed way up the road to the great pyramid trailed only by local guides leading their donkeys. There were no other tourists about; perhaps it was too early. While at the Sphinx, which was not fully dug out from the sand until 1913, and which sat in a depression surrounded by dunes, they posed the Little Corporal atop one of the sand hills. Afterwards they joined two European women and a boy to sit on the guides' camels for a formal portrait. Drake, who sports a white handkerchief in his suit coat pocket, looks every inch the successful American businessman. Hanlon, with his arms across his chest, looks as though he could ride the humped beast no-handed. Jones seems to be wondering why he is perched on this thing in ferocious heat in the middle of nowhere.[6]

Hanlon, whose memories of the trip's details grew confused as the years went by, told his daughter that he had met the king of England at the pyramids; but no one else mentions the royal encounter. If it had taken place, Hupp would have promoted it as one of the journey's highlights, as it did with the sultan of Sulu, the emperor of Japan's former retainer, the U.S. ambassador to Japan, Aguinaldo, Sun Yat-sen, and various minor nobility. Perhaps Hanlon's subconscious harbored the memory that George V had been *scheduled* to visit Egypt and vast preparations were under way when the Hupmen were there. The king left Portsmouth on November 13, 1911, on his way to his Durbar in India, and arrived in Port Said on November 20. He left his yacht, however, only to visit the khedive on his boat; Britain's monarch was in port only twenty-four hours before he departed for Aden, and he is not reported to have gone anywhere near the Sphinx, the pyramids, or the Hupmobilists.[7]

In 1930, Hanlon said he and his fellow travelers had spent two months touring

Egypt; he probably meant two weeks. In that short time, however, they may have squeezed in a side trip to Jerusalem by camel, because, as Hanlon later said, "no car could travel over those roads." Given some of the paths and trails they pushed their Hupmobile over, the Holy Land must have had no roads at all.[8]

The *Detroit Free Press* announced the Hupmobilists' next destination was Italy. To get there, they planned "to skirt the Mediterranean Coast on their way to Naples" on the North African side, steam through the Straits of Messina, which separate Sicily from the boot, and turn north to Naples. They were in such a hurry to finish their trip that they only infrequently sent the company and the press shorthand accounts of where they went and what they saw.[9]

They arrived in Italy by November 14 or 16, depending on which date scribbled on their health form is to be believed. The *Detroit Free Press* reported, however, that the Hupmobilists had docked in Naples "early in the week" before November 26, therefore somewhere around November 20 or 21. Hanlon was even vaguer and more confused; he alleged that they had driven from Cairo to Alexandria "and then toured back to Calcutta and Bombay over some terrible roads." They did not return to India, but they did take some photographs of Alexandria's harbor, indicating that they shipped from there to Naples, their Italian port of entry.[10]

Only seven weeks after landing in Naples, the Hupmobilists off-loaded their car from the ill-fated *Lusitania* in New York City. In those few weeks, they toured Italy, Monaco, France, England, and perhaps Germany and the Low Countries They stopped in major cities to perform their promotional duties but spent most of their time sightseeing and photographing the little Hupp in front of Europe's tourist attractions. The Hupmobilists absorbed an intensive course in classical history during their short stay in Italy and connected the little Hupp in the American public's mind with the greatness that once was Rome's.

When they debarked from their ship at Naples, they met a contingent of Italian cavalry on the dock preparing to leave with their horses and provisions for North Africa, where Italy was in the process of acquiring Tripolitania and Cyrenaica in the Italo-Turkish War. As soon as Hupp's motormen freed their car from the ship's hold, they fled the hubbub and drove into Naples, where they checked into the Grand Hôtel du Vésuve, a six-story hostelry located on the coast. Hanlon bought a postcard of the hotel that pictured Vesuvius in the background emitting copious amounts of smoke and ash. Naples boasted both Italy's largest opera house and the great tenor Enrico Caruso, who was at the very pinnacle of his career in 1911. It also had a castle

built in 1282, which had become a Carthusian monastery. The Americans took in these sights and drove down the shore road, where they posed, in dark suits and hats, in front of the famous volcano.[11] They then motored to nearby Capua, where they posed on the city's Roman bridge and toured its ninth-century cathedral.[12]

At Pompeii, a few miles down the coast, they spent hours, either in early morning or late afternoon, judging from the long shadows in their pictures, poking their heads everywhere among the ruins. Again, they seem to be the only sightseers. They were unable to drive the Little Corporal into the ruins; it is conspicuously absent from their photographs.[13]

After leaving Pompeii, the *Detroit Free Press* reported, the Huppers "made a picturesque trip to the eternal city over the historic road of the Appian Way." Upon their arrival in Rome, "they were welcomed with a splendid reception by Count Pec[c]orini, the Hupmobile distributor for Italy." As soon as they had finished their official duties in the capital, the Huppers checked into the Hotel Flora on the Via Veneto. Hanlon, who collected hotel postcards, dutifully bought one of the Flora. It is in German and depicts a decidedly upscale establishment *gegenüber*—opposite—

The Little Corporal outside an Italian customshouse. HPA/DJC.

Above: "On the Appian Way, with our friend the Friar, near the tomb of Lucile Metellers" shows Drake behind the wheel and perhaps Count Peccorini with the friar. A Hupp Torpedo is on the left.
Right: The old Roman roads put those in the United States to shame. HPA/DJC.

the Villa Borghese, ancestral home of Prince Scipione Borghese, who had won the Peking-to-Paris race just four years earlier.[14]

Rome was a driver's city, with many wide main thoroughfares. The Detroit tourists' photographs show few automobiles but numerous animal-drawn carts and trams. They passed so close to the Colosseum that they could almost touch it from the moving car. So few vehicles were on the road that they were able to park the Hupp at an angle across the bridge spanning the moat to the Castel Sant'Angelo. They also managed to snap a picture of the Hupp in the main portal of the Arch of Constantine, although construction crews had left mounds of dirt in front of the monument that partially obscured it. The Pantheon was right on the street, so they had no trouble driving up to it for a picture.[15]

Even on Rome's narrower streets, the paucity of traffic enabled the Americans to drive very close to the landmarks they wanted to capture photographically for corporate posterity; they shared a street with a horse cart and a tram to get a photo of the Hupp in front of Trajan's Column. Everywhere crowds gathered to ogle their car. They took short trips out of town to see the "Palace of the Caesars," which had been converted into

The little Hupp dwarfed by the Colosseum in Rome. HPA/DJC

Right: The Little Corporal in front of the Castel Sant'Angelo in Rome, built A.D. 135–39 by the emperor Hadrian.
Below: Rubble in the foreground partially obscured the Hupp and its crew in front of the Arch of Constantine. HPA/DJC.

a restaurant, to drive under the ruins of an aqueduct that had once provided Rome with its water, and to detour past the ruins of "Emperor Augustus's castle."[16]

The Hupp threads its way toward Trajan's Column. HPA/DJC.

Their audience with Pope Pius X, whom Hanlon persisted in calling Pope Leo (perhaps confusing him with his predecessor, Leo XIII), was the high point of their visit, however. Jones reported that "Count Peccorini, our Italian representative, arranged an audience at the Vatican [where] we also met the Misses Sarto, the sisters of the Pontiff." Almost twenty years later, Hanlon said, "[W]e were presented to Pope Leo who was greatly interested in both the car and our achievement. While at the Vatican we were vested with the honorary title of Count." No picture of them with the pontiff has survived, but the counts took numerous shots of their car in St. Peter's Square. They drove up almost to the cathedral's steps and the colonnades that embraced the square. No other cars appear in their photos.[17]

After touring Rome, they pointed their little Hupp inland toward Perugia, driving through numerous small towns, all of which seemed located upon steep hills designed to challenge the Hupp's climbing abilities. The world tourers also discovered that Italian local laws were sometimes quite independent of national ones; at numer-

Above: A stunning tri-
umph of Roman engineer-
ing and an example of
American transportation.
Right: The three intrepid
corporate representatives
stopped near "Emperor
Augustus's Castle."
HPA/DJC.

In Vatican City, the honorary counts pose in front of the colonnade around St. Peter's Square. HPA/DJC.

The Americans drove as close as they dared to the steps leading up to St. Peter's Basilica. HPA/DJC.

A well-composed picture accentuating the tower's lean with the Hupp as garnish. HPA/DJC.

ous towns, they had to stop at the city limits to allow local customs authorities to search the car. On a larger scale, the motorcar was so new that nations had not yet agreed to licensing reciprocity. The Hupp prominently displayed its Italian license plate on its rear, and when the Hupmobilists drove their last leg across Canada on their way back to Detroit, they had to buy a Canadian plate. By then they were so weary of attaching licenses to the Hupp that they put it on a chain and cavalierly hung it over their radiator cap.[18]

They spent the night in the Umbrian town of Perugia at Brufani's Grand Hotel, which, from Hanlon's postcard, appears to have been at the highest point in the city, next to the church. Leaving Perugia, the trio drove back toward the coast to Pisa, where they positioned the car in front of the Leaning Tower for its obligatory photograph. The three Americans then drove downtown to the Royal Hotel, where they attracted a crowd large enough to almost obscure their vehicle.[19]

Determined to see as much of Italy as their diminishing time allowed, the three turned their Hupp northeast to Florence. A decal they affixed to the Hupp indicates that they stayed at the Hotel Italie; their surviving photos affirm that they drove about the city to pose the Little Corporal in front of its monuments, at locations such as Neptune's Fountain and in front of the home of Amerigo Vespucci, for whom America, the world's leading motorcar producer, was named. The city's streets were empty; only in front of Vespucci's house did the Hupp draw a small crowd.[20]

Customs officials inspect the little Hupp. Only later in their Italian tour did they have to procure an Italian license plate. HPA/DJC.

Neptune towering over the Hupp in Florence on a dreary, wet day. HPA/DJC.

The countryside grew more mountainous as the Hupp motormen approached France. Hanlon entitled this view, "Climbing along the Italian Riviera." HPA/DJC.

The Hupmobilists left Florence, a city still swathed in its Renaissance glory, and headed for Genoa. Time was pressing, and they stepped up their pace. They lingered fewer hours at historical curiosities, venerable cities, and scenic views. If Hanlon's scrapbook is any indication, they took fewer pictures as well. Only a few clues indicate their probable route north to Paris. Hanlon claimed that they left Pisa and drove through Germany to Bremen, where they spent "four delightful days." After that, he alleged, "we drove back over our trail to Monte Carlo, spending five days at this popular resort, and then proceeded to Paris for a three week stay." It must have been at least the end of November when they reached Genoa and more likely early December. If they had followed Hanlon's route, they would have been in Paris when the *Lusitania* sailed from England.

Fragmentary evidence indicates that they followed the coastal route up through the Italian Riviera and into the French Riviera and Monaco. They stopped long enough to take a half a dozen photographs of their Hupp perched in spectacular mountainous terrain, one of which Hanlon labeled "climbing along in the Italian Riviera." Curiously, in a couple of the photos, the Hupp is not wearing its Italian li-

Left: The roads were good even in the Italian mountains. *Below:* The winding, hilly roads were beguiling, but death lurked for the unwary driver. HPA/DJC.

Hanlon, Jones, and two Frenchmen in a "view of Nice taken when leaving the city." HPA/DJC.

cense plate on the back, yet a clear rear view in Paris shows the oval identification tag attached. In all the Riviera pictures, however, the car is packed the same way and the three are wearing the same clothes, an indication they were taken within a few days of one another. The Americans are garbed in heavy overcoats and thick gloves for traversing high country in the late fall. The roads were some of the best of their trip; they might not have been paved, but they seem to have been smooth and had drainage ditches alongside them. They were perilous, however; lined with precipitous drop-offs, they must have made Hanlon, with his two-wheel brakes, wary on the long downhill grades, where the heavily laden car must have attained frightening speeds.[21]

Hanlon's driving skills were equal to the challenge, however, and he later told a hometown reporter that they had "entered France over the perfect roads of the world's most beautiful resort, the Riviera, and then descended into the beautiful valleys of the south of France" to Monte Carlo. It is unlikely that they spent "five days at this popular resort," as Hanlon later asserted. A close reading of the decals the tourers plastered all over their car indicates that they drove a couple miles down the road and stayed at the Majestic Hotel in Nice.[22]

The Hupmobilists probably did not linger long in the southern French paradise. Eight months earlier, another American, John C. Wetmore, had made the same trip in a French De Dion. Wetmore drove eighty-six miles along the same route, the Corniche d'Or road, which he allowed was the "most sensational and spectacular automobile road in the world." The highway had an interesting provenance; it was a collaborative effort by the Paris-Lyon-Marseille Railway, the French department through which the road ran, and the Touring Club of France, which contributed the substantial sum of 200,000 francs toward its construction.[23]

For their first twenty-four miles, Hupp's representatives drove from Cannes to Saint-Raphaël through the Esterel mountains, "skirting the shore and following its constant indentations all the way." The road, Wetmore remembered, was "actually carved from the rock for most of the distance." He noted that "hairpin turns abound in great numbers . . . and it requires a good and cautious driver to negotiate" them. "As a fool-killer," the American warned, "it would be without rival; for a reckless pilot would be punished by being dashed over the cliff into the sea, several hundred feet below."[24]

The Hupmobilists drove past several intriguing places, such as the island of Sainte-Marguerite, where Alexandre Dumas père's man in the iron mask was confined. The Touring Club of France had erected all the road's signage, "pointing out the danger spots" and giving "the motorist information as to the interesting histori-

A scenic vista in the Esterel Mountains in southern France. HPA/DJC.

Just north of Toulon, the three Americans drove through Avignon to see the Old Vatican, established in 1378 when the College of Cardinals split and elected two Popes. The opulence of the Avignon Papacy outshone most European royal courts. HPA/DJC

cal spots and how to reach them." In its attempt to offer motorists unexpected amenities, the club even went "so far as to provide benches where there are particularly fine views." West of Fréjus, about a morning's drive from Cannes, the corporate tourists entered vineyard country "where the going was level most of the way" except for an eight-mile stretch of mountains covered with cork trees. The vineyards stretched as far as the Americans could see, and they bought local wine for as little as three cents a quart.[25]

Further down the Côte d'Azur, the three men drove through Hyères, whose biggest industry was raising and supplying violets for European capitals. It was popular with English expatriates in search of sun and warmth; some 2,000 of them lived there when the Little Corporal chugged through. Just west of violet country, Wetmore ended his jaunt in Toulon, a town the Hupmobilists likely enjoyed because it featured "swell restaurants" and a vaudeville show "where petits chevaux gambling furnishes the entre acte attraction." Wetmore explained that the audience bet on one of nine toy horses "that are sent whirling around a course."[26]

Although the autoists could have stabled their car in Toulon for just two dollars a month, they quickly passed through the city and turned northward up the Rhône

The Hupp motormen enjoyed a welcome repast somewhere in rural France on their way to Paris. HPA/DJC.

Valley toward Lyon. South of that city, they entered the Loire Valley and stopped at Nevers, a town of about 25,000, where they spent the night at the Hôtel de France, which judging from Hanlon's postcard was closer to being a country inn than a grand national hotel. All through France, they stopped in small villages to look about and eat. In one they posed at a cafe seated at an outdoor table, with a couple of bottles of three-cent wine. Jones is smiling broadly, holding an oversized bread loaf.[27]

The Hupmobilists followed the Loire a few miles north of Nevers and then cut across country to enter Paris, where Hupp already had a distributor. Hanlon was struck by the "many automobiles, the first encountered in any quantity since leaving the United States, and [that] many of them were *Hupmobiles*." Paris certainly was not afflicted with traffic jams; a photo of the little Hupp crossing the Alexandre III bridge includes two other cars and a horse-drawn dray. Likewise, when they visited the Invalides to see Napoleon's tomb, there was one other car out front. In a classic snapshot of the Hupp posed under the Eiffel Tower, however, no other cars are in evidence.[28]

Above: The Little Corporal in front of the Invalides in Paris, where its namesake is entombed. The accompanying car is also a Hupp, probably the local distributor's guide car. *Right:* Only the gendarme and maybe Drake seem to be aware that they are being photographed under Alexandre-Gustave Eiffel's tower. HPA/DJC.

The railroad crane looked almost too small to lift the Hupp aboard a channel steamer at Calais. HPA/DJC.

Hanlon claimed they visited Bremen, Germany. When Drake took his next tour around the world, starting in 1912, he visited German Hupmobile dealers and appears to have known them personally. If he met them on the trip with Hanlon and Jones, they probably drove from Paris through the Low Countries, through Essen to Bremen, some 300 miles. It would have been a relatively easy jaunt for them to return from Bremen to Calais, where they boarded a ship for England.[29]

The Hupmobilists reported that their "visit to England was in many ways the most interesting of the trip, because there, for the first time they consorted everywhere with people who spoke their native tongue." Hanlon remembered: "We visited London and toured through England where the car was eagerly watched, and again we saw quite a few *Hupmobiles*." Their car was "particularly an object of interest in London," because "the Briton has just begun to take the invasion of American motor cars quite seriously." Drake believed the British realized that "light compact cars, of low price, can be made to perform practically all of the duties that a motor car may be called upon to do."[30]

Hupp Motor Car Company had worked hard to market its cars on the island. Three months earlier, William Truscott and E. E. Hipwell, representatives of Whitings Limited, London, had visited Detroit, where, the *Free Press* announced, they "closed a contract to represent the Hupmobile throughout Great Britain for another year." They pronounced themselves "very well satisfied with our first season's experience with the Hupmobile" and said they had had "no difficulty in disposing of our liberal quota and could have sold more had we been able to get them." Hupp's officials, who were struggling to build larger, more expensive cars, must have been unsettled when their two English distributors told the *Free Press* that "a decided demand has arisen abroad for an automobile of light, sturdy construction that is easy on tires and low on gasoline consumption," adding "we chose the Hupmobile because it conforms more closely to European ideals of design and mechanism than any other small American car that we know of." On "the splendid roads that one finds throughout the United Kingdom," they said, the Hupmobile could "average 30 miles to a gallon" of petrol, which in England cost "the equivalent of 28 cents a gallon in American money."[31]

That estimate was close to the twenty-eight miles a gallon the Little Corporal actually attained on its trip around the world, a point the three Americans made to English customers who came by Whitings to inspect the well-traveled Hupp. While in London, the Hupp motormen stayed at the Hotel Russell, a hulking Romanesque pile, whose postcard depicts two horse-drawn open carriages in the streets around it.[32]

The Hupmobilists probably arrived in Britain about the second or third week of December 1911. In 1930, Hanlon said that they "drove to Liverpool and shipped across the Irish Sea, spending quite some time touring the beautiful Emerald Isle. Our stay included visits to Belfast, Dublin, and a number of other cities" before they returned to Liverpool to ship out for home. No contemporary newspaper reports mentioned that they went to Ireland, and Hanlon's daughter denied he had visited the island. Dublin newspapers, in the months they might have been there, did not mention their visit. The capital was still small enough—New York City had twice as many Irish as Dublin—so that if the Americans had arrived with their famous car, Dubliners would have splashed it across their papers. Moreover, Hanlon's scrapbook contains no photographs that he identified as taken in Ireland. It is possible that Drake and perhaps Hanlon made a quick trip to Ireland to stir up some business and quickly returned to England to catch their ship.[33]

Near New Year's Eve, the three men were at the Liverpool docks, to oversee their little Hupp stowed aboard the *Lusitania*. They looked forward to returning to their native shores and basking in the adulation at New York's auto show. They also realized that their adventure was far from over; they still had to complete their global circuit. They were determined to drive to Pontchartrain Square to return the American flag, and they feared that their run from New York City through upstate New York and across Ontario in the dead of winter would be arduous. But all that lay in the future as they relaxed aboard the luxurious liner and anticipated their raucous welcome in New York City.[34]

THE SELLING OF
THE HUPP

11

The world tour was a working trip. Drake, Hanlon, and Jones were enthralled by the cultural differences they experienced, stunned by the natural and man-made wonders they saw, and fascinated by the famous people they met, but they never forgot that they were on a mission to sell Hupps. They were sent out to arouse enthusiasm for the Hupmobile with their daring global venture, laud its advantages, charm people, and recruit local notables to establish Hupp corporate outposts.

Drake was the point man for Hupp's dollar diplomacy. He worked the introductions he carried and used international banks to identify creditworthy businessmen who could be trusted to handle Hupp's affairs at such a remove. Later, he depended upon freight-forwarding houses to handle his transport and billing; firms such as H. W. Peabody & Company in New York City took delivery of factory-fresh cars and made the shipping and insurance arrangements to send them overseas. Hupp had no end of trouble with these middlemen, who frequently had difficulty securing steamship cargo space and meeting shipment dates within months of those that Drake and the company had promised.[1]

Joseph Drake spent fifteen months in the little Hupp's left-hand seat establishing and servicing different types of sales outlets. Although Drake often referred to all of the company's overseas representatives as agents, only a few technically were; mostly they did not work out of a sales outlet. They used their social, professional, or political connections to tout Hupmobiles, took deposits on cars, forwarded orders to the factory, and reimbursed the company before it shipped the vehicles. Dealers, by contrast, had "premises," displayed a Hupp sign, employed mechanics, and maintained a line of bank credit to guarantee their drafts to Hupp. The world tourers made a special effort to visit towns and cities where Hupp already had dealerships, have their picture taken in front of such establishments, and add snap to their dealers' advertising by taking potential customers for a ride.

Drake sought out prominent men with influence, rank, or wealth to sign as distributors to wholesale Hupps to dealers and agents within a stipulated territory. Hupp allowed distributors, who often were also the largest dealers in their area, a 25 percent discount on their cars. The arrangement meant that the company only dealt with one distributor in each region and that he was likely to command the necessary funds to pay for the cars in advance. Most of Hupp's agents, dealers, and distributors also handled other makes of cars. In the auto industry's first decade, car firms entered and departed the lists all too frequently and salespeople were notoriously fickle about pledging their loyalties to a single brand. They profited more from handling several names, covering every price range. Contracts with numerous motorcar manufacturers also gave them some leverage over the manufacturing companies. Drake's task was to woo special consideration for his cars and excite Hupp's sales representatives with well-limned pictures of the company's future prosperity.

Unfortunately, Drake's diary and business ledger for the journey have not survived, but his later correspondence indicates that he spent a great deal of time during the trip on his business responsibilities. He was adept at mixing entertainment with business; he enjoyed social affairs where he mingled with men likely to become "useful" business contacts. Like all good salesmen, he had an eye for the personal—children's and wives' names, hobbies, and memories of shared good times—and employed such tidbits to smooth over the inevitable trials of doing business a half a globe away.

It was through such social contacts that Drake met T. K. Oguri, who, on behalf of his Tokyo Motor Car Company, signed on as Hupp's dealer in that city. Drake spent three weeks with Oguri and appears to have been satisfied with his choice at the time. He later wrote to another American auto executive that Oguri "seems to

Hupp's traveling salesmen contacted their dealers everywhere to pose for pictures in their new touring car in front of their outlets, such as this one outside the Straits Motor Garage Syndicate in Singapore. HPA/DJC.

have financial backing and is well connected socially," two important considerations in choosing a corporate representative.[2]

Drake's enthusiasm did not last long, however. When the assistant sales manager of Detroit's Motor Wagon Company wrote him to ask about Oguri, who had applied to become that company's "foreign dealer," Drake was lukewarm. "I would state," he replied, "that I would hesitate very much in placing an agency with him." "Mr. Oguri," he continued, "is a very young man and has very vague ideas of business. . . . He was rather flighty in his ideas and did not seem to be able to settle down to steady application to business." Like most Americans, Drake did not have a high opinion of Japanese businessmen; Oguri "seems to be a little more irresponsible than the usual Japanese," he concluded.[3]

Although Drake probably did not want Oguri to represent another automobile line, the truth was that only a few weeks after his return home, his relationship with his Japanese dealer soured. Oguri's business style was not what most American corporate officials considered normal. He wrote Drake in late February 1912 to explain

192   THREE MEN IN A HUPP

that he had "been ill quite a lot and have not been working very hard." Without consulting Drake or anyone at Hupp, Oguri had "turned over the agency contract to Mr. Takata" at another company. Oguri had not done his homework, however; he apologized to Drake "because I have found afterwards that this company's business standing is not very good (this must be kept secret) and is not able to have cars in stock." Oguri told Drake that he was thinking of the coming to the United States in March and asked him to "arrange for me to get a position at your factory, as I would like to be in the motor business over there." Drake replied that Hupp officials would "do what they can for you if there is any opening at all," but pointed out the company's employees had "been brought up in the business and are well trained for their duties."[4]

Three months later, Oguri informed Drake that he had "sold one car"—to the "president of the Kitahama Bank of Nagoya, whom the world touring Hup party met . . . and whom we gave a ride in the W. T. Hup." Oguri was especially proud that he was now known as "Hupp san." His sales success had reinvigorated his enthusiasm for motordom, he wrote Drake; "I have made up my mind to put all my power for introducing Hupmobile."[5]

China was a bigger prize than Japan, however, and Drake constantly reassured and prodded his Shanghai distributor, C. J. Butsch of the Oriental Automobile Company, who was responsible for the entire country. He pushed Butsch to order at least fifty cars by the end of 1912 and offered to come to China to help him sell them. Drake promised by the time he and Butsch left China, Butsch would be begging for another fifty.[6]

Butsch was less enthusiastic than Drake. He reminded Drake that his initial order of November 1911 had not arrived in Shanghai until June 1912. His second order, cabled to Detroit in June, had not been shipped by October. Moreover, the Chinese revolution was killing his sales. "Money is tight," he explained, "and there is practically no business that leaves sufficient profit for foreigners or Chinese." The political upheavals had scared wealthy Chinese, who "retired to a lonely spot, where they cannot be traced by the new Republicans who are in power, as otherwise they would be sucked dry or kidnapped." Nevertheless, Butsch said, "we have made considerable efforts all over China to create a market for your car," and he believed the company might be successful in "Northern ports and . . . [along] the Yangtze River."[7]

Dollar diplomacy was never a simple proposition. Taking the larger diplomatic view, Butsch refused to sign for another fifty Hupps. He would have to sell them in a country that "wants money, money, and again money" and could only get it "from European and American financiers." He watched events unfold in the "awkward Balkan business" and predicted that "if a European war should develop . . . China will be unable to get one dollar from foreign financiers, and trade will be absolutely dead in China thereafter."[8]

Hupp's decision to drop out of the low-price field did nothing to help its sales in China and other Oriental markets. Butsch bluntly noted in late 1912 that the 1913 model Hupmobile had been raised in price to $975 and warned Drake that "we cannot get a higher selling price here for your cars, than that at which we are selling at the present." This meant that "the increase in price will simply come out of our commission."[9]

By the fall of 1913, after Hupp ended Model 20 production, Drake realized that that decision had priced its cars out of many of the world's countries; everywhere he was pestered for more Model 20s. He wrote J. Walter asking "if there is any possibility of our getting out a small car again." Drake needed an updated version of the Model 20, with a small, long-stroke motor to reduce European auto taxes (which were based on an engine's horsepower), an improved oiling system, a somewhat longer wheel base, a three-speed transmission, and a "tank under the seat and a carry space at the back, with nice graceful lines," which, he promised, would give him "a car that would sell." By then Drake understood the irony inherent in Hupp's decision to drop the Model 20; on New Year's Day 1913, he wrote a friend at Federal Truck Company that "my trip of two years ago . . . put a lot of cheap car people on to the opportunities out here and now . . . American cars are the topic of motor conversation." Hupp had, however, abandoned the market it had helped create.[10]

It was difficult, Drake discovered, to excite anyone in the Orient about any model Hupmobile when they never seemed to get delivered. He worked hard in the Philippines, for example, to nourish a business relationship with Leopold Kahn in Manila. When Drake returned home from his first trek, he found several letters from Kahn asking where his Hupps were and pleading for him "to do everything in [his] power to get" them shipped. Drake sent him a litany of the factory's woes and assured Kahn that "several cars" were on their way. A month later, Kahn mentioned that he still had "none on hand just now." He knew how to grab Drake's attention, however. He casually mentioned that the R.C.H. was "getting to be one of the most popular cars around here."[11]

Kahn's complaints were so numerous that in November 1912, Hupp's export

The Little Corporal in front of the monument to Java's first governor. HPA/DJC.

manager, C. H. Dunlap explained to Drake, who was in Bombay, that the shortage of ocean shipping due to worldwide prosperity made it difficult for Hupp to ship to anyone. He suspected that shipping company representatives gave Kahn "the usual song and dance to the effect they can handle without delay goods which we are shipping for a/c [account] Manila." Dunlap asked Drake when he arrived in Manila to "tell the clerk, office boy, or whoever it is that writes the above mentioned insulting letters, where he gets off at." Dunlap could not do it himself, because Kahn was a "valued representative" and he had to "be as gentle with [him] as Mary's little lamb."[12]

Throughout 1912, Drake labored to keep the distributors, dealers, and agents he had recruited on the world tour happy despite factory and shipping problems. His Indonesian and Malaysian distributor, the Straits Garage Syndicate in Singapore, was pestering Dunlap to send it cars. Drake alternately stroked its manager—"I see that you have been doing a wonderful business in Hupmobiles"—and apologized for being unable "to ship them to you as fast as you have ordered them." As always, he promised that Hupp would soon "be in a position to handle any business you can send us." Toward the end of the year, Dunlap did find cargo space to ship thirty-four Hupps to Singapore.[13]

Drake also worked to protect Hupp's competitive position abroad. Like other auto firms, Hupp allowed its dealers to carry several makes, as long as they did not compete in price with Hupps. Drake discovered that the Straits Garage had "taken on" the Briggs Detroiter and wrote that he was "very much disinclined to have the 'Hupmobile' represented by the same agents." He told his distributor that the Hupmobile would "answer all purposes" that the Briggs Detroiter "possibly could, and as you know, is far better value for the money." He was serious and stern. He told the Straits Garage that Hupp would "not be at all kindly disposed to your handling it, if you should keep on the agency with us."[14]

Drake was also wrangling with his representative in India. On his world tour, he had appointed dealers in Rangoon and Calcutta and a distributor in Bombay. As in Japan, the Hupp's small size was its strongest selling point: the crowded, chaotic conditions and choked, narrow streets in India were good advertisements for a "small, easily-handled car," he told reporters everywhere on the trip. The Hupp was "bound to be popular" and hence a good business proposition. The company could not get its cars out to the subcontinent, however, and its Indian representatives had no vehicles to demonstrate.[15]

Drake had signed a contract with Harry P. Gibbs, a consulting engineer with a British firm that had a connection in Bombay with the Tata Hydro-Electric Supply Company. Hupp's new distributor handled his cars through the Bombay Motor Company, which evidently had no formal business relationship with Hupp. The American firm allowed Gibbs the usual 25 percent discount on cars and 20 percent off on all accessories.[16]

Gibbs seemed to be an excellent choice; he was a car enthusiast with social connections among the British colonials. His wife spent the hot season "in the Hills," and he wrote Drake in February 1912 that he was preparing for "the event of the season, the fancy dress dance at the club." He also wanted Drake to recommend an American motorboat that he could buy to become "a member of the Yacht club." Ever the entrepreneur, he hinted to Hupmobile's secretary that "it might be the means of introducing the firms [sic] good[s] that supplies [sic] it."[17]

Only a few weeks after the trio left India, Gibbs wrote Drake that he had "landed the first lot" of cars and sold them all. He sent two to Calcutta, one to Bangalore, and took two to Bombay. Gibbs sold his own runabout and kept a new tourer just like the Little Corporal for his personal car and demonstrator. "I can sell more if I can only get them," he said.[18]

Selling cars overseas was fraught with cultural problems. Drake learned, for example, that social customs dictated automotive styles. "I am not able to do much with runabouts or coupes on acct. of no outside seat for a boy, which people here must have," Gibbs explained. He could sell all the touring cars he could get, but complained he had to use the coupe for his own transport—evidently Gibbs was unwilling or unable to display a "boy."[19]

Even when Hupp did ship socially appropriate body styles to colonial India, it had a difficult time getting them there unharmed. Drake's Bombay agent complained constantly of damage problems. The windscreen on one car arrived broken because the vehicle was "loose in the chocks" that were supposed to hold it securely inside its wooden crate. Furthermore, "the mud guards were under the car body and jammed by it." Gibbs complained that "the cases are not as strong as they should be and when the Steamship people sling them they bend the casing in and it takes the paint off the edge of the guards." After carefully unpacking the cars in his own yard, he found only one undamaged.[20]

Drake had no solution to offer; he wrote Gibbs that "there is always a certain amount of breakage . . . in cars that are shipped such great distances." He apologized, saying, "If you feel justified in coming back at the Company for inefficient packing I should certainly do so."[21]

Just getting the cars ordered, built, and delivered overseas was more vexing, however. The Bombay agent complained after four months that he had heard nothing about his initial July 1911 order for six cars. Hupp would not reply to his telegrams, and Gibbs grumbled that the company was "letting [him] down." He finally cabled his Boston banker, who interceded with Hupp and at least learned when his order was scheduled to be shipped. Two months later, however, the cars had still not arrived. Moreover, Dunlap showed "annoyance . . . on acct. of my cables," Gibbs complained. He asked that Drake "make satisfactory arrangements for the handling of my affairs at that end."[22]

Information did not flow much more freely than cars. Gibbs was peeved with Drake, because although he was its "agent for India," the company had told him nothing about its new Model 32; he had only learned of it from outsiders. "Really, your foreign department ought to have a live man at it's [sic] head," he told Drake. Hupp finally wired him news that "some advertising has been sent," and he received his July order in February 1912; by then, however, his second order was already late.[23]

Back in Detroit only three weeks, Drake struggled to solve Hupp's foreign delivery problems and placate his distributors. He explained to Gibbs that the company had shipped his cars in time to catch a ship leaving New York on November 10, 1911,

Drake was not simply making excuses for Hupp's production delays. The tents shown here covered the area that became the administration building. The company claimed that despite outside temperatures of zero, the workers labored at a comfortable 65°F inside the tents. Hupmobile, *The Man, the Machine, the Material* (Detroit, 1913).

"but [it] refused to take the cars." They found another ship that loaded them fifteen days later. But the real difficulties were at the factory, where "we are working night and day to get out the new car," Drake noted. "Our new factory," he wrote, "has taken longer to build than expected on account of the very severe winter." Things were so bad that "one part of the building was built in more than zero weather under a tent." The weather had also affected domestic transport, "tying up . . . all freight lines throughout the country . . . [and] thousands of carloads of freight have been side tracked." In a classic understatement, Drake asserted "this has seemed to be working against the running of the business in a proper and smooth manner." He sought, however, to placate Gibbs with the information that "some days ago a Touring Car was shipped you and it was one of the first that we were able to get out. . . . I practically stole this car to get it away to you," even before Hupp had "supplied all our American dealers." To appease Gibbs further, Drake had the busy Hastings write India explaining the problems he had getting his cars out in a timely manner.[24]

Gibbs was less interested in the new models than he was in securing shiploads of Model 20s. Drake finally admitted that he could not "ship you any more of the old model Touring Car because we are bending every effort to get out the new car." With no Model 20s available, Drake had to try to generate enthusiasm in Bombay for the Model 32, which nobody there had seen yet. It was "going to be the car that will set them all talking in India," he wrote his distributor.[25]

Drake also gave Gibbs a financial incentive to promote the unseen new car. Like most car companies, Hupp allowed its agents and distributors a fee per car to cover their advertising costs. Soon after Drake returned to Detroit, he allotted Gibbs an extra $10 per Hupp, which, he hoped, "gives you a little extra help in getting your cars before the public over there." Conspiratorially, Drake added, "this is a rather special thing for you Harry, so please do not make it generally known."[26]

By the fall of 1912, barely a year after the Hupmobilists had left India, Gibbs was threatening to sever his relationship with Hupp. Drake agreed that "you have been in a very embarrassing position and [I] suppose you have had some financial loss at the way things have been going," and he admitted that it had all been Hupp's fault. Gibbs had already talked to Speyer & Co. of Calcutta about assuming his contract. Drake had met H. R. Speyer on his tour and was impressed with him, especially after Speyer mentioned that he wanted fixed monthly Hupp shipments. By Christmas 1912, Drake was convinced that he should contract with Speyer and let Gibbs go; Gibbs had already instructed his bankers not to pay for any more Hupps the factory consigned to him in preparation for exiting the business.[27]

Drake gave the contract to Speyer and was upset at the outcome of his time-consuming relationship with Gibbs. "India is a nightmare to me in a way, as far as business is concerned," he wrote Dunlap. Upon further reflection, he added, "I do not believe there is anyone in India that can get out and hustle enough to do business, it all has to come to them." He professed, "I did the best I could" and concluded that it was impossible to "get any enthusiasm started up about Motor cars unless they come from England or France," although he did not understand how anyone could get excited about those countries' cars.[28]

His conviction that American cars were superior to European ones spurred Drake to step up his efforts to promote Hupps more energetically in Europe. In Italy, for example, he reached into the social hierarchy for a distributor, contracting with Count Peccorini, who was affiliated with R. d'Isola & Company in Rome. He and the count struck up a firm friendship during the Hupmobilists' short stay in Italy. Soon after Drake arrived home, the count penned him a chatty note alluding to the "throngs with wild excitement" who had lined Rome's streets to meet Hanlon, Drake, and Jones and requesting a photo of Drake, which he promised to keep "in my own private study—and only show it to worthy people." Peccorini hoped that Drake had not forgotten "the Pope, his sisters, [and] the Baron."[29]

Like Gibbs and Butsch, Peccorini had had little contact with the company after the trio departed, however, and he was not pleased. Less direct than his Asian counterparts, Peccorini asked Drake "to let us know all that we don't know about the Hupp Co., the new car, what chance there is of ever getting it, if it is true that there is a new car, etc." Even an Italian count was unable to break through the factory's silence while Drake and his two colleagues were still on the road struggling to get back to Detroit.[30]

Six weeks after shoveling his way home across Ontario, Drake replied that despite all the difficulties the factory had had building the Model 32s, he had shipped the count a new model "some days ago." He added: "We hope very soon to be able to send them along to you in any quantity you may require." Drake vowed he would return to Rome in October 1912, when they would "have a good time and . . . scare up some business."[31]

The Italian distributor's contract was up for renegotiation in 1912, and Drake wanted to avoid the haggling and the avalanche of minutiae that cascaded over him in dealing with all his European representatives—such negotiations threatened his working friendships. He therefore persuaded the company to hire a middleman, "Mr. J. L. Poole, a gentleman of a great deal of experience in foreign motor car business and a man of very pleasing personality," located in Paris, to "have charge of our business in Continental Europe." Drake told his overseas agents that they would "reap a great deal of benefit" from the new arrangement.[32]

Count Peccorini's reaction to the organizational change has been lost, but Drake's Paris distributor, J. Archer, was less than thrilled. Two weeks after Drake explained the change, Archer shot a note back to Detroit wondering "if Mr. Poole is the same gentleman who has been agent of the Oldsmobile Company in France and also of the Buick automobile." If he was, Archer wanted Drake to know that "he has not succeeded in France in launching these two companies." Drake reassured his French connection that indeed it was the same Poole and explained that it was not his fault Buick and Oldsmobile had failed there, "particularly Buick, . . . as we understand the company did not stand back of him as it properly should."[33]

Archer faced the same problems as Hupp's agents in Italy, India, and the Orient. "We would be very much obliged to you to make the necessary efforts with this Firm, in order that we may be able to have the touring cars we have ordered," he wrote Drake barely three weeks after the latter had returned to Detroit. To prod Hupp, Archer added, "we are very much bothered, all of our customers are howling for ever so long and we are not able to know what to reply to them." Drake sent his Paris representative his standard letter about manufacturing problems, saying that he had already shipped him one touring car and assuring him "that Mr. Poole will be of great assistance to you in placing cars throughout France. . . . [and] will greatly advance our mutual interests." Archer was skeptical but said that "if the Hupp Motor Car Company delivers its cars punctually, we are certain we can do some interesting business."[34]

After meeting Hupp's new European middleman, Archer was satisfied, however, that he was a "man of business affairs" with whom he was "in almost perfect accord." Lack of cars had cost the French agency "the loss of almost the entire season," but Archer wrote Drake that Poole's acceptance was guaranteed when he "faithfully promised us that we would have [cars] passed over to us before any other agents."[35]

In Berlin, Drake had set up a distributorship with Theodore Tietz, with whom he had immediate problems. Hupmobiles' clutches were defective, Tietz discovered, and he had to repair them at his own expense. After he complained, Drake wrote him from England that "we will frankly admit having some trouble with [them] in our earliest cars, but have now corrected that, and can assure you that the cars coming through from now on will give you no further trouble on that score." Tietz also informed Drake that continental automobile tastes demanded that Hupp change its offerings if it wished to sell well there. Drake wrote his brother "we are losing a lot of sales. All over the Continent they are crying out for landaulettes or limousines," and he insisted that J. Walter "get somebody busy on that." He promised his brother, "We will sell more of them over here—in fact twice as many—as we would in America," not much of an incentive for the factory to invest in additional tooling for a secondary market.[36]

Supplying parts, a problem that afflicted all auto companies in foreign markets, was as troublesome to Hupp as failing to build and ship an adequate number of appropriately styled cars. Almost a year and a half after the trio left India, G. W. Disney, a sanitary engineer in Ceylon, claimed that his crankshaft had broken while he was driving his Hupp slowly on a perfectly level road. He had hired a mechanic, who said that "the breakdown was due to an obvious flaw visible in the metal." Not one to suffer in silence, Disney began writing an almost daily flow of letters to everyone in the Orient associated with the company demanding that his car be temporarily fixed until Hupp could replace it free of charge. He also demanded compensation for his carriage, horse, coolie hires, and complaining telegrams. Drake, pulled into the dispute, scoured the globe from the Suez to Hawaii looking for a crankshaft, to no avail. After six months of increasingly belligerent correspondence, Disney was still crankless and Drake was decidedly cranky.[37]

To alleviate supply difficulties everywhere, Drake proposed to his brother that

Hupp create regional parts warehouses around the globe. He felt strongly enough about it to write from England that it was "absolutely necessary" that the company establish "a spare parts depot at Hamburg." Unused to taking a hard line with his younger brother, he was agitated enough to demand, rather than ask. "For Heaven's sake use the arguments you have in your head and get a Spare Parts Depot over there as soon as possible, or sooner," he wrote. He appealed to J. Walter's practical side, reasoning, "it is not a question of our expending a few thousand dollars without making anything on it, but it is a question of our being able to sell cars in Europe." Hupp had learned that successful dollar diplomacy required a global infrastructure to support its efforts. Sending the world tourers, and later Drake, around the world every few years to cultivate personal business relationships was not enough. Hupp had to station company employees at strategic overseas points to support its ambitious sales expectations.[38]

When the Hupmobilists left England, Drake was certain Hupp's sales on the island would probably exceed his expectations. That had not happened, however, because Hupp could not supply the British market with cars. Before he visited London again, ten months later, Drake assured his distributor, Harry Whiting of the Whiting Company, that although it had been "nip and tuck with us all this year, another year will see us all [the] way out of the woods, yourself included." He wrote J. Walter that his London representative was "certainly enthusiastic, and has lost no courage through the experience he has had during the last season." Drake was certain Whiting would take 600 cars for 1913 in regular shipments "unless he gets cold feet before I get his signature on the contract."[39]

To compete in Britain, Hupp had to cater to tastes there. Drake wrote his president that Hupp's tops would not sell in England. Whiting had had some made locally, and Drake shipped one home, suggesting J. Walter try it on his own car. Worse, Drake had "stood in the sales room and heard people refuse to consider our car with the nickel trimmings." In England, he explained, "everything is polished brass on all the cars . . . and they won't have anything else." Hupp's sales were also not helped by shipping only black cars; Britons called the new Hupmobile the "Funeral Car." To make the company's cars more appealing, Whiting painted white striping along their sides. Drake advised the factory that Whiting "would very much prefer the Blue Body" and noted that he "did not complain that the colour is not always even." Drake told his brother that Whiting was "now spending part of his profit in putting finishing touches on the body, and we get very little complaint from him."[40]

Newly promoted to vice president, Drake also kept a close eye on competitors' overseas sales, especially those of R.C.H. With some glee, he noted that R.C.H. had raised its prices in England and warned his brother "from the looks of things they are doing some tricky business." R.C.H. advertised two engine sizes, which reduced one of its cars to a tax level lower than Hupp's Model 32. Drake was certain R.C.H. had only one engine and asked J. Walter to have someone check, for "Mr. Whiting is very anxious to put a stop to it." Robert Hupp had let it be known that he had a contract with an English distributor for 1,000 cars, which Drake was happy to report "is all rot." R.C.H. did have many "cars down at the docks, that have not been taken up yet . . . [but] they are certainly not selling to any great extent." He noted parenthetically that "Overland and Flanders are the ones that are making competition, the other fellow is only making the moss."[41]

On his second circle of the globe in 1912 and 1913, and possibly on his tour in the Little Corporal as well, Drake did personal business on the side. He and J. Walter were stockholders in the Federal Motor Truck Company, whose secretary-treasurer was Garvin Denby, probably a brother of Edwin Denby, one of Hupp's largest financial backers. Just after Drake left on his second world tour, J. Walter wrote that Federal had paid a dividend of 10 percent on "old capital," money the initial investors had put in, and an astounding 90 percent on its stock. Walter need not have added, "It is doing splendidly."[42]

The Drakes, however, were more than passive investors. While on his second trip, Joseph established Federal dealerships overseas, as he may have done on his earlier trek with Hanlon and Jones. On January 1, 1913, Drake wrote Denby, "India are very much interested in motor trucks and I have been having some talk on the subject with them." Drake asked Denby to send Hupp's dealers in India truck literature and "tell them I requested you to do so and that I and others of the Hupp Motor Car Co. are large stockholders in the federal." Drake, however, counseled Federal to cut out distributors and sell directly to its dealers, advice perhaps gleaned from his own experiences with Gibbs.[43]

Everywhere he went, Drake looked for truck sales outlets. When he arrived in Singapore, he "began to sound the praises of the Federal Truck." He tried to get the Straits Garage syndicate there to handle the line, because they were "making money out there so fast they do not know what to do with it." Phizackerley of Sydney, Australia, also wanted to handle trucks, and Drake suggested that when Phizackerley arrived in the states, Denby, J. Walter, and Dunlap give him and his party the royal treatment, because if "you put them up at the Club and show them every attention, they will appreciate it." Drake suggested prospects for Federal dealerships across Australia and New Zealand, along with suggestions as to how Federal should carve out its sales territories. His efforts on behalf of Federal Truck were not a conflict of interest—Hupp only made a half-hearted foray into truck production in 1913–14—but Federal was a drain on his time and diverted his attention from Hupp's affairs. Federal's astounding dividends, however, helped the Drakes and their friends buy control of Hupp after Robert Hupp decamped.[44]

While Drake worked to make money for his brother and other Hupp officers overseas, J. Walter helped out at home. In June 1913, the two Drakes were trying to "wipe out their debts to Co. for Hupp purchase." J. Walter Drake bought $19,000 worth of stock in "John E.," a code name for an unidentified firm, putting only $9,000 down. A month later, the new shares paid a 33.3 percent dividend, plus another 12.5 percent on the newly raised $1 million in capital. Moreover, "John E." promised another 10 percent dividend the following month, which J. Walter declared "will fix us both in fine shape." After the second dividend, J. Walter wrote his brother that he had paid for their Hupp shares with $370,000 earned from these transactions. The Drakes also invested with Dunlap in "Nelson stock," at two for one, and Walter promised to "swing all I can for you & me & sell bal. to friends." Hupp harbored a nest of calculating capitalists.[45]

The Drakes' brother Harry lived in California and was perpetually short of cash, because he was trying to start a fruit farm. Joseph Drake sent him money whenever he could, and after J. Walter's financial machinations in mid 1913, he was feeling generous. After explaining that the "trouble we had in Detroit in getting things into shape, and buying Hupp stock took most of the money we had," he told Harry to ask for twice what he really needed, for "I believe we are pretty well fixed financially now." Joseph Drake was also something of a plunger on his own account. In 1915, he came across a new "deep sea exploring apparatus" and wrote a friend in Brisbane that it might be just "what we will need in our business when we take the pearl fishing business over." Always the optimist, Drake observed that the pearls they were getting at one and two hundred feet were pretty good and believed "there must be some pretty fine pearls in oysters 500 or 600 feet down."[46]

The company's management shakeup, new factory, the severe 1911–12 winter weather, and the aggravations attendant upon bringing out a completely new Hupp could not have come at a worse time for Drake. The instability and delays threatened to undo everything the three Hupmobilists had accomplished in their fifteen months of travel, socializing, and negotiating. The world tour, however, enabled Drake to sign prominent overseas businessmen to represent the company. Although Hupp claimed that the trip had increased its foreign orders 400 percent, it could not fill them. The company's failures strained its relations with its new overseas distributors, dealers, and agents and lured Drake back on the road in the fall of 1912. He planned to demonstrate the new Hupmobile to representatives he had signed on his first tour to encourage them to stay within Hupp's corporate fold. Drake never considered such exertions would be necessary, however, when he, Hanlon, and Jones celebrated their return at New York City's auto show and fought their way back to Detroit through near-record snowfalls and bitingly cold temperatures.

THE LAST LEG

12

The three world travelers had followed the internal corporate changes that convulsed their company from afar. Drake must have been apprehensive about his and his brother's futures, and Hanlon, whose personal friendship with Charles Hastings had earned him his trip ticket, was equally concerned about his own job. They quickened their pace to get home to family, friends, and work. The celebrations in New York and Detroit that enfolded them, however, dispelled most of their fears about their future prospects with Hupp.

Officials of the recast Hupp Motor Car Company had laid elaborate plans to greet their adventurers at New York's dock. The *Detroit Journal* announced on December 30, 1911, that the company had paid for a "special car attached to 'The Detroiter,' carrying a delegation from this city . . . for New York to welcome the homecoming Hupmobile world-tourists." The New York Central Railroad sped "J. Walter and George A. Drake, Edwin Denby, Milton A. McRae, the head of Detroit's Chamber of Commerce, a number of prominent Motor City businessmen," and a Detroit Board of Commerce representative in sumptuous comfort to take part in the formal dockside celebrations. The firm seized the chance to reassure the public and its dealers with an open demonstration of its newfound unity and portents for continued success after its well-advertised split with Robert Hupp.[1]

As the *Lusitania* sliced through the icy North Atlantic waters bearing the Little Corporal and its crew home, Motor Dealers' Association officials worked overtime to mount the Twelfth National Automobile Show, which would showcase the Hupmobilers and their car. The 1912 motor extravaganza sprawled over 125,000 square feet in Madison Square Garden. Some five hundred craftsmen overran "the place from cellar to rafters" to finish the displays as the tugboats nudged the *Lusitania* into its berth. The show's sheer size was enough to overwhelm the three men who had preached the practicalities of littleness to the world, a theme they continued to emphasize as they walked down the gangplank on January 4, 1912. Joseph Drake told the welcoming crowd that the trio had "convincingly demonstrated the value of the light and low-priced American car," which had led to "a 400 per cent increase in their foreign trade in a few months." Hupp's officials must have been ill at ease as they listened to their official representative rhapsodize about a car and market they had decided to abandon.[2]

Two days later, the National Auto Show threw open its doors to the public. The three travelers could not in their wildest dreams have envisioned telling their stories on such a stage. The show's gross ostentation elevated their homecoming to the level of a Louis XIV fête. Despite the outside temperature of zero and an inside one not much higher, because exhibitors kept the outside doors open to bring in their cars and paraphernalia, a reporter pronounced it "the most brilliant automobile exhibit ever seen in the Garden—in fact, that structure in all its career has never held a more artistically arranged exposition."[3]

The dealers' association spared no expense. The Garden's foyer was "decked out on each side with thick boxwood hedges, in the recesses of which marble figures sculptured by the eminent Martini and standing on tall pedestals" greeted the crowds. Past the hedges, the newsman continued, "the visitor is confronted by a large fountain casting up sparkling streams of water," behind which was located a "statue representing the 'Era of Motors.'"[4]

In the main hall, a huge "canopy-like oriental rug," 100 by 200 feet, which weighed almost three tons, stretched overhead from wall to wall, fringed by twenty-four smaller panels. An "impressive female figure with arms outstretched," representing the "Triumph of the Industry," dominated the big rug's center. Garlands of flowers from the canopy to the floor completed the tableau. Around the main floor, decorators had constructed a balcony supported by "twenty-five ornate crimson and gold steel columns," to create more floor space. For guests too overawed to remain standing, dealers spread more than 1,000 chairs around the main floor.[5]

The show overflowed into the Exhibition Hall, Concert Hall, and basement. The Exhibition Hall "had been transformed into a California Patio," with a "grape arbor setting," "huge pergola," and "mammoth landscape painting by Pal representing a golden sunset in Southern California." The Concert Hall had been converted "into a veritable Japanese cherry garden." The ceiling was festooned with real cherry branches, to which "artificial blossoms . . . scented with dainty perfume" had been attached. A painted landscape "depicting the 'Land of Flowers' in all the glory of full bloom with Fuji Yama, the sacred mountain of Japan, towering in the distance" encircled the room. Even the basement restaurant "in the form of a Spanish Bodega in a California setting," bespoke the American auto industry's aspirations to conquer the world.[6]

The United States, short on history and full of immigrants, was in search of itself. At the new century's onset, Americans embraced foreign art, culture, and royalty; the more alien the better. Asian, Near Eastern, and especially Egyptian influences were everywhere. The juxtaposition of such exotic motifs with the auto sales booths was symbolic; America was hell-bent on mechanizing these lands and hinted that in return, it wished to adopt selected aspects of their cultures to cloak the premier industrial nation with a patina of agelessness and scent of these former empires' grandeur.

The show was a major social event of the winter season. Two special "society nights" when "the smart set" turned out in full force, rivaling the "Horse Show" and "famous Metropolitan Opera premiers," according to the *New York Times,* were especially noteworthy: "The visitors walking around the huge amphitheater form a show in themselves—plenty of beautiful women in beautiful gowns." And in the background, the soft strains of the Madison Square Garden Band's music helped put the visual delights in perspective.[7]

The show advertised $2,500,000 worth of automobiles, trucks, and accessories on view among the grape arbors and cherry blossoms. Sixty manufacturers of "pleasure cars," thirty-four "commercial car" or truck makers, and twenty motorcycle companies offered their wares in the Garden. The cars ranged in price from $350 to a hefty $7,500. Some 5,500 automobile men worked their exhibits and mingled with prospective buyers and dealers; the industry was booming.[8]

The Hupp explorers arrived before the workers had completed their decorations and for several days exhibited their world-traveled car in the showroom of H. J.

Koehler Company, Hupp's New York City distributor. When the show opened, Hanlon drove the Little Corporal, still proudly displaying its dirt, dust, decals, and dings, to the Grand Central Palace and parked it next to a display of the company's shiny, new larger models.[9]

The *New York Times*, despite its ample and enthusiastic coverage of the show, did not specifically mention Hupp's display. It covered the Hupmobilists' arrival in the city and ran several later articles on their departure into upstate's snowy wastes. The paper was careful not to mention any auto company by name, however, unless its new models exhibited technological novelties or were purchased on the floor by celebrities. The little Hupp probably attracted much attention nonetheless, if simply because it was the only dirty automobile in the hall.

Ironically, when compared to the 1912 display models, the Little Corporal was clearly a dated specimen. Although auto technology had not advanced greatly since it had left its native shores, public preferences had changed dramatically, and automakers responded quickly to the new demands. A thoughtful newspaperman put the 1912 automotive improvements into perspective when he observed that they were necessary because people used their cars more often and all adult family members drove.[10]

As cars became more essential, Americans motored more frequently in bad weather. "One of the evidences of progress is seen in the increased use of closed bodies," one writer said. Only a few years earlier, he observed, most cars were "utterly without top," but he predicted that those would no longer sell. Some enterprising manufacturers, he noted, had provided glass windows that could be "let down" into the sides of the body. By 1912, even touring cars came equipped with a top, a "Glass front," and side curtains, which made them "capable of being completely closed and thus defy the weather."[11]

Drivers, once buttoned into a car in miserable weather, hated to crawl out into the elements to crank their motors or light their lights, and self-starters, both electric and acetylene, were popular at the show, as were inside and outside electric lights. Kerosene lamps were "mussy," and women particularly wanted to just "push a button or turn a knob" to illuminate the road, especially in bad weather. The dirt-encrusted Hupp was also surrounded by cars with less easily discernible technical improvements. Quieter sliding or rotary valves, improved clutches, larger wheels, bigger and heavier springs for better stability and a softer ride, wider and lower bodies, improved mufflers, and simpler oilers were all ballyhooed.

After examining competitors' cars at the show, Hupp Motor Car Company officials were convinced that they had made the right decision to bring out their long-stroke Model 32 so as to stay with industry leaders and satisfy the more affluent motoring public's demands. Although Hupp continued to manufacture Model 20s into 1913, they steadily became less important to its product mix. They fell from 24 percent of the 7,640 cars Hupp manufactured in 1912 to only 7 percent of the 12,543 it built in 1913. Those who braved the subfreezing cold and blizzards to see the show expected more from their motors than the Model 20 offered. Henry Ford, who was there, did not even bother to exhibit his cars; he knew that the likes of the duke of Newcastle, William K. Vanderbilt, Norman Armour, Griswold Lorillard, Mrs. Craig Biddle, Frank Jay Gould, Percy Rockefeller, and Worthington Whitehouse, who came to be seen and buy display cars in the Garden, would not give his Model T's a nod. He came to check the "competition," to see how to improve his cars without increasing their price. Ford could afford to stand above the fray—he outproduced his nearest rival, Willys-Overland, by better than 600 percent in 1912.[12]

As Hanlon, Drake, and Jones prepared to drive their final leg back to Detroit, they no doubt fervently wished they could be cocooned in a closed motorcar with an electric starter and lights. New York's weather during the show had been frightful, and forecasts predicted the same along their route home. The temperature hovered at zero on January 8 as crowds gathered to enter Madison Square Garden at eight o'-clock in the evening, and it did not warm up much the following week. A snowstorm buffeted the city on January 12 and lingered into the following day, "Theatrical Matinee Day" at the Garden. Nevertheless "there were stars in abundance and any number of mere chorus and show girls." One actress, Kitty Gordon, appeared "encased in huge white bearskin furs" to stroll among the automotive industry's delights.[13]

Drake missed most of the motor show. The day after he arrived in New York City, he caught a train to Detroit, where he remained until January 12, three days before the trio was scheduled to depart. Upon his return to New York, he complained that "my time was so taken up with hustling to get the car ready . . . that I saw no one except on business." The three remained at the show long enough to fret about the portents of even worse weather ahead, make plans to have Hupp's local distributor give the car "a preliminary trial to find out if all its parts were in good running order," and prepare to leave on January 15. In the presence of reporters, however, they were cocky. One of them said that since they had been "*par-boiled* in Java," he figured "they might as well finish it up by being half-frozen at home." Drake chimed in to

remind the newsmen that he had been on the winter trip to New York City back in 1910 and thought "there can't be any worse conditions encountered than those." He reminded the press that the snow that winter "was reported the worst in many years" and admitted that "there will be no sorrow if it holds its record for a while longer."[14]

The following day, the *Times* reported that "one of the party" proclaimed "we started out to go around from Detroit to Detroit, and we are going to make it, if it takes a month to shovel our way the rest of the route." The paper added as an aside, "and it surely looks as if there was [*sic*] going to be some snow shoveling to do." Had the Hupmobilists left for Detroit as soon as they had arrived in New York City, the press happily reminded them, "their task would have been a comparatively easy one. There would have been cold weather, but not a great deal of snow." Instead, while the veteran travelers reveled in their accolades at the show, "there have been all kinds of blizzards along the route."[15]

Despite their bravado, however, the adventurers made careful preparations for the bleak task ahead. They spent the day before their departure "in laying in supplies

Hanlon wheels the Little Corporal out from Hupp's New York City distributor, H. J. Koehler Company, after it tuned and examined the car in preparation for its run home. HPA/DJC.

The world tourers, swathed in fur, leather, and wool, in New York in January 1912. HPA/DJC.

of fur coats, sweaters, woolens, and boots," a reporter noted. The next day, they arrived at Koehler Company's headquarters at Broadway and Fifty-fourth Street in their new togs, which made them "resembl[e] Arctic explorers." The Hupp Motor Car Company, as usual, laid on festivities. A large crowd of well-wishers and some twenty-five "Hupmobile enthusiasts" attended to escort them out of the city. The *Times* reported that Hanlon, Jones, and Drake "were stalling around, finding excuses to stay close to the fire for just a few minutes longer." They evidently found a few, because they left well over an hour after their scheduled 10 A.M. start.[16]

They planned to drive up the Hudson River Valley to Albany, turn west through the Mohawk Valley to Utica, Syracuse, and Buffalo, and cross over to Ontario for the dash home. The *Detroit Free Press* predicted that "if they are not storm-stayed by the deep snows through the Mohawk Valley or held up by admiring throngs in the various cities through which they pass," they would reach the Motor City in time for the opening of its auto show on January 20, only six days away.[17]

Accompanied by "Hupmobile enthusiasts," the little Hupp chugged northward

212   THREE MEN IN A HUPP

In parts of New York State the trio spent more time shoveling than driving. HPA/DJC.

toward Yonkers and the upstate New York winter wonderland. The roads to Albany were fairly clear, however, and the crew made the capital city by nightfall. Their struggle began in earnest when they drove into the Mohawk Valley, a perennial funnel for snow storms. They encountered "heavy snow with many drifted stretches and much practically unbroken road," which they had to shovel their way through. They took most of the day to get to Canajoharie, where a local newsman put the best face on their slow progress, writing, "it was hard going but the little car did its work nobly."[18]

Bundled in their furs, the three men left early on Wednesday, January 17, hoping to make Rochester or Buffalo in two days. It was not to be; "the moderation of the zero weather which has worried the tourists thus far," wrote a Syracuse reporter, "was followed by heavy snows, and particularly on the run through the Mohawk Valley the boys were kept busy with the shovels fighting off the drifts that blocked their way." They shoveled all day and covered only about fifty miles to Utica. The Detroit newspaper bragged that Utica gave Jones, its home-town boy, and his colleagues "a royal reception." Even in the lousy weather, his brothers in "the local lodge of Elks . . . met them at the outskirts of the town with several automobiles and a

When the travelers met with a decent, clear road they were so surprised they stopped to take a picture of it. HPA/DJC.

truck containing a band and escorted them into town." The *Utica Daily Press*, however, was a good deal more subdued, mentioning only that Jones drove through there and printing a short biographical sketch of him. Perhaps the cold, snowy weather kept the paper's reporter from attending the welcoming festivities.[19]

The groggy Huppers dragged themselves out into the icy blasts early the next morning and barely made Syracuse before nightfall "after the hardest day's battle of the trip." A Detroit scribe, however, from the cozy comfort of his office, predicted that "unless something unforeseen happens there is no doubt that they will arrive in Detroit in time for the opening of the automobile show Monday."[20]

The "unforeseen" was everywhere, most of it piled up to the top of the Hupp's doors. On Friday, the trio, all of whom must have yearned for their balmy days in Fiji, dug their way to Batavia, after "another strenuous day's battle with snowdrifts" and a stop in Rochester, where they "held an impromptu reception in the lobby of the Powers Hotel," probably in a vain effort to get warm and dry. A local newspaperman pointed out that "many cars starting to make trips between towns east of here have turned back rather than buck the snow," but observed proudly, "the Hupmobilists keep plugging toward Detroit." On Saturday, the temperature rose, and they endured "almost steady rain which made the going heavy," but they made pretty good

The land on the other side of the bridge was the last remaining country between them and the comforts of home. HPA/DJC.

time to Buffalo, always a winter chokepoint, and up to Niagara Falls, where they crossed the river into Ontario. At nightfall, they stopped in Hamilton, where a local scribbler described their tour as "the globe-grueling trip" and noted that "something over 200 miles remains to be done before the long journey is ended."[21]

They were the longest 200 miles they had faced. They fought over snowy roads, sometimes tearing down farmers' fences to cut across their fields to avoid snowdrifts clogging the road, and putted into London, Ontario, by Sabbath evening for a pretty good day's work of about 75 miles, at an average speed of less than seven miles per hour. "They were well nigh exhausted with their efforts against the elements," a local reporter observed—and warned that there was worse to come. The next morning "they recruited an auxiliary force of men from local dealers" to help them out. "With two Hupmobiles and a snow gang to fight their way through the drifts," they made only twelve miles to Mount Bridges, still a long 120 miles from home. The *Detroit Journal* proclaimed it the "shortest run of the trip." From Mount Bridges, Drake called Hupp's headquarters and promised his bosses that "with luck" he hoped "to get to Detroit soon, but [I] will stick to the job and bring the car in on its own power if it takes the rest of the month." His brother feared it might; Hupp's president indefinitely postponed the Monday welcoming ceremonies.[22]

The Little Corporal shared the road with sleighs on the Canadian side of Niagara Falls. HPA/DJC.

Even in the terrible conditions, the Hupmen did not lose their sense of humor. HPA/DJC.

All day Tuesday, the weary crewmen dug their way through drifting snow, sometimes five and a half feet deep—higher than the car. To make their lives even more miserable, temperatures plummeted to −30°. They shoveled and plowed their way the last miles across western Ontario throughout that day and most of the next, keeping headquarters informed of their progress so that it could schedule their welcoming party.[23]

After noon on Wednesday, January 24, the trio wired that they had "floundered through the last snowbanks at Maidstone and had found a comparatively clear road for the last ten miles." A reception party that included J. Walter Drake, his brother George Drake, John E. Baker, Hupp's Canadian Branch manager, and the firm's Windsor agent left Windsor in four cars at about 2 P.M. to meet the weary world travelers. The greeting party "went on, mile after mile, through the nipping cold, and still saw no signs of the three men."[24] "At last," a newsman reported, "a speck appeared far down the frozen pike." Someone in the back of one of the Detroit cars

The welcoming party crowded around the little Hupp to greet its ambassadors. J. Walter Drake, Hupp's president, stands fourth from the right wearing the Santa Claus hat. HPA/DJC.

shouted "It looks like 'em." "The spot grew larger. Finally there loomed up three huge figures almost obscuring in their bulk the little car that bore them. . . . A shout went up from the waiting Hupmobiles" and there was furious waving from both sides. Finally, they "drew alongside the strangest motoring party that ever amazed the natives of Essex county." Hupmobile's executives piled out of their cars and began "a scramble in the snow and a rush for the world-stained little Hupmobile and a race to see who was to be the first to shake the hands of the three huge bundles of fur who . . . looked like a trio of Esquimaux on a polar expedition." The *Free Press* noted that they were "so swathed in furs that only their noses and eyes were visible."[25]

"There were shouts of hilarity, handshakes, and affectionate embraces" all around. "The men looked like hardened explorers returning from some extraordinary adventure," and when they removed their hats and gloves, their "faces [were] browned and stained with travel. Their hands were puffed and blue with cold, roughened and callused by tough labors," all proof, the reporter thought, that they "were apparently as hard as nails."[26]

In fifteen months on the road, the crew had come to resemble its car. A newsman remarked that "the Hupmobile that has made this record, covered with its hieroglyphics and scars of battle, the dents left by portagings in the Philippines, bumping over the cobble stones of Shanghai, and the out-wearing of sandstorms of China" indicated that the crew were as tough as Hupp's auto. The reporter further noted the weather-beaten "car was plastered from end to end with hotel labels from every quarter of the globe and "Tour of the World" was painted on it in four languages." It also bore trophies from the last leg; "it was covered with snow, and, if other evidence of hard travel was needed, there were two large snow shovels in the impedimenta." Photographs of the meeting also show heavy chains on the Little Corporal's rear tires and baggage on its running boards.[27]

The little parade of five Hupmobiles turned west toward the Windsor ferry. It was greeted at the dock by "hundreds of people" who had braved the biting cold to see "the world-bespattered Hupp" and "to study its strange evidences of travel and to stare at the intrepid trio." Suddenly, out of the din "piped a shrill voice, . . . there's my papa." When Hanlon's son, five-year-old Wilfred, came closer, however, he "was at first reluctant to accept the uncouth driver of the world-touring Hupmobile as his father." Not until Hanlon removed his "helmet" did the child believe; "with a cry of delight Wilfred sprang into his father's arms." He "had to get into the car and hold the wheel before he could be satisfied."[28]

Above: The little Hupp's next-to-last stop was at Hupmobile's headquarters in Windsor. Hanlon's son Wilfred sits astride the hood. *Left:* Wilfred takes his turn at the wheel on the ferry. HPA/DJC.

The real "doings" began on the Detroit side of the river. As the ferry neared, a band struck up "Home Sweet Home" and "there was a din and clamor of greetings." The newspaper reported "the dock was black with people and the windows of the neighboring buildings were filled with the faces of the curious." The noise was deafening, "there was a band playing, banners flying and cheers long before the ferry docked." Some thirty Hupmobiles were scattered throughout the crowd. After Hanlon steered the car off the boat, the "little Hupmobile, still sturdy and fit, passed up the avenue with its fur-covered heroes inside, while the escort tailed the rear."[29]

As the parade passed up Woodward Avenue, "the word was passed, 'Here they are,' and the crowd swarmed out to the street and surrounded the car that has seen strange sights and roads." The adventurers fought their way through the throngs to the Hotel Pontchartrain, where they had started their journey. Joseph Drake formally presented Mayor William B. Thompson with the little silk American flag that the former mayor had given the crew when it departed in 1910. Mayor Thompson gave a short address, in which he "said an achievement such as theirs was a credit not only to the Hupp Motor Car company and the car that had borne them 27,000 [*sic*] miles, but to the enterprise and pluck of the whole automobile industry and Detroit." Afterwards, when the crowd asked the three how they liked the rest of the world, they replied in unison "Detroit for mine," which prompted an ovation. Later, they drove their car to the Hupmobile Sales Company at 730 Woodward Avenue, "where it was placed on exhibition." Only then did "the trio of travelers, weary but happy, hasten . . . home for a bath and a shave and the other creature comforts of which they had so long been deprived."[30]

The next day, when Drake sat down to catch up on his correspondence, the rigors of his just-completed trek were fresh in his mind. "I wore out three gross of snow shovels personally on the trip home," he wrote his London agent. The last lap was pure misery, he continued; "we dug the car out of drifts five feet deep; we pushed it through drifts fully as deep; we lived on sardines and crackers; we slept when we could; we swore all the time, but here we are." One letter was insufficient to relieve his frustrations. He followed up with another, still complaining, "in the nine days it took to drive through I think I shoveled snow 48 hours of each day, and pushed the car through drifts for another 60 hours each day." The exertions took their toll on him: "My back is broken, my spirits are broken, but my nerve is still with me."[31]

The final segment of the world tour had been a "fearful trip," Drake said. "I never imagined it could be so hard, and after we got into it I did not imagine we

The homecoming parade, led by a truck carrying a band, made its way up Woodward Avenue. Crowds were noticeably absent in the bitterly cold weather. HPA/DJC.

could get out of it. . . . but we did, and the papers here have made a big fuss about it." All the "fuss," however, did not lift his spirits much. "Now I hope I am done with brass bands, and spectacular motor car expeditions for some time to come," he wrote his London agent. To another friend he was more direct; it had been "a trip I will never take again as long as I am in my right senses." Little did he know.[32]

Hanlon, Drake, and Jones did not have long to rest. The Detroit auto show was already in full swing, and they were its featured guests. It had opened on January 21, the day before they were scheduled to return, in the Wayne Gardens and an annex across the street, connected by a specially built covered walkway. Many of the companies that had exhibited in New York had rushed out to the Detroit show on their way to Chicago's exhibition, due to begin the following week. While Detroit's show was only about half the size of New York's, it was decorated "to delight the eye even of the man or woman who knows little or nothing about motor cars."[33]

The Wayne Gardens had been entirely "walled and ceilinged with tissue paper that has been variously colored and fireproofed," the *Detroit Journal* noted. Following New York's lead, "great festoons of greenery and flowers are arched across the roofs, and flags and bunting assist in the decorations." Interior decorators had learned to work electricity into their designs, and "the lighting effect is beautiful," the paper said. On the second floor of the Gardens, "the ceiling is arched with dozens of rows of green incandescents. Between them are bright white lights and hanging from the ceiling in various places are clusters of globes of soft white light."[34]

Across over 50,000 square feet of floor space, manufacturers displayed seventy-three "distinct lines of pleasure cars, motor trucks, and electric cars," some of which were "comparative infants in the field." The firms came, the newsman proclaimed, bursting with local pride, because "those in search of novelties . . . [and] newly designed cars that will shortly appear on the market always head for Detroit." Besides, he wrote, those in the trade who wanted "inside information in the automobile industry invariably head to Detroit and not Cleveland, Indianapolis, Buffalo or other centers of the industry." Detroit, he confidently asserted, was "the hub of the industry with its two score automobile factories and almost uncountable factories where component parts of the major motor car are manufactured."[35]

The eleventh annual Detroit auto show broke all previous attendance records, attracting 40,000 guests during the week. Attendees who paid their half dollar could look the little Hupmobile over and shake its crew's swollen, callused hands. In a quarter-page ad, otherwise devoted almost entirely to praising its new Model 32, Hupmobile announced that it would exhibit the world-touring Little Corporal in its booth at the auto show on Thursday. It did so only in the morning, however; that afternoon, it held an open house for the car and its crew at its Woodward Avenue showroom.[36]

The press reported that "hundreds of Hupmobile enthusiasts were in to have a look at and admire the much labeled, dirty, sturdy little car that had just completed the longest tour ever undertaken in an automobile." Hanlon, Drake, and Jones answered questions and told tales about "what the party had to contend with in the way of bad road conditions." Also on display at the showroom was "an interesting set of photographs, which attracted almost as much attention as the little car itself." The company artfully set the stage for the afternoon by hiring the appropriately named Pekin Trio to provide background music. The Little Corporal was on display in Detroit for only a short time; four days after arriving home, it was shipped to the Chicago auto show. The globe-girdlers were not quite finished with their journey.[37]

THE AFTERMATH

13

The Hupp Motor Car Company was anxious to milk as much publicity as possible from its three adventurers during the auto show season, and it hustled the trio back on the road for two more months. The Detroit exhibition closed on January 27, 1912, only four days after the Hupmobilists shoveled their way out from under Ontario's snows. In a final fanfare in which "horns of all sorts grunted, honked, and shrieked their good-bye," the other companies moved their autos out of the hall to ready them for display in Chicago.[1] The *Detroit Journal* noticed that "there is to be no rest for the Hupmobile world-touring car and the men who drove it around the world." By closing night, the Little Corporal had already been loaded aboard a train, along with "the men who girdled the globe," and whistled off to Chicago where, the newsman was confident, they "will be the unique feature of the Hupmobile exhibit." He predicted that the crew would "tell just how it was done" and speak of lands "so remote that a lad fresh from a geography course could not recognize the names . . . while the car itself, with its foreign labels, will be studied by the curious crowds."[2]

The Little Corporal's moment in the Windy City's sun, however, was brief. It went on exhibit on Saturday, January 27, where it "was a distinct attraction . . . and

Little did the three global travelers know when they posed for this picture, half-frozen, displaying their collection of decals, outside of Windsor, Ontario, that they had two more months of touring for Hupp ahead of them. HPA/DJC.

hundreds of persons read the tags from every country and land which the tourists visited." A reporter also overheard guests comment "on the size of the car and its doings." The following day, he announced, however, that "it was necessary to take the world-touring Hupmobile from the building to make room for newer models." Hupp's salesmen were caught in a bind; the little car drew crowds and created interest in the Model 20s, but they wanted to promote their newer Model 32s. The Little Corporal was a paean to Hupp's past, not a harbinger of its future.[3]

Company officials devised a clever solution to their marketing quandary. They parked the tourer in front of the show building for the balance of the week, where it reminded visitors of the Hupmobile's merits, perhaps enticing them to stop at the company's booth inside. Lest anyone overlook the Little Corporal, Hupp's "advertising and publicity promoter," Frank J. Mooney, arranged a reception, probably at the Annex Hotel, "the one place headquarters" for the show, where he hosted a luncheon to honor Hanlon, Jones, and Drake and invited "all of the local automobile newspapermen, advertising men and visitors" to see the car and listen to the crew recount its exotic adventures. Perhaps tired of covering Hupp's world promotion, the *Detroit Free Press* reporter appears to have been underwhelmed; it was a "well conducted reception" that had "passed off very nicely," he conceded.[4]

The auto show circuit was an extension of the three men's trip. When the Chicago show closed, they set off with "their travel-stained Hupmobile" for St. Louis, where they were on the floor when its exhibition opened on February 5. Five days later, they graced Hupp's exhibit at the Indianapolis show. From there, they accompanied their automobile to the Cincinnati and Cleveland car shows. When the latter closed on the last day in February, they were finally free to return to Detroit and their families. The Cleveland festivities marked the formal end of their sixteen-month trip; it was the last recorded time they all appeared with the Little Corporal.[5]

The show did not mark the end of Hanlon's driving marathons, however. Just eight months later, he made national headlines with a cross-country dash to join a rally organized by Charles J. Glidden, who had amassed a fortune in the telephone business before becoming obsessed with automobiles. Starting in 1904, he held yearly "tours" throughout the United States to demonstrate the cars' durability and promote road improvements. Auto manufacturers took advantage of the tours' publicity and entered specially prepared cars to increase their chances of winning favorable publicity. As corporate competition grew fiercer, the tours lost their raison d'être, and Glidden hosted his final rally in 1914.[6]

The 1912 Glidden tour, much discussed at the Chicago auto show that welcomed the Hupmobilists home, was projected to run from Duluth, Minnesota, to New Orleans. Cleverly planned, it was routed through "the important automobile centers of the middle west. . . . taking in the Mississippi River valley and also much of the Ohio valley as well." By February, over eighty cars had been entered, including a new Hupmobile. By the time the 1,700-mile tour began in October 1912, however, its starting point had been moved to Detroit.[7]

Hanlon was Hupp's driver of choice, but when the Glidden autos left Detroit, he was, perhaps for publicity purposes, in Cleveland, Ohio, with his Model 32 roadster. Two days later, he set out to catch up. The "automobile enthusiasts of Cleveland did not take the matter seriously," the *Detroit Free Press* reported, "for they believed it impossible for Hanlon to cover the two days' handicap enjoyed by the Glidden party." Accompanied by Howard J. Watrous of Detroit, Hanlon madly drove 700 miles in two days and caught up with the caravan in Nashville, "ending one of the most remarkable runs ever recorded in this country," rhapsodized the Detroit reporter.[8]

The Motor City newsman was not surprised at Hanlon's feat, because he was "one of the best tour drivers in the United States [who] holds his own with many of the European drivers." At Nashville, Hanlon and Watrous joined the procession of cars and enjoyed the celebrations at every city through which they passed. When the tour reached New Orleans on November 1, the mayor hosted the drivers at a formal dinner in the Grunewald Hotel. The report sent back to Detroit reminded readers that Hanlon "enjoys the distinction of having covered more ground in one particular car than any other driver in the United States."[9]

The Hupp company used Hanlon to promote its cars while he was in the South. He was met in Nashville by "Uncle" Abner Powell, the firm's distributor "in New Orleans and the territory surrounding." Uncle Abner announced that Hanlon's run "fully demonstrates the possibilities of the Hupp make." Hanlon and Watrous remained in New Orleans "the better part of a week," where they played "the role of salesmen" to help Powell's advertising campaign. A local reporter added, tongue in cheek, that he hoped the two men would use some of their time "to clean up."[10]

Four years later, Hanlon again became Hupp's traveling representative, thanks to Pancho Villa and the ongoing Mexican political chaos. In 1910, the Mexican dictator Porfirio Díaz had been overthrown, and three years later Victoriano Huerta seized power in a military coup. President Woodrow Wilson refused to recognize a "government of butchers," cut off military supplies to the country, and supported a rebel leader, Venustiano Carranza, on the condition that he hold American-sponsored elections. He refused, but Wilson, with no other options, supported him anyway. After Huerta resigned in 1914, Carranza formed a new government but refused to call an election. Wilson then threw United States's support to Pancho Villa, "a wily peasant-born general." In a turnabout in 1915, however, Wilson recognized the Carranza government, which turned Villa against the United States. On January 10, 1916, a detachment of his troops took eighteen Americans from a Mexican train in Chihuahua and shot them. That March, Villa crossed the U.S. border and attacked Columbus, New Mexico, killing seventeen Americans and setting fire to buildings. Thousands of U.S. troops under the command of General J. J. "Black Jack" Pershing subsequently invaded Mexico to hunt Villa down.[11]

Thomas Hanlon rode in "Black Jack's" train. The U.S. Army was experimenting with cars and trucks, including many Hupp vehicles. The company sent Hanlon along as a driver, to oversee maintenance and repairs, and to report on the Hupmobiles' performance. Mustered into the army's quartermaster's corps as a chauffeur on September 20 at Columbus, New Mexico, Hanlon was paid $100 a month, plus a "subsistence" expense account, not to exceed $2.00 per day, "upon proper receipts." He signed on for a tour of "three months unless longer required."[12] Hanlon enjoyed every minute of his short military career. Outfitted in an army uniform, complete with knee-high boots and a campaign hat, he posed for pictures among his cars and newfound friends, especially a group he labeled "the comedy four." He loved the masculine camaraderie, photographed his fellow troopers on guard duty, pushing trucks out of mud, bathing, shaving, clowning around, and loafing in places such as Camp el Villa.

General Villa eluded Pershing's pursuit and in early 1917 Wilson pulled the army out of Mexico. Hanlon, however, had already been mustered out. He spent a glorious fifteen days gallivanting about Mexico in his Hupmobiles and was discharged on October 4, 1916, due a half month's pay. The Hupp company paid his travel expenses from Detroit to New Mexico and back. He turned in his uniform and returned to domesticity.[13]

Hanlon's long absences had unsettled his home life. Mary Hanlon, whom he married on August 1, 1901, endured his periodic absenteeism for twenty years, until they formally separated in the spring of 1921, although they continued "living under the same roof." Mary sued for divorce and Hanlon filed a "cross-bill" contesting the property settlement. The whole mess ended up in the newspapers, where Mary accused Hanlon of "keeping late hours and associating with another woman." Furthermore, she charged him with "cruelty," testifying "he abused her" and "threw potatoes at her, choked her and once threatened to break a plate over her head." In his countersuit, Hanlon accused Mary of nagging.[14]

The legal tussle was finally settled out of court when Hanlon withdrew his countersuit; the two sides reached a property settlement in which Mary got the house but became responsible for its outstanding $2,000 mortgage. Very soon thereafter, on December 27, 1923, Hanlon married Mildred Emerick, and four years later they adopted Mariann. Some family members believed that Mariann was really Hanlon's daughter by a woman other than Mary or Mildred, which had precipitated his divorce.[15]

Hanlon's name periodically turned up in the press afterwards, usually in conjunction with stories recounting his trip around the world. At the Society of American Engineers' annual 1930 spring meeting in French Lick, Indiana, the Hupp Motor Car Company displayed the Little Corporal and a 1910 runabout that had been Detroit's first police car. Hanlon accompanied the cars to the resort and Hupp published his remarks in a pamphlet that was riddled with errors. The company dated the Little Corporal to 1910, claimed it had been called a "Sport Phaeton," and even got the three men's departure date wrong by eight days. Hanlon's memory was not sharp either; while he related specific tales well, he could not recall his exact itinerary and had only the haziest recollection of how much time the trio had spent in various places. His enthusiasm for travel, however, remained undimmed. When a reporter asked if he would take another such trip, the irrepressible Hanlon shot back, "You bet your sweet life. I'd start today—right this minute." And always alert for a chance to promote Hupmobiles, he declaimed, "I would probably make such a trip with infinitely greater ease and comfort and far less worry in a modern *Hupmobile*." But after a moment's hesitation, he confessed, "I still think, all other things being equal, that I'd prefer to enjoy the glamour, the romance, the beauty and intense curiosity of many of the world's peoples by making the trip again in that old Model 20 *Hupmobile*."[16]

Three years later, Hupmobile, by then on the financial skids, entered two floats in Chicago's Century of Progress parade that marked the opening of the exhibition's Automotive Week. One featured Old Tom and his weathered little Hupp and the other a shiny 1933 silver anniversary Hupmobile roadster. Whereas newspapers had addressed him as "Thomas Hanlon" or "Mr. Hanlon" back in 1910–12, by 1933, as he approached his mid fifties, he became "Tommy." The *Chicago Herald-Examiner* described Tommy seated in "the history-making Hupmobile garbed in linen duster and goggles," clothes like those he wore when "he drove in those pioneering days." The *Chicago American* introduced "Tommy Hanlon" and "the car that made the 48,600-mile tour and rolled up 150,000 additional miles since its now historic journey from 1910–1912." The reporter was close to the trip's actual mileage; over the years, the figure given in newspaper accounts ranged from 28,000 to about 50,000 miles. They eventually settled on 48,000 land miles and used the earlier figure of 28,000 miles to estimate the distance the car had traveled aboard ships. The Hupp's odometer, added for the trip and now a Hanlon family treasure, registers 47,777 miles and appears to be the best evidence of how far the globe-girdlers drove. Where the newspaperman conjured up the alleged 150,000 "additional miles" remains something of a mystery.[17]

The parade was Hanlon's last brush with fame. He did not talk about his trip very much, because his new wife "did not care to hear about his life before she married him," although he frequently told stories about it to his daughter. Three years after the Century of Progress festivities, Hupmobile was moribund and Hanlon was out of a job. Too young to retire, he found employment working under the Scott Fountain on Belle Isle, where he was responsible for keeping it running. When both

Hanlon and a cast of extras aboard Hupmobile's float in Chicago's 1933 Century of Progress Parade, which featured an idealized version of the trio's route. HPA/DJC.

dried up, he worked for a firm that owned a number of apartments as a "fixer" of everything from electrical wiring to plumbing.[18]

He still enjoyed himself, however; he stayed in contact with some former Hupp colleagues, and his daughter recalled that Charles Hastings had visited him frequently in the late 1930s. A lifelong Democrat, although his second wife was a staunch Republican, Hanlon applauded President Franklin Roosevelt's New Deal. He enjoyed the company of a wide circle of friends, one of whom was Detroit's chief of police, who was always careful to woo the city's Irish constituency. Mariann Hanlon recalled that the chief had been involved in rum running during prohibition and occasionally called on Hanlon to help him "dump liquor" that the cops had intercepted. Hanlon eagerly volunteered, because "some bottles fell into his hands." His journey ended on April 12, 1949, when at age seventy-two, he died of a massive coronary thrombosis. He was survived by Mildred, his two children, two brothers, and two sisters.[19]

Tom Jones too remained busy, although his post-tour life was tragically cut short. He was never a permanent Hupp employee, and after the trio finished working the

1912 auto show circuit, he took a job as advertising manager for the Empire Motor Car Company in Indianapolis. Empire had been founded in 1909 to build a car similar to Hupp's Model 20 runabout. Sold under the name "Little Aristocrat," it cost about $200 more than a Hupmobile. Empire stuck with the small car concept until 1912, when, like Hupp, it decided to build larger, more expensive vehicles. That year, the firm moved its manufacturing to Greenville, Pennsylvania, where it manufactured two-, four-, and five-seat autos, with four- and six-cylinder engines, and wheel bases up to 122 inches. Like many of its competitors, Empire was an "assembler"; always a marginal proposition, it went out of business in the 1919 recession.[20]

By that time, however, Jones was long gone. The U.S. Department of Commerce hired him, probably on J. Walter Drake's recommendation, and sent him back to China and Japan as a trade commissioner to compile a report on industrial conditions in those countries, paying especial attention to their automobile manufacturing. He is also reported to have been affiliated with J. B. Crockett & Company, an export firm.[21]

When the United States declared war on the Central Powers on April 6, 1917, the government recalled Jones from China. He returned to the states and in May enlisted in the Navy's aviation branch. It sent him to the Boston School of Technology for his "ground training" and then posted him to Long Island for his initial flight instruction; in mid 1918, the Navy sent him to Pensacola, Florida, to finish his training. On September 24, 1918, a week before he was to receive his ensign's commission, just shy of thirty-one years of age, and less than two months before the war's end, he took a "hydroaeroplane" up with five fellow aviators. "Within a short distance of the training station," the plane crashed, killing three, including Jones. No cause for the accident was ever reported, and only "after persistent search" was his body finally recovered and sent home to New Hartford for burial. The *Utica Daily Press,* which had promised that "a naval funeral will be held here, one of the most impressive that can be imagined," did not in the end cover the burial.[22]

Like Jones, Drake did not settle down after he finished his stint in the Little Corporal. In fact, he too revisited many of the places the three had toured earlier. On October 9, 1912, just before Hanlon made his dash from Cleveland to Nashville, Vice President Drake set out on another trip around the world; he had been home only eight months. This time, he circled the globe the other way around. He attended the 1912 Olympia auto show in London, drove through France and Italy, sailed from Naples to Ceylon, and proceeded from there to Bombay, from where he drove a

Hupmobile 5,000 miles around the subcontinent, "mostly over roads which he describe[d] as being some of the finest in the world." He also visited the Malay states, Australia, the Philippines, China, Japan, New Guinea, Tasmania, New Zealand, and the Hawaiian Islands before returning to the United States on February 3, 1914.[23]

On his second world tour, Drake met "a very nice young lady on the boat" from Naples to Ceylon. It was love at first sight; "before I left the boat I had practically finished the deal," he wrote, and he and Gladys Markwell set a wedding date for September 11, 1913, in her native Brisbane, Australia. A month before his marriage, he ruminated that "it seems rather queer that after travelling practically all over the world, I should find a young lady way out here in Australia at the other side of the world from home."[24]

He pitched Hupp sales everywhere and used his travel accounts to stump for road improvements at home. After his return, he told an automobile trade press representative that he took great pride in "the way American cars—the Hupmobile in particular, of course—are standing up abroad and the reputation they are making." But he had nothing but disgust for American roads when compared to their foreign counterparts. He told of meeting a dealer in the Antipodes who had just returned from the United States. He had been in Toledo and could not decide whether to take the train or drive back to Detroit. A local man advised him to go by rail, because "no automobile could get him to Detroit over the roads." By contrast, Drake emphasized, islands such as Ceylon and Tasmania had "magnificent roads as fine as any boulevard." Hupp's vice president could not understand the disparity; other nations, he said, "are older than our country, and labor is cheaper, but we have many times as much money as they have, besides greater energy and greater resources in every way." With many other Americans, especially those active in the better-roads movement, he remained perplexed at how the commercially dominant United States could conquer foreign markets that enjoyed a more sophisticated public infrastructure.[25]

Drake made another trip around the world in Hupp's service between 1914 and 1916 to promote its overseas sales. In 1919, however, he retired and moved to the balmier climes of Santa Barbara, California. Family lore related that he had made his fortune and moved to the warmer area to savor his hard-earned winnings. He bought a large house, hired servants, and lived the good life throughout the prosperous 1920s.[26]

The stock market crash in October 1929 blighted his fortunes; he lost most of his money. Earlier, however, he had divided his assets with his wife, and she came through the debacle in better financial shape. Even so, they had to sell their house and moved to Santa Ynez, where they owned a ranch. They offered their servants the choice of staying on at half salary and most moved out to the ranch with the Drakes. At Santa Ynez, Drake "indulged in raising prize turkeys and chickens." By the depression's end, he had recouped some of his lost fortune and became active in local philanthropic circles. With two sons, he was especially active in the Boy Scouts, who named their camp for him. He was also an avid golfer, belonged to two local clubs, and kept his membership in a Detroit golf club.[27] Drake died suddenly on Saturday morning, August 25, 1944, and was buried the following Monday in the Santa Barbara cemetery. He left his wife Gladys, two sons, Walter and Harry, and two daughters, Joan and Doris. His brother J. Walter had died three years earlier, but two other brothers survived him.[28]

By April 1949, then, all three men were dead. For fifteen months, they had lived in intimate proximity and shared the thrills of discovery and fears of disaster, but they came to rest almost as far away from one another as possible within the continental United States: Jones in New York's Mohawk Valley, beneath 200 to 300 inches of snow each winter, Hanlon in Detroit, with its extremes of midwestern weather, and Drake, "the rich one," "the boss," in sunny Santa Barbara, where only the balmy Pacific breezes ruffled his resting place.

Two of the three world travelers outlived the man who had dreamed up their odyssey and his original company. After his R.C.H. venture failed, Robert Hupp formed the Monarch Motor Car Company in Detroit in 1914 and brought out an "assembled" car, buying virtually all the parts from outside suppliers. His automobiles used Continental engines, and electric lights and starter were standard. In 1915, he offered Monarchs with V-8 engines to power the 3,000-pound cars. By World War I, he had moved well into the mid-price range, where competition was fierce. He ran into raw material problems after the United States entered the war in 1917 and later blamed that conflict for Monarch's demise that year. His electric auto production survived the war, only to fall victim to the declining demand for such cars and the 1919 depression. Hupp served as a captain in the U.S. Army's engineering corps during World War I, and after the armistice, he joined the Four Wheel Hydraulic Brake Company, which later became the Lockheed Company. Hupp persuaded Walter Chrysler to adopt hydraulic brakes, and all Chryslers were equipped with them from the outset; it took General Motors twelve years to catch up. Hupp worked as a consulting engineer until December 7, 1932, when, at the age of fifty-three, he was felled by a massive cerebral hemorrhage at the Detroit Athletic Club as he prepared to play squash.[29]

After Hupp left the Hupp Motor Car Company, it continued to prosper. It was flush enough at Christmas 1911 to give every employee a week's extra pay, at a time when other, more established firms gave their workers turkeys or other "useful articles." Even Henry Ford played the grinch, promising that his company would "await the new year before making its annual distribution of awards for good work." He was only a couple of years away, however, from promising his workers the unheard-of wage of $5 a day.[30]

When the Hupp Motor Car Company sued "Bobby" Hupp, it was building a new factory at Mt. Elliott and Milwaukee avenues in Detroit to bring all its production facilities under one roof. It broke ground the third week of September 1911 for a plant with 125,000 square feet of floor space, three times larger than its Jefferson Avenue facilities. The company hoped to produce between 15,000 and 20,000 Hupmobiles a year.[31]

The firm did not reach its maximum capacity until 1923, but Hupmobiles sold well enough to make the company the sixth-largest auto manufacturer in the nation in 1912, with 7,640 cars. Sales flagged in 1915, however, and Hupp skirted bankruptcy by selling a majority interest to outside investors, who rechartered the firm as the Hupp Motor Car Corporation. It built solid, good-looking, if unexciting, mid-priced automobiles, which commanded a loyal following. Hupmobile prospered in the 1920s, setting a production record in 1929, when it turned out almost 66,000 cars, to place fourteenth in the American automobile manufacturing standings.[32]

That year, Hupmobile purchased 95 percent of Chandler-Cleveland Motors, located in Cleveland, Ohio, a takeover that gave the merged firm $40,000,000 in assets, securities valued at $135,000,000, and the capacity to build 100,000 automobiles a year. Hupp stopped producing Chandlers and used one of its new Cleveland plants to build bodies and another to manufacture a new, lower-priced Hupmobile. The company's timing could not have been worse; the depression slashed auto sales; its output fell to 22,000 in 1930 and 5,000 fewer the following year. Hupp retrenched and consolidated all its manufacturing in Detroit.[33]

The company lost money in the 1930s and grew progressively weaker as its sales declined to the 9,000-per-year range in 1934 and 1935. Like many other hard-pressed automobile manufacturers, Hupp built some of its most striking cars when it was collapsing. It hired the noted industrial designer Raymond Loewy and brought out stylish, aerodynamic cars. It was to no avail, however; in 1935, the firm temporarily ceased production and then reopened in fits and starts. For a short time, it built the Hupmobile Skylark, using the old Cord automobile dies with some alterations. After manufacturing more than a half a million automobiles, Hupp built its last car in 1940, although employees cleaned out the parts bins to produce a few more, which they sold as 1941 models.[34]

Fifteen years later, the Bonded Wrecking and Salvage Company tore down Hupmobile's Detroit plant, purchased by Midland Steel Products Corporation to make way for a parking lot. It was a huge job—the factory had grown to one million square feet. The newspaper's obituary for the demolished factory noted that Hupp had manufactured automobiles worth $600,000,000 in it through 1935.[35]

The Hupp Motor Car Corporation refused to die, however. In 1946, it moved to Cleveland where it manufactured freezers, air-conditioning units, and soft-drink dispensers until 1955, when it was purchased by John O. Ekblom, who, in that era of business consolidations, merged it with seven other companies. Under Ekblom's ministrations, the number of Hupp employees rose tenfold, from 400 to 4,000. By 1960, air conditioning and heating systems constituted 45 percent of its business, appliances 35 percent, and aviation, auto parts, and hydraulics the remaining 20 percent.[36]

In 1967, White Consolidated Industries bought Hupp. For decades, White had manufactured sewing machines, sold under the Sears brand name. By 1956, competition from cheaper imported machines forced White to reorganize as a sewing machine importer, contracting its production out overseas. In the 1960s, White initiated a calculated acquisitions program. Strong in the appliance field, it prospered with more than $2 billion in sales in 1986, when it merged with AB Electrolux of Sweden.[37]

The merger spun Hupp off to Blaw-Knox Corporation of Pittsburgh, which had once been a part of White. Hupp, still located in Cleveland, employed about 340 workers in the late 1980s, who manufactured automotive climate control systems and light commercial air conditioning equipment. Blaw-Knox sold Hupp in 1990 to Sunderland Industrial Holdings Corporation, a financial holding company headquartered in Washington, D.C. Hupp soon encountered financial difficulties, reportedly because of "improper pricing of its products," and it filed for bankruptcy under Chapter 11 in November 1991. It declared assets of $27,300,000 and liabilities of $28,900,000.[38]

Hupp still would not die. On February 8, 1993, CPT Corporation, which had purchased a part of Sunderland, acquired an 80.1 percent stake in Hupp and renamed it H. Industries. Still manufacturing heating, ventilating, and air conditioning equipment for commercial and military applications, Hupp also owned a subsidiary, DCM Corporation, which made fractional horsepower electrical motors. Hupp was still in financial trouble, however, and in the fall of 1994, its lenders foreclosed. On October 27, they sold its assets "to an unrelated party." Hupp no longer had any assets or employees, but its remains lingered on. Hupp's unions sued CPT to fully fund their members' pension plan, a case they won in mid 1999. With that last twitch Hupp slipped, unnoticed, out of existence.[39]

The Little Corporal, or at least most of it, outlived them all. Hupp stored it in its Detroit factory and brought it out for infrequent public showings and parades. Over the years, some of its parts disappeared; Hanlon took the speedometer/odometer assembly, headlamps and side lamps vanished, and the gas generator and piping were probably removed when the lamps were taken. The two spare tires mounted on the left-hand side for the journey were taken off and never replaced. Otherwise, the little Hupp remained in the same condition it had been in when it returned to the Motor City, with "world tour" emblazoned in four languages, English, Japanese, Chinese, and French, across its sides and rear end and the numerous decals the three travelers had plastered all over their vehicle. Before World War II, someone sprayed the car with a varnish-like substance that covered the decals and made them almost impossible to read. A few fell off and the sprayed material aged, turned brown, cracked, and flaked off in places. The Hupp escaped wartime metal drives and was still housed in the factory when Hupp ceased car production in 1941. There it remained until 1946, when the company moved its headquarters to Cleveland, Ohio. On January 7 of that year, Hupp's president, Ralph Geddes, wrote to Frederick Crawford, who had opened his world-famous auto and airplane collection to the public in Cleveland, asking if he were interested in having the Little Corporal. Geddes said he thought it was "one of the first cars built by Hupp" and believed it was "the first American car to make a trip around the world." Hupp's president admitted that "the car would require some restoration" but said that it was "in reasonable condition." He also offered to "assemble some of the newspaper clippings of the time" and added, "I am told the man who drove the car still lives in Detroit and often recounts the trip to his friends." Crawford replied that he "would be thrilled to have the Hupp in our museum." Crawford's technical consultant followed with a letter to

Dusty, jacked up, its left headlamp still canted upward, stripped of its spare tires and center spotlight, and with the Chicago mayor's silk flag propped up in front of it, the little Hupp sat in Hupp's trophy room along with a dead fish and a stuffed horned beast, which probably had their own stories. The man behind the wheel may be Wilfred Hanlon; he bears a striking resemblance to Thomas Hanlon. HPA/DJC.

Geddes promising that "the car, standing on its own merits, would be a gem, but the added interest of its 'round-the-world-flight' promises to lend real distinction to our museum display." Geddes accordingly shipped it to Cleveland, where it arrived on February 19, 1946.[40]

The Little Corporal has been on display since and has not been restored. Over the years, its upholstery has frayed and rotted; it has grown dusty and dirty, pieces are scattered about it, and its tires long ago lost their Detroit air. The Crawford Museum's present assistant curator describes it as an "archaeological site." The Crawford hired a consultant in 2000 to examine the car and report on preservation options, but the museum had no definite plans to restore it to its 1910 condition. The Little Corporal sits in a corner of the Crawford Museum's basement awaiting its next challenge.[41]

The fruits of its earlier efforts, however, continue to reverberate throughout the world. The "little Hupp," which exemplified the virtues of smallness, helped to make the world a smaller place, with its markets and economies tied more closely together. William Howard Taft's dollar diplomacy, designed to promote America's conquest of the world's markets, continued apace long after he stepped down from the presidency in 1913. The history of the twentieth century attests to the fact that the increase in world trade did not proportionally decrease armaments, but in and around the wars, American businessmen relentlessly continued to carve out global markets. The same impulses that prompted the Huppmen to undertake their sales adventure induced other companies to imitate Hupp's boldness.

If the three men set out to duplicate their feat in their Hupp in the twenty-first century, they would find it almost impossible to go anywhere and not feel at home. American retail and fast food outlets, soft drinks, automobiles, technology, fashions, UPS trucks, architecture, and English are everywhere. In the automotive world, General Motors, Ford, and Daimler-Chrysler realized Robert Hupp's 1910 dreams to make, sell, and service his products in every country and colony on earth. His three intrepid corporate missionaries with their little car helped blaze the trail for other companies to eventually achieve the world automotive dominance Robert Hupp sought.

POSTSCRIPT

All five years I worked on this book, I had a gnawing desire to drive a 1911 Model 20 touring car to see what it must have been like to circle the globe in one ninety years ago. Hupp did not make many tourers that year, perhaps as few as one hundred, and it proved difficult to find one in running condition owned by someone brave enough to allow a novice in the driver's seat. The Hupmobile Club's 2001 listing identified five members who owned 1911 touring motorcars, and I called one, Steve Speth, a Daimler-Chrysler engineer who lives in Orchard Lake, just north of Detroit, to ask if his car was running, would he give me a ride and, even better, let me drive it. Speth said of course his car ran and, even though we had never met, enthusiastically agreed to both my requests.

Fittingly, I had an opportunity to drive the car in Detroit, where it had been manufactured and where the Hupmobilists' started and ended their odyssey. In June 2001, I, my wife, Roberta, my daughter Anne, who teaches high school history, and her husband, Tom, a history professor at Albion College, descended upon Speth and his car. We found his immaculately restored 1911 Model 20 tucked into his garage alongside a vintage Chrysler 300, a Viper, a Triumph TR 6, and a 1912 R.C.H., the car Robert C. Hupp built after he left the Hupp Motor Car Company.

Speth's car is not perfectly identical to the world touring model. He is unsure whether it was manufactured in 1911 or 1912, but it is a later model, as evidenced by its two front doors. His Hupp also features a windshield and top. In all other respects, however, his is a copy of Hanlon's steed. Both have outside, kerosene-fueled driving

lamps and carbide headlights, although Speth's car has no carbide generator. His auto is also a great deal more sporty. He painted its body royal blue, accented with white pin striping, applied by a man he found who did a perfect freehand job. Its body contrasts beautifully with the car's black fenders and white wooden wheels accentuated by brass hubs and nipples.

We rolled the car out of the garage, and Speth cranked it with care. Despite the factory's claim almost a century ago that Hupps were safe to crank, Speth knows firsthand that the crank can "kick" hard. The company was correct, however, in its claim that the motor was exceptionally easy to turn over. After several spins, it caught and settled into a nice even idle. I was struck by all the noise it made; it had the typical four-cylinder chuff, but I was not prepared for all the valve noise. Speth pointed out, however, that the valve stems and springs are exposed. I was less surprised by the engine's smoke, because I knew that it was designed to burn oil to keep the top of the engine lubricated.

Speth has wound his Hupp up to a munificent twenty-two miles an hour, which meant that we did not venture out on Detroit suburban roads; we remained in the residential area around his home. My first impression getting into the car was that it was much higher than it appeared. It may have been low-slung for its day, but it has to be entered much like a present-day SUV. Anne, who rode in the back seat, discovered that it was higher than the front seats—it is located over the rear wheels—and said she felt like royalty chugging through the neighborhood; "poohbahesque" was the way she put it. She declared the Hupp smelled of oil, rubber, leather, and exhaust, like the miniature antique cars she used to ride at fairs, and that it was "prissy" and "feminine" and the experience of riding in it "unreal." Tom, who thinks "real" history ended with America's Early National Period, about sixty years before the Hupmobile was born, and who has chided me for years for writing this book, smiled broadly through his rides and kept muttering that the car looked as if it had just come from the factory showroom floor.

Roberta was surprised she sat so high in the venerable Hupp and was impressed by the amount of wind that buffeted her at such low speeds, even with the windshield. She also noted that what everyone called the "little Hupp" looked much bigger, longer, and sleeker. Inside, however, she found it "snug," especially since Speth and the Wards are tall. The two front bucket seats are so close together that the occupants rub shoulders; this was certainly true for Speth and me.

After taking the Ward clan for rides, Speth got out of the car and told me to "take it for a drive." Behind the wheel, I was surprised to see how short the shift lever was. I shifted into first at the rear of the quadrant and slowly released the clutch, which was a bit spongy and had more vibration than I am used to. With only 16 advertised horsepower pulling close to 2,000 pounds, a weight-to-horsepower ratio of 125 to 1, the car accelerated surprisingly well. The real trick was to shift into "high," or second gear. The shift lever has an inordinately long throw, and its shortness meant that I had to lean far down and forward to get it into second. Speth had never mastered double clutching and advised me to forget it as well. The shift, therefore, was accompanied by a gnashing of gears, although thankfully of brief duration. During the time it took to throw the gearshift and engage the gear, the engine and car both slowed, and when I let the clutch out, the motor sputtered momentarily and then accelerated very slowly, emitting its typical four-cylinder pulse. On the perfectly flat roads I drove on, that was no real problem, but in rolling countryside, shifting must have been an art. That was probably why Hanlon often went out of his way to prove his and the car's abilities in hills and mountains. I can only imagine how difficult it was for him to downshift the Little Corporal ascending steep hills.

Reversing the car also posed problems. The reverse notch on the top center of the quadrant is fairly deep, and when in it, the shift lever pushed my thigh toward the center of the car, which made it difficult to reach the brake pedal, located on the far right, and even to use the accelerator in the middle. I had to shift my body leftward to enable my foot to reach the pedals. Such an ungainly arrangement may have been exacerbated by the fact that I am tall; perhaps a shorter man would have had less trouble. It went into reverse easily enough, however, where the clutch and accelerator action mimicked that of being in first gear.

Even though every day I drive a thirty-six-year-old car whose brakes, by modern disk brake standards, are so primitive that I have to make an appointment to stop, I was stunned to find that the Hupp's braking ability was almost nonexistent. Even at speeds of about fifteen miles per hour, after I applied the brakes hard, it took me about half a city block to bring the car to a rest. The Model 20's drivers always had to be aware of what was way down the road to allow plenty of time to avoid problems. Even if Hanlon's brakes were twice as effective as Speth's, their inefficiency must have made touring in the mountains a terrifying experience. Driving Speth's Hupp gave me a much greater appreciation for the early automobilists' talents; it took a professional like Hanlon to coax a car up to the Continental Divide, and all his fortitude and finesse to bring it down safely.

At speed, the little Hupp, which is very hard-sprung, is a most flexible machine. Everything on it vibrates and moves. The headlights bob about, not always in unison, the front end sways, and passengers jounce about, hanging on. Despite its ladder frame, the Hupp squirms, flexes, and bends in conformity with the road conditions, speed, wind, and load. It is like driving a load of wet pasta.

The Hupp's big wooden steering wheel is comfortable and just the right size. With its rack-and-pinion steering, its turning ratio is quick and the car is responsive. It is harder to turn than I would have expected, given its weight, but it provides a nice feel of the road—the Hupp at any speed is never divorced from road feel; it is too tightly sprung.

The full leather bucket seats are initially very comfortable. Under way, however, they are less so. Under the horsehair-filled, tufted leather are wooden boards, which make the seats feel very hard, especially over bumps and rough spots. I can only imagine what they must have felt like after a full day of thrashing through Wyoming gullies or bouncing up volcanoes in Hawaii, or after sitting on them for 47,000 miles. The Hupp's automotive adventurers must have been a hard-bottomed lot when they returned.

The Hupp that circled the world was certainly a durable machine. What was less obvious to me until I drove Speth's was that it was also a fragile one, which required not only a great deal of tinkering to keep it in shape but far more driving skills than are common today. The car could take punishment, the terrain Hanlon drove it over proved that, but it had to be meted out by a driver skilled at determining just how far he could push it. Had Hanlon exceeded those limits, this book would have been much shorter. I cannot imagine how he drove it through creeks, swamps, mudholes, snow, and dust for fifteen months and still paraded it down Woodward Avenue when he returned home. But thanks to Speth's willingness to let me drive his blue beauty, I do know why Hanlon said in 1930 that he would not hesitate to drive the car around the globe again; after my stint behind the Model 20's wheel, I agree that, without hesitation, I would try it tomorrow.

NOTES

Introduction

1. Odometer in possession of Thomas Hanlon's grandson, Don Jeffery, Jr., Livonia, Michigan.

2. *Detroit Free Press*, Mar. 19, 1911.

3. *The American Car Since 1775: The Most Complete Survey of the American Automobile Ever Published,* by the editors of *Automobile Quarterly* (New York: L. S. Bailey, 1971), pp. 139, 491.

4. *Detroit Free Press*, July 23, 1911.

5. Thomas A. Bailey, *A Diplomatic History of the American People* (New York: Appleton-Century-Crofts, 1964), p. 529; John M. Dobson, *America's Ascent: The United States Becomes a Great Power, 1880–1914* (De Kalb: Northern Illinois University Press, 1978), p. 204; p. 205, quotation; J. A. Hobson, *Imperialism: A Study* (London: K. Nisbet, 1902).

6. Unidentified newspaper clipping, n.d., in Mariann Hanlon Jeffery's collection, Livonia, Michigan (henceforth cited as MJC).

7. *Detroit Free Press*, Dec. 18, 1910.

8. Ibid., Apr. 23, 1911, two quotations; unidentified newspaper clipping, n.d., MJC, quotation.

9. Unidentified newspaper clipping, n.d., MJC, quotation; Hupp Motor Car Company, *Round the World in a Hupmobile: Detroit to Manila* (Detroit: Hupp Motor Car Co., 1911), n.p., two quotations.

10. Unidentified newspaper clipping, n.d., MJC.

11. Ibid.

12. Ibid.

13. Vincent P. De Santis, *The Shaping of Modern America, 1877–1916* (Boston: Allyn & Bacon, 1973), p. 123.

14. Unidentified newspaper clipping, n.d., MJC.

Chapter 1. The Genesis

1. *Detroit Free Press*, Jan. 21, 1912.

2. Ibid.

3. Curt McConnell, *Coast to Coast by Automobile: The Pioneering Trips, 1898–1908* (Stanford: Stanford University Press, 2000), p. 311; John Rae, *The American Automobile* (Chicago: University of Chicago Press, 1965), pp. 24–25, 40; *American Car Since 1775*, pp. 138–39.

4. Menno Duerksen, "The Story of Hupmobile," *Hupp Herald,* Summer 1979, pp. 18–19.

5. G. N. Georgano, *The Complete Encyclopedia of Motorcars, 1885 to the Present* (New York: Dutton, 1972), pp. 575–76.

6. William W. Cuthbert, "Hupmobile," *Horseless Carriage Gazette,* Nov.–Dec. 1971, p. 18; Duerksen, "Hupmobile," p. 19; Rae, *American Automobile*, p. 61; *Detroit Free Press*, Jan. 21, 1912.

7. Duerksen, "Hupmobile," pp. 10–20.

8. Charles K. Hyde, "National Architectural and Engineering Record: Hupp Motor Car Company Plant" (typescript, Apr. 1981), National Automotive History Collection, Detroit Public Library; Rae, *American Automobile*, pp. 24–26; Hupp Motor Car Company, *The Man, the Machinery, the Material* (Detroit: Hupp Motor Car Co., ca. 1912), p. 1; Duerksen, "Hupmobile," p. 20.

9. Donald Finlay Davis, *Conspicuous Production: Automobiles and Elites in Detroit, 1899–1933* (Philadelphia: Temple University Press, 1989), p. 92, quotation; *Detroit News*, Nov. 28, 1941.

10. *Detroit News*, Nov. 28, 1941; Davis, *Conspicuous Production*, p. 92; U.S. Congress, *Biographical Directory of the American Congress, 1774–1927* (Washington, D.C.: GPO, 1928), p. 897.

11. Hyde, "National Architectural and Engineering Record," n.p.; *Detroit Free Press*, Oct. 29, 1911; Duerksen, "Hupmobile," p. 19.

12. *Detroit Free Press*, May 3, 1911.

13. Duerksen, "Hupmobile," p. 17.

14. Ibid., p. 20; Davis, *Conspicuous Production*, p. 92.

15. Hupp Motor Car Company, *The Man, the Machine, the Material*, p. 1.

16. Cuthbert, "Hupmobile," p. 18.

17. Ibid., p. 19.

18. Ibid., p. 18; *Detroit News*, Mar. 6, 1956, quotation; Hupp Motor Car Company, *The Man, the Machine, the Material*, p. 1.

19. *Detroit Free Press*, May 3, 1911.

20. *American Car Since 1775*, p. 139.

21. Ibid.; Duerksen, "Hupmobile," p. 21.

22. *Detroit Free Press*, Jan. 15, 1911.

23. Ibid., Dec. 18, 1910.

24. Ibid., Mar. 19, 1911.

25. Ibid., Apr. 23, 1911.

26. Ibid., June 27, 1911; ibid., Feb. 13, 1911.

27. Duerksen, "Hupmobile," p. 21.

Chapter 2. The Send-off

1. Hupp production figures are from Jeffery Godshall, "Hupmobile: The Twilight Years," *Antique Automobile,* July–Aug. 1968, p. 40.

2. Hupp Motor Car Company, *Hupmobile: One Thousand Miles Through Snowdrifts* (Cleveland: Corday & Gross, 1910), n.p.

3. Ibid., quotation; unidentified newspaper clipping, n.d., MJC.

4. Hupp Motor Car Company, *Hupmobile: One Thousand Miles Through Snowdrifts,* pp. 2, 5, 7, quotation, 10, 11.

5. Ibid., pp. 11–13; p. 12, quotations.

6. Ibid., p. 15.

7. Ibid., p. 17, three quotations; unidentified newspaper clipping, n.d., MJC, four quotations; Hupp Motor Car Company, *Hupmobile: One Thousand Miles Through Snowdrifts,* p. 2, quotation; p. 5.

8. Unidentified newspaper clipping, n.d., MJC; *Detroit Free Press*, Oct. 6, 1910, four quotations.

9. *Detroit Free Press*, Oct. 6, 1910.

10. Ibid.

11. Unidentified newspaper clipping, n.d., MJC, quotation; *Hupp Herald* 1, 3 (1972), n.p.

12. Unidentified newspaper clipping, n.d., MJC.

13. Unidentified newspaper clipping, n.d., MJC, all quotations; David Burgess Wise, *The New Illustrated Encyclopedia of Automobiles* (Edison, N.J.: Wellfleet Press, 1992), p. 320; Georgano, *Complete Encyclopedia of Motorcars,* pp. 671–72.

14. *Detroit Free Press*, Nov. 3, 1910.

15. Ibid.

16. Ibid., Nov. 4 and 6, 1910.

17. Ibid., Nov. 4, 1910.

18. Thomas Hanlon's photo album, in possession of Don Jeffery, Jr., Livonia, Michigan, DJC.

19. *Detroit Free Press*, Nov. 4, 1910.

20. Ibid.

21. Ibid., Nov. 5, 1910.

22. Ibid., Nov. 6, 1910.

23. *Goshen Daily Democrat*, reprinted in *Detroit Free Press*, Nov. 6, 1910.

24. *Detroit News Tribune*, Nov. 6, 1910.

25. *Detroit Free Press*, Nov. 7, 1910.

26. Ibid., Nov. 4, 1910.

Chapter 3. The Predecessors

1. Photograph, "Century of Progress" parade, DJC.

2. Wise, *New Illustrated Encyclopedia of Automobiles*, pp. 14, 343; Michael Scott, *Packard: The Complete Story* (Ridge Summit, Pa..; TAB Books, 1985), p. 16; Rae, *American Automobile*, pp. 30–31.

3. Luigi Barzini, *Pekin to Paris: An Account of Prince Borghese's Journey Across Two Continents in a Motor-Car,* trans. L. P. de Castelvechio (London: E. Grant Richards, 1907), reprinted as *Peking to Paris: A Journey Across Two Continents* (New York: Liberty Press, 1973), p. 16.

4. Ibid., pp. xvii, 80–81.

5. Ibid., pp. 173–76 ff.; Ferdinand Hediger, "Itala," *Automobile Quarterly* 38, 1 (July 1998): 30–31. See the story of the race in *Automobile Quarterly* 4, 2.

6. Dermot Cole, *Hard Driving: The 1908 Auto Race from New York to Paris* (New York: Paragon House, 1991), passim; Georgano, *Complete Encyclopedia of Motorcars,* p. 672.

7. Harriet White Fisher, *A Woman's Tour in a Motor* (Philadelphia: J. B. Lippincott, 1911).

8. "Andrew, Harriet White Fisher," in *The National Cyclopedia of American Biography* (New York: James T. White, 1927), B: 215–16.

9. Fisher, *Woman's Tour,* p. 15.

10. Ibid., p. 18.

11. Ibid., passim.

12. Ibid.

13. Edith Townsend Kaufmann, "A Woman's World Tour in a Motor," in *Around the World with a Camera,* ed. John Sleicher (New York: Leslie-Judge Co., 1915), n.p., all quotations.

14. Ibid.

15. "Globe-Girdling: 85 Years Ago," *The Packard,* no. 36 (Mar. 1913), reprinted in *The Packard Cormorant,* no. 93 (Winter 1998–99): 28.

16. Melvin A. Hall, *Journey to the End of an Era* (New York: Scribner, 1947), p. 13.

17. Ibid., p. 14.

18. Ibid., p. 15, quotation; p. 16, remainder of quotations.

19. Ibid., p. 16, quotation; p. 17.

20. Ibid., p. 19.

21. Ibid.

22. Ibid., p. 21.

23. Ibid., p. 22.

24. Ibid., pp. 22, 25.

25. Ibid., p. 25, two quotations; p. 26, remainder of quotations.

26. Ibid., p. 28.

27. Ibid., p. 28, quotation; p. 32, quotation.

28. Ibid., p. 33.

29. Ibid., p. 35, quotation; p. 36, quotation.

30. Ibid., p. 36.

31. Ibid., p. 37.

32. Ibid., p. 37; p. 38, two quotations; p. 39, two quotations.

33. Ibid., p. 39.

34. Ibid., p. 40.

35. Ibid.

36. Ibid., p. 41.

Chapter 4. The American West

1. *Detroit Free Press*, Nov. 8, 1910.

2. Ibid.

3. Ibid., Nov. 20, 1910.

4. Omaha newspaper article reprinted in *Detroit Free Press*, Nov. 12, 1910.

5. *Detroit Free Press*, Nov. 20, 1910.

6. Ibid., two quotations; Columbus news article reprinted in ibid., Nov. 15, 1910, remainder of quotations.

7. *Detroit Free Press*, Nov. 17, 1910.

8. Ibid., Nov. 18, 1910.

9. Ibid., Nov. 19, 1910, all quotations; unidentified newspaper clipping, MJSB.

10. *Detroit Free Press*, Nov. 20, 1910.

11. Unidentified newspaper clipping, MJC, quotation; *MoTor,* Nov. 26, 1910, p. 524; *Detroit Free Press,* Nov. 24, 1910; Gregory Franzwa, *The Lincoln Highway,* vol. 3: *Wyoming* (Tucson: Patrice Press, 1999), p. ix.

12. *Detroit Free Press,* Dec. 4, 1910, two quotations; Franzwa, *Wyoming,* p. 23, quotation; *Detroit Free Press,* Nov. 24, 1910, two quotations.

13. *Detroit Free Press*, Nov. 24, 1910.

14. Ibid., Dec. 4, 1910, two quotations; anon., typescript for Hupp article on the 1933 Century of Progress Celebration in Chicago, n.d., n.p., MJC, quotation; anon., typescript of tour highlights, n.d., n.p., MJC, two quotations.

15. *Detroit Free Press*, Nov. 4, 1910.

16. Ibid., all quotations except final; Hupp Motor Car Company, *Round the World in a Hupmobile,* n.p., final quotation.

17. *Detroit Free Press*, Nov. 4, 1910.

18. Ibid.

19. Anon., Century of Progress typescript, p. 1; *Detroit Free Press*, Dec. 4, 1910, quotation.

20. *Detroit Free Press*, Dec. 4, 1910.

21. Ibid., Nov. 23, 1910, quotation; Franzwa, *Wyoming*, p. 27; *Detroit Free Press*, Nov. 23–27, 1910; *Honolulu Evening Bulletin*, Dec. 24, 1910, quotation.

22. *Honolulu Evening Bulletin*, Dec. 24, 1910.

23. Franzwa, *Wyoming*, p. 45; *Detroit Free Press*, Nov. 27, 1910, all quotations.

24. *Detroit Free Press*, Dec. 4, 1910, five quotations; Hupp Motor Car Company, *Round the World in a Hupmobile*, n.p., quotation.

25. *Detroit Free Press*, Dec. 9, 1910; *Honolulu Evening Bulletin*, Dec. 24, 1910, quotation.

26. *Detroit Free Press*, Dec. 18, 1910, two quotations; ibid., Dec. 9, 1910, quotation.

27. Ibid., Dec. 13, 1910.

28. Ibid., Dec. 17, 1910, quotation; ibid., Dec. 18, 1910, two quotations.

Chapter 5. The Men

1. Interview with Mariann Hanlon Jeffery, July 20, 1998.

2. Unidentified newspaper clipping, n.d., MJC.

3. Interview with Don Jeffery, Jr., July 20, 1998; Georgano, *Complete Encyclopedia of Motorcars*, p. 168; unidentified newspaper clipping, Nov. 2, 1902, MJC, quotation.

4. Interview with Mariann Hanlon Jeffery, July 20, 1998, quotation; unidentified newspaper clipping, n.d., MJC, two quotations.

5. Unidentified newspaper clipping, n.d., MJC.

6. Interview with Mariann Hanlon Jeffery, July 20, 1998.

7. Ibid.; card in MJC.

8. Interview with Mariann Hanlon Jeffery, July 20, 1998.

9. *Utica Daily Press*, Sept. 25, 1918; telephone conversations with Mrs. Holly Broadbent and David Owens, June 24, 2001.

10. *Detroit Free Press*, Sept. 26, 1918, quotation; *Automobile Topics*, Oct. 29, 1910, p. 255.

11. *Automobile Topics*, Oct. 1918, p. 854, quotation; *Utica Daily Press*, Sept. 25, 1918, quotation.

12. *Detroit Free Press*, Sept. 25, 1918, two quotations; *Automobile Topics*, Oct. 1918, p. 854, quotation; *Detroit Free Press*, Sept. 26, 1918; *Utica Daily Press*, Sept. 25, 1918.

13. Drake to Arthur Pomeroy, Aug. 27, 1913, Joseph R. Drake Papers, American Heritage Center, University of Wyoming, Laramie, Wyoming (henceforth cited as JRDC), quotation; Drake to George Shaw, Feb. 5, 1912, JRDC, quotation.

14. *Santa Barbara News-Press*, Aug. 27, 1944; *Detroit Free Press*, Oct. 16, 1910; *Detroit News*, Nov. 28, 1941, quotation.

15. Hanlon photo album, DJC.

16. Drake to William Truscott, Feb. 9, 1912, JRDC, two quotations; Drake to Dr. J. J. Strohmeyer, Feb. 28, 1912, JRDC, quotation.

17. Drake to Thomas Graham, Feb. 5, 1912, JRDC, two quotations; Drake to Truscott, Feb. 9, 1912, JRDC, two quotations.

18. *Detroit Free Press*, May 3, 1911; Nov. 30, 1911; Oct. 16, 1910.

19. *Detroit Free Press*, Oct. 16, 1910.

20. *Santa Barbara News-Press*, Aug. 27, 1944.

Chapter 6. The Pacific

1. "Base Ball Lineup," *Manchuria* (shipboard newspaper), Dec. 17, 1910, MJC; *Detroit Free Press*, Jan. 8, 1911, all quotations.

2. *Honolulu Evening Standard*, Dec. 24, 1910.

3. *Detroit Free Press*, Mar. 5, 1911; *Honolulu Evening Standard*, Dec. 24, 1910, quotation.

4. Interview with Mariann Hanlon Jeffery, July 20, 1998, first quotation; Hupp Motor Car Company, *Round the World in a Hupmobile*, n.p., remainder of quotations.

5. Hupp Motor Car Company, *Round the World in a Hupmobile*, n.p., three quotations; anon., typescript of tour highlights, p. 1, final quotation.

6. *Detroit Free Press*, Feb. 26, 1911, quotation; ibid., Apr. 3, 1927, four quotations.

7. Ibid., Apr. 3, 1927.

8. Anon., typescript of tour highlights, p. 1.

9. Hupp Motor Car Company, *Round the World in a Hupmobile*, n.p.

10. Anon., typescript of tour highlights, p. 1, three quotations; interview with Mariann Hanlon Jeffery, July 20, 1998.

11. Anon., typescript of tour highlights, p. 2.

12. Ibid.

13. *Detroit Free Press*, Apr. 9, 1911; unidentified New Zealand newspaper clipping, MJC.

14. *Detroit Free Press*, Apr. 23, 1911.

15. Hupp Motor Car Company, *Round the World in a Hupmobile*, n.p.

16. Ralph S. Tarr, *New Geographies: Second Book* (New York: Macmillan Co., 1912), p. 396, first quotation; anon., typescript of tour highlights, p. 2, quotation.

17. *Detroit Free Press*, Apr. 27, 1911, two quotations; anon., typescript of tour highlights, p. 2, two quotations; Hupp Motor Car Company, *Round the World in a Hupmobile*, n.p.

18. Hupp Motor Car Company, *Round the World in a Hupmobile*, n.p.

19. *Detroit Free Press*, Apr. 27, 1911, two quotations; Hupp Motor Car Company, *Round the World in a Hupmobile*, n.p., quotation.

20. Unidentified Christchurch newspaper, MJC.

21. Ibid.

22. *Detroit Free Press*, Apr. 27, 1911, four quotations; Hupp Motor Car Company, *Round the World in a Hupmobile*, n.p., quotation; unidentified Christchurch newspaper, MJC, quotation.

23. Hupp Motor Car Company, *Round the World in a Hupmobile*, n.p.

24. *Detroit Free Press*, Sept. 3, 1911; ibid., Oct. 29, 1911, quotation.

25. Unidentified Hobart, Tasmania, newspaper, MJC.

26. Ibid.

27. Hupp Motor Car Company, *Round the World in a Hupmobile*, n.p., quotation; unidentified Hobart, Tasmania, newspaper, MJC, two quotations.

28. Unidentified Hobart, Tasmania, newspaper, MJC.

29. Ibid.

30. Hupp Motor Car Company, *Round the World in a Hupmobile*, n.p., quotation; *Detroit Free Press*, Apr. 9, 1911, quotation; *Japan Times*, May 13, 1911.

31. Anon., typescript of tour highlights, p. 2.

32. Hupp Motor Car Company, *Round the World in a Hupmobile*, n.p.; *Detroit Free Press*, Apr. 11, 1911; ibid., June 18, 1911.

33. *Detroit Free Press*, Apr. 11, 1911, two quotations; ibid., May 28, 1911, quotation.

34. Ibid., May 28, 1911.

35. Ibid., Apr. 11, 1911.

36. Ibid., June 18, 1911, four quotations; ibid., June 19, 1911, quotation.

37. *Detroit Free Press*, June 18, 1911.

38. Ibid., quotation; ibid., Apr. 11, 1911; anon., typescript of tour highlights, 2.

39. *Detroit Free Press*, May 28, 1911, quotation; Hupp Motor Car Company, *Round the World in a Hupmobile*, n.p., quotation; *Horseless Age* 29 (Feb. 7, 1912): 308, three quotations; Hupp Motor Car Company, *Hupmobile's Old Car Exhibit: S.A.E. Spring Meeting, French Lick, Indiana, May 25–30, 1930*, n.p.; *Detroit Free Press*, June 18, 1911; anon., typescript of tour highlights, p. 2, quotation.

40. *Detroit Free Press*, June 18, 1911.

41. Ibid., quotation; ibid., May 28, 1911, quotation.

42. Ibid., June 18, 1911, quotation; anon., typescript of tour highlights, p. 2, quotation.

43. Tarr, *New Geographies*, 159.

44. "Non-Christian Peoples of Philippine Islands," *National Geographic Magazine* 24 (Nov. 1913): 1199, quotation; p. 1201, quotation.

45. Ibid., p. 1204, quotation; *Detroit Free Press*, Sept. 10, 1911, quotation.

46. "Non-Christian Peoples of Philippine Islands," p. 1201, quotation.

47. Anon., typescript of tour highlights, p. 2, quotation; *Detroit Free Press*, May 28, 1911, remainder of quotations.

48. *Detroit Free Press*, May 28, 1911, quotation; *Japan Times*, May 13, 1911; Hupp Motor Car Company, *Hupmobile's Old Car Exhibit*, n.p.; id., *Round the World in a Hupmobile*, n.p., three quotations.

Chapter 7. The Car

1. *Detroit Free Press*, Oct. 9, 1910; William Cuthbert (technical advisor on the Model 20 for Hupmobile Club members) to author, Apr. 22, 2000.

2. Barzini, *Peking to Paris*, 251–54; unidentified Hupp advertisement, 1910, MJC; Hupp Motor Car Company, *Hupmobile, the Four Cylinder 20 H.P. Car Extraordinary* (Detroit: Hupp Motor Car Co., 1910), p. 12.

3. Hupp Motor Car Company, *Hupmobile . . . Car Extraordinary*, p. 8.

4. Cuthbert to author, Apr. 22, 2000, quotation; Hupp Motor Car Company, *Hupmobile . . . Car Extraordinary*, p. 15, quotation.

5. Ibid., p. 15.

6. Ibid., p. 15, quotation; p. 16, quotation; p. 17, two quotations.

7. Ibid., p. 17.

8. Unidentified Hupp advertisement, Auto Sales Company, Cleveland, Ohio, WRHS; William W. Cuthbert, "Hupmobile," *Horseless Carriage Gazette,* Nov.–Dec. 1971, pp. 17–18.

9. Hupp Motor Car Company, *Hupmobile Instruction Book* (Detroit: Hupp Motor Car Co., 1910), p. 16, two quotations; p. 8.

10. Unidentified Hupp advertisement, WRHS.

11. Hupp Motor Car Company, *Hupmobile . . . Car Extraordinary,* p. 10.

12. Cuthbert, "Hupmobile," 21.

13. Unidentified Hupmobile advertisement, WRHS.

14. Harold Whiting Slauson, "Automobile Touring at Night," in *Around the World with a Camera,* ed. Sleicher, n.p.

15. Hupp Motor Car Company, *Hupmobile Instruction Book,* p. 5.

16. Ibid.; Cuthbert to author, Apr. 22, 2000, last quotation.

17. Hupp Motor Car Company, *Hupmobile Instruction Book,* p. 7, quotation; p. 8, quotation.

18. Ibid., p. 8, quotation; p. 9, quotation.

19. Ibid., p. 10.

20. Ibid., p. 11.

21. Ibid., pp. 11–12.

22. Ibid., p. 13.

23. Ibid.

24. Ibid., p. 15; p. 16, quotations.

25. Ibid., p. 17.

26. Ibid., p. 19.

27. Ibid., two quotations; p. 20, three quotations; p. 18, two quotations; p. 19, three quotations.

28. Ibid., p. 22.

29. Unidentified Hupp advertisement, WRHS, quotation; unidentified Hupp advertisement, Auto Sales Company, WRHS, quotation.

Chapter 8. The Far Side of the Globe

1. *Detroit Free Press,* June 25, 1911.

2. Ibid., two quotations; Melvin Hall, "Around the World by Motor," *Literary Digest* 46 (Apr. 12, 1913), quotation.

3. *Detroit Free Press,* Apr. 30, 1911, quotation; ibid., May 2, 1911, quotation.

4. *Detroit Free Press,* June 25, 1911.

5. Ibid., three quotations; *Celestial Empire* (Shanghai), May 6, 1911, two quotations.

6. *Detroit Free Press,* Jan. 21, 1912, quotation; ibid., June 25, 1911, quotation; ibid., Jan. 21, 1912, quotation; ibid., June 25, 1911, quotation; ibid., Jan. 21, 1912, quotation.

7. *Japan Times,* May 17, 1911; interview with Mariann Hanlon Jeffery, July 20, 1998.

8. *Detroit Journal,* Sept. 4, 1911.

9. *Detroit Free Press,* Apr. 2, 1911.

10. Ibid., Mar. 18, 1911, quotation; David Burgess-Wise, "Ford in Japan," *Automobile Quarterly,* Oct. 1998, p. 112, two quotations; Jan Norbye, "Rising of the Sun: Birth of the Japanese Auto Industry," *Automobile Quarterly,* Oct. 1998, p. 33.

11. *Japan Times,* May 17, 1911; *Detroit Free Press,* Feb. 12, 1912, six quotations.

12. *Automobile Topics*, Feb. 11, 1911, p. 1209.

13. *Japan Times*, May 17, 1911; *Hupp Herald*, Fall 1972, p. 4; *Detroit Journal*, July 10, 1911, quotation; *Japan Times*, May 16, 17, 18, 1911.

14. *Japan Times*, May 17, 1911, quotation; *Detroit Journal*, July 12, 1911, five quotations.

15. Unidentified manuscript, MJC, p. 2; *Detroit Journal*, July 10, 1911, all quotations.

16. *Straits Times* (Singapore), July 22, 1911, three quotations.

17. Ibid.

18. Ibid., six quotations; Hall, "Around the World," two quotations.

19. *Detroit Free Press*, July 9, 1911, all quotations; Hall, "Around the World."

20. Unidentified manuscript, MJC, p. 2.

21. Ibid., quotation; interview with Mariann Hanlon Jeffery, July 20, 1998.

22. Interview with Mariann Hanlon Jeffery, July 20, 1998; unidentified manuscript, MJC, p. 2.

23. *Japan Times*, June 3, 1911, ten quotations; ibid. June 4, 1911, quotation; ibid., June 8, 1911, two quotations.

24. *Detroit Free Press*, July 9, 1911.

25. *Detroit Journal*, Aug. 5, 1911, two quotations; *Detroit Free Press*, July 9, 1911, quotation; *Detroit Journal*, Aug. 8, 1911, three quotations.

26. Hupp Motor Car Company, *Hupmobile's Old Car Exhibit*, n.p., all quotations; *Hupp Herald*, Fall 1972, p. 4.

27. *Detroit Free Press*, Sept. 17, 1911.

28. Hupp Motor Car Company, *Hupmobile's Old Car Exhibit*, n.p.; unidentified manuscript, p. 2, MJC; *Detroit Free Press*, July 9, 1911, and Jan. 6, 1912; *Horseless Age*, Feb. 7, 1912, p. 309; *Automobile Topics*, Jan. 13, 1912, p. 592; *Detroit Journal*, Sept. 4, 1911.

29. *Detroit Free Press*, July 1, 1911, two quotations; *Straits Times* (Singapore), July 22, 1911, quotation.

30. Unidentified manuscript, p. 2, MJC, quotation; *Automobile Topics*, Jan. 13, 1912, p. 592, quotation.

31. Unidentified manuscript, p. 2, MJC.

32. Hall, "Around the World."

33. *Detroit Journal*, Sept. 4, 1911, quotation; *Detroit Free Press*, Sept. 10, 1911, three quotations.

34. *Detroit Free Press*, Sept. 10, 1911.

35. Ibid., July 2, 1911.

36. Ibid., quotation; ibid., Jan. 21, 1912, quotation.

37. Hanlon photo album, DJC.

38. Ibid.; Tarr, *New Geographies*, p. 359.

39. Menu aboard ship *VILLE-DE-LA-CIOTAT*, Aug. 28, 1911, MJC; Hall, "Around the World," all quotations.

40. Hanlon photo album, DJC.

41. Ibid.

42. Ibid.

43. *Detroit Free Press*, Mar. 26, 1911.

44. *Detroit Journal*, Jan. 6, 1912; *Detroit Free Press*, Jan. 21, 1912, quotations.

45. Unidentified manuscript, p. 2, MJC, three quotations; postcards in MJC.

46. Hanlon photo album, DJC.

47. Harry Gibbs to Joseph R. Drake, Nov. 3, 1911, JRDC.

Chapter 9. The Corporate Home Front

1. *Detroit Free Press*, May 3, 1911, two quotations; ibid., Nov. 30, 1911, quotation; ibid., Dec. 25, 1910, three quotations.

2. Ibid., Dec. 11, 1910, quotation; ibid., Apr. 2, 1911.

3. Ibid., Jan. 21, 1912; ibid., May 13, 1911.

4. Ibid., May 7, 1911.

5. Ibid., May 13, 1911.

6. Ibid.

7. Ibid., four quotations; ibid., July 16, 1911, quotation.

8. Ibid., Oct. 25, 1911, three quotations; Duerksen, "Hupmobile," p. 26.

9. *Detroit Free Press*, Sept. 10, 1911, quotation; ibid., Nov. 19, 1911, four quotations; R.C.H. advertisement, in ibid., Oct. 8, 1911.

10. *Detroit Journal*, Sept. 21, 1911, two quotations; *Detroit Free Press*, Sept. 22, 1911, four quotations.

11. *Detroit Journal*, Jan. 31, 1912; *Detroit Free Press*, Feb. 1, 1913, quotation; *Detroit Free Press*, May 3, 1911.

12. *Motor World*, Feb. 12, 1913, quotation; Joseph Drake to Frank Mooney, Nov. 9, 1912, JRDC, two quotations; J. Walter Drake to Joseph Drake, Nov. 30, 1912, JRDC, quotation.

13. Davis, *Conspicuous Production*, theme.

Chapter 10. The Continent

1. *Detroit Free Press*, Nov. 12, 1911.

2. Hupp Motor Car Company, *Hupmobile's Old Car Exhibit*, n.p.; *Detroit Free Press*, Nov. 12, 1911, quotation.

3. Hupp Motor Car Company, *Hupmobile's Old Car Exhibit*, 1930, n.p.

4. *Detroit Free Press*, Dec. 3, 1911.

5. Ibid., three quotations; *Detroit Journal*, Dec. 6, 1911, quotation; *Detroit Free Press*, Dec. 3, 1911, two quotations.

6. Interview with Mariann Hanlon Jeffery, July 20, 1998, quotation; Hanlon photo album, DJC.

7. *The Times* (London), Nov. 11, 16, 21, 1911.

8. Hupp Motor Car Company, *Hupmobile's Old Car Exhibit*, n.p.

9. *Detroit Free Press*, Nov. 12, 1911.

10. "Folio di riconoscimento, Nov. 14 or 16, 1911," MJC; *Detroit Free Press*, Nov. 26, 1911, quotation; Hupp Motor Car Company, *Hupmobile's Old Car Exhibit*, n.p., quotation; Hanlon photo album, DJC.

11. Postcard, MJC; Hanlon photo album, DJC.

12. *Columbia Gazetteer of the World*, ed. Saul Cohen (New York: Columbia University Press, 1962), 1: 534.

13. Hanlon photo album, DJC.

14. *Detroit Free Press*, Jan. 21, 1912, quotation; ibid., Nov. 26, 1911, quotation; postcard, MJC.

15. Hanlon photo album, DJC.

16. Ibid.

17. *Automobile Topics*, Jan. 13, 1912, p. 592a, quotation; Hupp Motor Car Company, *Hupmobile's Old Car Exhibit*, n.p., quotation; Hanlon photo album, DJC.

18. Hanlon photo album, DJC.

19. Postcard, MJC; Hanlon photo album, DJC.

20. Hanlon photo album, DJC.

21. Ibid; Hupp Motor Car Company, *Hupmobile's Old Car Exhibit*, n.p., quotations; Hanlon photo album, DJC.

22. *Detroit Free Press*, Jan. 21, 1912, quotation; Hupp Motor Car Company, *Hupmobile's Old Car Exhibit*, n.p., quotation.

23. *Detroit Free Press*, April 9, 1911.

24. Ibid.

25. Ibid.

26. Ibid.

27. Ibid.; Hanlon photo album, DJC.

28. Interview with Mariann Hanlon Jeffery, July 20, 1998; Hupp Motor Car Company, *Hupmobile's Old Car Exhibit*, n.p., quotation; Hanlon photo album, DJC.

29. Hanlon photo album, DJC; letters to Germany from Joseph Drake's correspondence, JRDC.

30. *Detroit Free Press*, Jan. 21, 1911, quotation; Hupp Motor Car Company, *Hupmobile's Old Car Exhibit*, n.p., quotation; *Detroit Free Press*, Jan. 21, 1912, two quotations.

31. *Detroit Free Press*, Sept. 17, 1911.

32. Postcard, MJC.

33. Hupp Motor Car Company, *Hupmobile's Old Car Exhibit*, n.p., quotation; interview with Mariann Hanlon Jeffery, July 20, 1998; Hanlon photo album, DJC.

34. *Detroit Journal*, Dec. 28, 1911; unidentified newspaper clipping, MJC.

Chapter 11. The Selling of the Hupp

1. Harry Gibbs to Drake, Nov. 3, 1911, JRDC.

2. Drake to A. M. Lawrence, Jan. 26, 1912, JRDC.

3. A. M. Lawrence to Drake, Jan. 23, 1912, JRDC, quotation; Drake to A. M. Lawrence, Jan. 26, 1912, JRDC, five quotations.

4. T. K. Oguri to Drake, Feb. 27, 1912, JRDC, three quotations; Drake to Oguri, May 2, 1912, JRDC, two quotations.

5. Oguri to Drake, May 5, 1912, JRDC.

6. Drake to C. J. Butsch, Oct. 9, 1912, JRDC.

7. Butsch to Drake, Oct. 16, 1912, JRDC.

8. Ibid.

9. Butsch to Drake, Nov. 13, 1912, JRDC.

10. Drake to J. Walter Drake, Sept. 2, 1912, JRDC, two quotations; Drake to Garvin Denby, Jan. 1, 1913, JRDC, quotation.

11. Drake to Leopold Kahn, May 2, 1912, JRDC, two quotations; Kahn to Drake, June 8, 1912, JRDC, two quotations.

12. Dunlap to Drake, Nov. 20, 1912, JRDC.

13. Drake to Straits Motor Garage Syndicate, Sept. 16, 1912, JRDC, three quotations; Dunlap to Drake, Feb. 6, 1913, JRDC.

14. Drake to Messrs. Straits Motor Garage, Sept. 2, 1913, JRDC.

15. *Detroit Free Press*, Nov. 12, 1911.

16. Drake to Dunlap, Dec. 18, 1912, JRDC; Dunlap to Drake, Jan. 24, 1913, JDRC.

17. Gibbs to Drake, Feb. 5, 1912, JRDC.

18. Ibid., Nov. 3, 1911.

19. Ibid., Jan. 15, 1912.

20. Ibid., Feb. 5, 1912.

21. Drake to Gibbs, Mar. 7, 1912, JRDC.

22. Gibbs to Drake, Nov. 3, 1911, JRDC, quotation; ibid., Jan. 15, 1912, three quotations.

23. Gibbs to Drake, Jan. 15, 1912, JRDC, quotation; ibid., Feb. 5, 1912, quotation.

24. Drake to Gibbs, Feb. 12, 1912, JRDC; Drake to Gibbs, Mar. 1, 1912, JRDC, eight quotations; Charles Hastings to Gibbs, Feb. 27, 1912, JRDC, final quotation.

25. Drake to Gibbs, Feb. 12, 1912, JRDC.

26. Gibbs to Drake, Nov. 3, 1911, JRDC; Drake to Gibbs, Mar. 1, 1912, JRDC, two quotations.

27. Drake to Gibbs, Sept. 16, 1912, JRDC, quotation; Dunlap to Drake, Nov. 18, 1912, JRDC; Speyer & Co. to Drake, Oct. 2, 1912, JRDC; Drake to J. Walter Drake, Dec. 12, 1912, JRDC; Drake to Dunlap, Dec. 18, 1912, JRDC.

28. Drake to Dunlap, Mar. 31, 1913, JRDC.

29. Count D. Peccorini to Drake, Feb. 7, 1912, JRDC.

30. Peccorini to Drake, Feb. 7, 1912, JRDC.

31. Drake to Peccorini, Mar. 5, 1912, JRDC.

32. Drake to R. d'Isola & Co., Mar. 5, 1912, JRDC.

33. J. Archer to Drake, Mar. 20, 1912, JRDC, two quotations; Drake to Archer, May 2, 1912, JRDC, two quotations.

34. Archer to Drake, Feb. 10, 1912, JRDC, two quotations; Drake to Archer, Mar. 5, 1912, JRDC, quotation; Archer to Drake, Mar. 30, 1912, JRDC, quotation.

35. Archer to Drake, May 28, 1912, JRDC.

36. Drake to Theodore Tietz, Nov. 4, 1912, JRDC, quotation; Drake to J. Walter Drake, Nov. 8, 1912, JRDC, three quotations.

37. G. W. Disney to Messrs. Speyer & Co, Feb. 3, 1913, JRDC, quotation; ibid., Feb. 6, 1913; ibid., Jan. 31, 1913; Speyer & Co. to Drake, Feb. 4, 1913, JRDC.

38. Drake to J. Walter Drake, Nov. 8, 1912, JRDC.

39. Drake to Harry Whiting, Sept. 16, 1912, JRDC, quotation; Drake to J. Walter Drake, Nov. 1, 1912, JRDC, two quotations.

40. Drake to J. Walter Drake, Nov. 1, 1912, JRDC, three quotations; Drake to Hupp Motor Car Co., Nov. 1, 1912, JRDC, two quotations.

41. Drake to Hupp Motor Car Co., Nov. 8, 1912, JRDC.

42. *American Car Since 1775*, p. 418; J. Walter Drake to Drake, Nov. 30, 1912, JRDC, two quotations.

43. Drake to Denby, Jan. 1, 1912, JRDC.

44. Drake to Denby, Mar. 31, 1913, JRDC, all quotations; *American Car Since 1775*, p. 423.

45. J. Walter Drake to Drake, June 5, 1913, JRDC, four quotations; ibid., July 17, 1913, two quotations.

46. Drake to Harry Drake, July 12, 1913, JRDC, two quotations; Drake to Ivan Bond, Apr. 7, 1915, JRDC, three quotations.

Chapter 12. The Last Leg

1. *Detroit Journal*, Dec. 30, 1911, quotation; unidentified newspaper clipping, n.d., MJC.

2. *New York Times*, Jan. 7, 1912; ibid., Jan. 3, 1912, quotation; unidentified newspaper clipping, n.d. two quotations.

3. *New York Times*, Jan. 8, 1912; ibid., Jan. 7, 1912, quotation.

4. Ibid., Jan. 7, 1912, three quotations; ibid., Jan. 10, 1912, quotation.

5. Ibid., Jan. 7, 1912.

6. Ibid.

7. Ibid.

8. Ibid.

9. *Detroit Journal*, Dec. 30, 1911.

10. *New York Times*, Jan. 7, 1912.

11. Ibid.

12. Ibid., two quotations; *Hupp Herald,* Dec–Feb., 1972, p. 10; *New York Times*, Jan. 13 and Jan. 10, 1912; *American Car Since 1775,* p. 139.

13. *New York Times*, Jan. 8, Jan. 13, 1912; ibid., Jan. 14, 1912, quotation.

14. Drake to Charles J. Campbell, Feb. 5, 1912, JRDC, quotation; *Detroit Free Press*, Jan. 16, 1912, quotation; *New York Times*, Jan. 15, 1912, five quotations.

15. *New York Times*, Jan. 16, 1912.

16. Ibid., Jan. 15, 1912, quotation; ibid., Jan. 16, 1912, three quotations.

17. Ibid., Jan. 15, 1912; *Detroit Free Press*, Jan. 16, 1912, quotation.

18. *Detroit Free Press*, Jan. 16, 1912, quotation; ibid., Jan. 17, 1912, two quotations.

19. Ibid., Jan. 19, 1912, four quotations; *Utica Daily Press*, Jan. 18, 1912.

20. *Detroit Free Press*, Jan. 19, 1912.

21. Ibid., Jan. 20, 1912, quotation; ibid., Jan. 19, 1912, quotation; ibid., Jan. 20, 1912, three quotations; ibid., Jan. 21, 1912, two quotations.

22. *Detroit Journal*, Jan. 23, 1912.

23. *Detroit Free Press*, Jan. 25, 1912.

24. Ibid.

25. *Detroit Journal*, Jan. 25, 1912, seven quotations; *Detroit Free Press*, Jan. 25, 1912, quotation.

26. *Detroit Journal*, Jan. 25, 1912.

27. *Detroit Free Press*, Jan. 25, 1912, two quotations; *Detroit Journal*, Jan. 25, 1912, two quotations.

28. *Detroit Journal*, Jan. 25, 1912, four quotations; *Detroit Free Press*, Jan. 25, 1912, three quotations; *Detroit Journal*, Jan. 25, 1912, quotation.

29. *Detroit Journal*, Jan. 25, 1912, three quotations; *Detroit Free Press*, Jan. 25, 1912, quotation; *Detroit Journal*, Jan. 25, 1912, quotation.

30. *Detroit Free Press*, Jan. 25, 1912, three quotations; *Detroit Journal*, Jan. 25, 1912, two quotations.

31. Drake to Harry Whiting, Jan. 26, 1912, JRDC, two quotations; Drake to Louis Calder, Jan. 26, 1912, JRDC, two quotations.

32. Drake to Calder, Jan. 26, 1912, JRDC, two quotations; Drake to Whiting, Jan. 26, 1912, JRDC, two quotations; Drake to Philip Frank, Jan. 26, 1912, JRDC, quotation.

33. *Detroit Journal*, Jan. 22, 1912.

34. Ibid.

35. Ibid., Jan. 21, 1912, two quotations; *Detroit Free Press*, Jan. 21, 1912, three quotations.

36. *Detroit Free Press*, Jan. 26, 1912.

37. Ibid.

Chapter 13. The Aftermath

1. *Detroit Free Press*, Jan. 28, 1912.

2. *Detroit Journal*, Jan. 27, 1912.

3. *Detroit Free Press*, Jan. 29, 1912.

4. Ibid., two quotations; ibid., Feb. 1, 1912, three quotations.

5. *Detroit Journal*, Jan. 27, 1912.

6. Rae, *American Automobile*, pp. 31–32.

7. *Detroit Free Press*, Feb. 1, 1912, quotation; ibid., Oct. 26, 1912.

8. *Detroit Free Press*, Oct. 26, 1912.

9. Ibid., quotation; unidentified newspaper clipping, n.d., MJC, quotation.

10. *Detroit Free Press*, Oct. 26, 1912.

11. James West Davidson et al., *Nation of Nations: A Narrative History of the American Republic,* 3d ed. (New York: McGraw-Hill, 1998), pp. 800–801.

12. Q.M.C. form 127, Sept. 20, 1916, MJC.

13. Hanlon discharge document, Oct. 4, 1916, MJC.

14. Unidentified newspaper clipping, n.d., MJC.

15. Interview with Mariann Hanlon Jeffery, July 20, 1998.

16. Hupp Motor Car Company, *Hupmobile's Old Car Exhibit*, n.p.

17. *Chicago Herald-Examiner*, Sept. 3, 1933, two quotations; *Chicago American*, Sept. 2, 1933, quotation.

18. Interview with Mariann Hanlon Jeffery, July 20, 1998, quotation; *Chicago American*, Sept. 2, 1933.

19. Interview with Mariann Hanlon Jeffery, July 20, 1998, two quotations; unidentified newspaper clipping, n.d., MJC.

20. *Automobile Topics*, Oct. 1918, p. 854; Georgano, *Complete Encyclopedia of Motorcars*, p. 278.

21. *Detroit News*, Nov. 28, 1941; *Detroit Free Press*, Sept. 26, 1918; *Automobile Topics*, Oct. 1918, p. 854.

22. *Detroit Free Press*, Sept. 26, 1918; *Utica Daily Press*, Sept. 25, 1918; ibid., Oct. 1, 1918; *Detroit Free Press*, Sept. 25, 1918, two quotations; *Utica Daily Press*, Oct. 1, 1918, quotation.

23. *The Automobile*, Oct. 10, 1912, p. 750; ibid., Mar. 19, 1914, quotation.

24. Drake to F. Rahnert, Sept. 2, 1913, JRDC, two quotations; Drake to A. W. North, Aug. 7, 1913, JRDC; Drake to Gibbs, Aug. 7, 1913, JRDC; Drake to C. B. Van Dusen, July 12, 1913, JRDC, quotation.

25. *Automobile Topics*, Mar. 21, 1914; ibid., Mar. 21, 1912, five quotations; Drake to Clare Beames, Jan. 27, 1916, JRDC; Drake to quarantine doctor in charge of San Francisco port, Aug. 4, 1916, JRDC.

26. Interview with Drake's grandson, Tracy Montee, May 25, 2000.

27. *Santa Barbara News-Press*, Aug. 27, 1944.

28. Ibid.

29. Duerksen, "Hupmobile," 23; Georgano, *Complete Encyclopedia of Motorcars,* pp. 574, 492, 372; *Detroit News*, Mar. 6, 1956; Duerksen, "Hupmobile, Part Five—A Venture Called Skylark," *Cars & Parts* (n.d., reprint), 25.

30. Joseph Drake to Harry Gibbs, Mar. 1, 1912, JRDC, quotation; *Detroit Journal*, Dec. 21, 1911, two quotations.

31. *Detroit Free Press*, Oct. 14, 1911; *Detroit Journal*, Oct. 20, 1911.

32. *American Car Since 1775*, pp. 138–41; Godshall, "Hupmobile: The Twilight Years," p. 33.

33. Godshall, "Hupmobile," p. 33; Richard Wager, *Golden Wheels: The Story of the Automobiles*

Made in Cleveland and Northeastern Ohio, 1892–1932 (Cleveland: J. T. Zubal, with the Western Reserve Historical Society, 1975), p. 190.

34. *American Car Since 1775*, p. 141; *Detroit News*, Feb. 16, 1956; Eric Johnson, "Experimental Skylark," *Hupp Herald,* Spring 2000, pp. 2–4.

35. *Detroit News*, Feb. 16, 1956.

36. *Encyclopedia of Cleveland History*, ed. David D. Van Tassel and John J. Grabowski, 2d ed. (Bloomington: Indiana University Press, with Case Western Reserve University and the Western Reserve Historical Society, 1996), "Hupp Corp." On line at http://ech.cwru.edu.

37. Ibid., "White Consolidated Industries."

38. Ibid.

39. CPT's 10K SEC filing, Sept. 28, 1999, http://www. secgov; telephone conversation with Mike Schenker, CPT corporate counsel, May 16, 2000, quotations.

40. Ralph Geddes to Frederick Crawford, Jan. 7, 1946, in Western Reserve Historical Society (WRHS), Cleveland, Ohio, six quotations; assistant secretary to Crawford, Jan. 11, 1946, WRHS, quotation; Norman J. Shibley to Geddes, Feb. 5, 1946, WRHS, quotation.

41. Phone conversation with Chris Grasso, assistant curator, Crawford collection (WRHS), June 5, 2000.

SELECT BIBLIOGRAPHY

Primary Sources

Anonymous. Typescript for Hupp article on the 1933 Century of Progress.
Automobile Topics, 1910–18.
Broadbent, Mrs. Holly. Interview, July 24, 2001.
Celebration in Chicago. N.d., n.p. Mariann Hanlon Jeffery collection.
———. Typescript of tour highlights. N.d., n.p. Mariann Hanlon Jeffery collection.
Celestial Empire (Shanghai), Apr.–July 1911.
Ceylon *Observer*, 1911.
Detroit Free Press, 1910–12.
Detroit Journal, 1910–12.
Detroit News, Nov. 1941.
Drake, Joseph R. Papers. American Heritage Center, University of Wyoming, Laramie. Cited as JRDC.
Hanlon, Thomas. Photo album.
Hyde, Charles K. "National Architectural and Engineering Record: Hupp Motor Car Company Plant." Typescript, Apr. 1981. National Automotive History Collection, Detroit Public Library.
Japan Times, 1911.
Jeffery, Don, Jr. Numerous interviews and collection, cited as DJC.
Jeffery, Mariann Hanlon. Interview, July 20, 1998, and collection, cited as MJC.
Montee, Tracy. Letters and interview.
National Automotive History Collection. Detroit Public Library. Hupmobile holdings.
New York Times, 1910–12.
Owens, David. Interview, July 24, 2001.
Santa Barbara News-Press, Aug. 1944.
Schenker, Mike. CPT Corporate counsel. Interview, May 16, 2000.
Straits Times (Singapore), July 1911.
The Times (London), 1911–12.
Utica Daily Press, January 1912, Sept.–Oct. 1918.
Western Reserve Historical Society. Hupmobile materials. Cited as WRHS.

Books and Articles

The American Car Since 1775: The Most Complete Survey of the American Automobile Ever Published. By the editors of *Automobile Quarterly.* New York: L. S. Bailey, 1971.

Bailey, Thomas. *A Diplomatic History of the American People.* New York: Appleton-Century-Crofts, 1973.

Barzini, Luigi. *Pekin to Paris: An Account of Prince Borghese's Journey Across Two Continents in a Motor-Car.* Translated by L. P. de Castelvechio. Introduction by Prince Borghese. London: E. Grant Richards, 1907. Reprinted under the title *Peking to Paris: A Journey Across Two Continents* (New York: Liberty Press, 1973).

Burgess-Wise, David. "Ford in Japan." *Automobile Quarterly,* Oct. 1998.

Cole, Dermot. *Hard Driving: The 1908 Auto Race from New York to Paris.* New York: Paragon House, 1991.

The Columbia Gazetteer of the World. Edited by Saul B. Cohen. New York: Columbia University Press, 1962.

Cuthbert, William W. "Hupmobile." *Horseless Carriage Gazette,* Nov.– Dec., 1971.

Davidson, James West, et al. *Nation of Nations: A Narrative History of the American Republic.* 3d ed. New York: McGraw-Hill, 1998.

Davis, Donald Finlay. *Conspicuous Production: Automobiles and Elites in Detroit, 1899–1933.* Philadelphia: Temple University Press, 1989.

De Santis, Vincent P. *The Shaping of Modern America, 1877–1916.* Boston: Allyn & Bacon, 1973.

Dobson, John. *America's Ascent: The United States Becomes a Great Power, 1880–1914.* De Kalb, Ill.: Northern Illinois University Press, 1978.

Duerksen, Menno. "Hupmobile, Part Five—A Venture Called Skylark." *Cars & Parts,* n.d.

———. "The Story of Hupmobile." *Hupp Herald,* Summer 1979.

The Encyclopedia of Cleveland History. Edited by David D. Van Tassel and John J. Grabowski. 2d ed. Bloomington: Indiana University Press, with Case Western Reserve University and the Western Reserve Historical Society, 1996. On line at http://ech.cwru.edu.

Fisher, Harriet White. *A Woman's Tour in a Motor.* Philadelphia: J. B. Lippincott Co., 1911.

Franzwa, Gregory. *The Lincoln Highway.* Vol. 3: *Wyoming.* Tucson: Patrice Press, 1999.

Georgano, G. N. *The Complete Encyclopedia of Motorcars, 1885 to the Present.* New York: Dutton, 1972.

"Globe-Girdling: 85 Years Ago." *The Packard,* no. 36 (Mar. 1913). Reprinted in *The Packard Cormorant,* no. 93 (Winter 1998–99).

Godshall, Jeffery. "Hupmobile in the Twilight Years." *Antique Automobile,* July–Aug. 1968.

Hall, Melvin A. "Around the World by Motor." *Literary Digest,* Apr. 12, 1913.

———. *Journey to the End of an Era: An Informal Autobiography.* New York: Scribner's, 1947.

Hediger, Ferdinand. "Itala." *Automobile Quarterly* 38, 1 (July 1998): 30–31.

Hupp Motor Car Company. *Hupmobile Instruction Book.* Detroit: Hupp Motor Car Co., 1910.

———. *Hupmobile's Old Car Exhibit: S.A.E. Spring Meeting, French Lick, Indiana, May 25–30, 1930.* Detroit: Hupp Motor Car Co., 1930.

———. *Hupmobile, the Four Cylinder 20 H.P. Car Extraordinary.* Detroit: Hupp Motor Car Co., 1910.

———. *Hupmobile: One Thousand Miles Through Snowdrifts.* Cleveland: Corday & Gross, 1910.

———. *The Man, the Machine, the Material.* Detroit: Hupp Motor Car Co., n.d. [1913?].

———. *Round the World in a Hupmobile: Detroit to Manila.* Detroit: Hupp Motor Car Co., 1911.

Johnson, Eric. "Experimental Skylark." *Hupp Herald,* Spring 2000.

Kaufmann, Edith Townsend. "A Woman's World Tour in a Motor." In *Around the World with a Camera,* ed. John Sleicher. New York: Leslie-Judge Co., 1915.

McConnell, Curt. *Coast to Coast by Automobile: The Pioneering Trips, 1898–1908.* Stanford: Stanford University Press, 2000.

"Non-Christian Peoples of Philippine Islands." *National Geographic Magazine* 24 (Nov. 1913).

Norbye, Jan. "Rising of the Sun: Birth of the Japanese Auto Industry." *Automobile Quarterly,* Oct. 1998.

Rae, John. *The American Automobile.* Chicago: University of Chicago Press, 1965.

Scott, Michael. *Packard: The Complete Story.* Ridge Summit, Pa.: TAB Books, 1985.

Slauson, Harold Whiting. "Automobile Touring at Night." In *Around the World with a Camera,* ed. John Sleicher. New York, 1915.

Tarr, Ralph S. *New Geographies: Second Book.* New York: Macmillan Co., 1912.

U.S. Congress. *Biographical Directory of the American Congress, 1774–1927: The Continental Congress, September 5, 1774, to October 21, 1788, and the Congress of the United States, from the First Through the Sixty-ninth Congress, March 4, 1789, to March 3, 1927, Inclusive.* 69th Cong., 2d sess. House document no. 783. Washington, D.C.: GPO, 1928.

Wager, Richard. *Golden Wheels: The Story of the Automobiles Made in Cleveland and Northeastern Ohio, 1892–1932.* Cleveland: J. T. Zubal, with the Western Reserve Historical Society, 1975.

Wise, David Burgess. *The New Illustrated Encyclopedia of Automobiles.* Edison, N.J.: Wellfleet Press, 1992.

INDEX

The authorized representative in the EU for product safety and compliance is:
Mare Nostrum Group
B.V Doelen 72
4831 GR Breda
The Netherlands

www.ingramcontent.com/pod-product-compliance
Lightning Source LLC
Chambersburg PA
CBHW062000090426
42811CB00006B/1000